Jo Smith is from Kāti Huirapa ki Puketeraki from Karitane, north of Dunedin. She is an experienced media educator and researcher with a persisting focus on the ways in which colonial histories and the power they wield impact on and inform contemporary media practices. She has published and presented extensively on her work in Indigenous and postcolonial media, at conferences and in journals and books both in Aotearoa and internationally, including chapters in edited collections such as *Reverse Shots: Indigenous Film and Media in an International Context*, *The Oxford Handbook of Postcolonial Studies*, *Huihui: Pacific Rhetorics and Aesthetics* and *The Fourth Eye: Māori Media in Aotearoa New Zealand*. She has published articles in journals such as *Arena, Continuum, Transnational Cinemas, Settler Colonial Studies* and *AlterNative: An International Journal of Indigenous Peoples*. Her research work has been supported by a number of grants, including a Royal Society Fast Start Marsden Grant in 2008–2009 for her project *Unsettled States: Settler-Native-Migrant Media*, and a 2012–2014 Standard Marsden Grant for *Onscreen Indigeneity: The Case of Māori Television*. She has a PhD from the University of Otago and was previously a lecturer at the Universities of Otago and Auckland. She currently researches and teaches in the Media Studies programme at Victoria University of Wellington.

Māori Television
The First Ten Years

Jo Smith

AUCKLAND
UNIVERSITY
PRESS

First published 2016

Auckland University Press
University of Auckland
Private Bag 92019
Auckland 1142
New Zealand
www.press.auckland.ac.nz

© Jo Smith, 2016

ISBN 978 1 86940 857 2

Supported by the Marsden Fund Council from government funding,
managed by the Royal Society of New Zealand.

A catalogue record for this book is available from
the National Library of New Zealand

This book is copyright. Apart from fair dealing for the purpose of private
study, research, criticism or review, as permitted under the Copyright Act,
no part may be reproduced by any process without prior permission of
the publisher. The moral rights of the author have been asserted.

Cover design by Spencer Levine
Back cover image by Gil Hanly

This book was printed on FSC certified paper.

Printed in China by 1010 Printing International Ltd

Contents

Acknowledgements	vi
Introduction: Five Frameworks for Understanding Māori Television	1
Chapter One: The Long Struggle for Māori Television	8
Chapter Two: Bringing Tikanga to Television	38
Chapter Three: To Zig Where Others Zag – Māori Television Programming Strategies	64
Chapter Four: Audience Engagements with Māori Television Programming	91
Chapter Five: Māori Television and a Politics of Culture Framework	120
Chapter Six: Putting the Five Frameworks to Use	144
Conclusion	161
Appendix One: The Māori Television Service (Te Aratuku Whakaata Irirangi Māori) Act 2003 Section 8	166
Appendix Two: Funding Channels	167
Appendix Three: Māori Television's Right of Reply	168
Bibliography	171
Index	182

Acknowledgements

This book owes much to the support and contribution of many individuals and organisations, particularly the interviewees and focus group participants whose thoughts, wisdom and experiences form the foundation of the book. I acknowledge the passion, commitment and expertise of those who work in the field of Māori media. I am extremely grateful for the time you gave to this project. Jim Mather enabled the research to proceed, Haunui Royal, Mahuta Amoamo and Coral Palmer offered ongoing assistance, and Paora Maxwell supported the completion of the research. Sue Abel worked with me in the first few years of the *Onscreen Indigeneity* project, out of which this book emerged. Thank you for all the work you did for the project.

Support in the early stages came from a range of people, including Diane Zwimpfer, Irene Wood, Charles Husband, Victoria University of Wellington (VUW) Women's Writing Group members Teresia Teaiwa, Sara Kindon, Deb Jones and Carol Harrington, as well as Richard Hill, Tracey McIntosh and Margaret Mutu. This book also benefited from the insights and generosity of VUW colleagues, including April Henderson, Maria Bargh, Ocean Mercier, Nicola Hyland, Minette Hillyer, Joost de Bruin, Peter Thompson, Trisha Dunleavy and Thomas Owen. I also acknowledge my project mentor Khyla Russell, the Rūnaka o Kāti Huirapa ki Puketeraki, as well as Angela Barnes and Nicola Bright for their expertise in relation to Māori research.

The book also benefited from the knowledge and insights of Jessica Hutchings whose expertise in the field of kaupapa Māori has helped to push my thinking in new directions. I also acknowledge the editorial comments offered by both Jessica and Jenny Lee on a book chapter I wrote for their edited collection, *Decolonising Education*. Their insights informed subsequent content for this book. Leah Gifford came on board at a significant moment in the project as both a project manager and research assistant. Thanks also to the many research assistants whose diverse expertise enriched the final work: Sarah Hudson, Coral Panoho, Ross Burden, Jani Wilson, Pania Lee, Katie Freeman-Tayler, Jono McLeod, Alicia Sudden, Jacqui Poutu, Chloe Manga and Emma Kelly.

I acknowledge the Royal Society Marsden Fund for supporting this project between 2012 and 2015. Thanks too to Jeannette Vine of the VUW Research Trust, and to former Research Trust adviser Christine Romanes. I acknowledge the following people who provided images for the book: John

Miller, Gil Hanly, Karen Waaka, Quinton Hita, Kay Ellmers and Hinewehi Mohi. Thanks to Sam Elworthy and his team at Auckland University Press, as well as Ray Prebble, Jennifer Garlick and Diane Lowther, and to Paul Diamond for reviewing the manuscript. Finally, thanks to Jess for your infinite patience, laughter and encouragement while this book was being made, and to my wider whānau, for their love and support.

Me tino mihi atu ki te huhua o ngā tāngata me ngā whakahaere nā rātou i tautoko, me te whai wāhi ki te whakaotinga o tēnei pukapuka, ina koa ki ērā i uiuitia, i whai wāhi anō hoki ki ngā rōpū arotahi. Ko ō rātou whakaaro, ō rātou mōhiotanga me ā rātou wheako te tūāpapa o te pukapuka nei. Kei te mihi atu ki a rātou e mahi ana i te rāngai pāpāho Māori mō tō rātou ngākaunui, tō rātou ū me tō rātou mākohakoha. Kei te tino whakamihi i a koutou mō tō whakapau wā ki tēnei kaupapa. Nā Jim Mather i whakaae kia haere tēnei rangahau, nā Haunui Royal rātou ko Mahuta Amoamo, ko Coral Palmer i whakarato i te āwhina haere tonu. Nā Paora Maxwell i tautoko te whakaotinga o te mahi tuhi. Aku mihi nunui ki a koutou katoa. I mahi tahi māua ko Sue Abel i te tōmuatanga o te kaupapa *Onscreen Indigeneity* i puta mai ai tēnei pukapuka.

I te tōmuatanga o te kaupapa ka whiwhi tautoko au i te whānuitanga o ngā tāngata, tae atu ki a Diane Zwimpfer, ki a Irene Wood, ki a Charles Husband, ki a Teresia Teaiwa rātou ko Sarah Kindon, ko Deb Jones, ko Carol Harrington nō te Rōpū Tuhutuhi o ngā Wāhine o Te Whare Wānanga o te Ūpoko o Te Ika a Māui, ki a Richard Hill, ki a Tracey McIntosh me Margaret Mutu hoki. I whiwhi hua tēnei pukapuka i te mātau me te ngākau makuru o ngā hoamahi nō Te Whare Wānanga o te Ūpoko o Te Ika a Māui, tae atu ki a April Henderson rātou ko Maria Bargh, ko Ocean Mercier, ko Nicola Hyland, ko Minette Hillyer, ko Joost de Bruin, ko Peter Thompson, ko Trisha Dunleavy, ko Thomas Owen. Kei te tuku mihi anō hoki ki tōku kaiakopono, ki tōku whanaunga, a Khyla Russell, ki te Rūnaka o Kāti Huirapa, ki a Angela Barnes rāua ko Nicola Bright mō tō rātou mōhiotanga me tō rātou mākohakoha e pā ana ki te rangahau Māori.

Kāore tēnei pukapuka i eke ki tōna taumata o nāianei ki te kore te mōhiotanga me te mātau o Jessica Hutchings. Nā ōna mākohakoha ki te rāngai kaupapa Māori i pei atu ōku whakaaro ki ngā ahunga hōu. Kei te whakamihi anō hoki i ngā tākupu whakatikatika i whakaratohia e Jessica rāua ko Jenny Lee mō tētahi wāhanga pukapuka nāku i tuhi mō tā rāua kohinga he mea whakatika ko *Decolonising Education*. He mea whakarei ngā ihirangi o tēnei

ACKNOWLEDGEMENTS

pukapuka e tō rāua mātau. I whai wāhi mai a Leah Gifford i tētahi wā hira o te kaupapa, ā, nā āna mahi hei kaiwhakahaere kaupapa me te kaiāwhina rangahau i tautoko te rangahau ka noho hei pou here mō tēnei pukapuka. Ngā mihi hoki ki te tokomaha o ngā kaiāwhina rangahau i mahi i tōku taha i tēnei kaupapa, nā te whānuitanga o ō rātou mākohakoha tēnei whakaputanga i whakarei: ko Sarah Hudson rātou ko Coral Panoho, ko Ross Burden, ko Jani Wilson, ko Pania Lee, ko Katie Freeman-Tayler, ko Jono McLeod, ko Alicia Sudden, ko Jacqui Poutu, ko Chloe Manga, ko Emma Kelly.

Me mihi anō hoki ki te Tahua Marsden o Te Apārangi, nāna tēnei kaupapa i tautoko i waenga i ngā tau 2012 ki 2015. Kei te mihi hoki ki a Jeanette Vine o te Tarahiti Rangahau o Te Whare Wānanga o te Ūpoko o Te Ika a Māui, ki te kaitohutohu o mua o te Tarahiti Rangahau, ki a Christine Romanes. Kei te whakamihi hoki i ēnei tāngata i whakarato whakaahua mō te pukapuka: ko John Miller rātou ko Gil Hanly, ko Karen Waaka, ko Quinton Hita, ko Kay Ellmers, ko Hinewehi Mohi. Ngā mihi ki a Sam Elworthy me tōna rōpū i te Auckland University Press. Ngā mihi ki a Ray Prebble, Jennifer Garlick ko Diane Lowther. Hei whakamutunga ake, ngā mihi ki a Jess mō tō manawanui mutukore, tō katakata me tō whakatītina i tēnei pukapuka e tuhia ana. He mihi aroha ki tōku whānau whēnui nā ratou ahau i tautoko kia whakaputaina tēnei pukapuka. E mihi ana, e mihi ana.*

Note on macrons: In this book the use of macrons is congruous with practices at the time of a source's publication.

---

* Aspects of chapter five draw on material developed with Sue Abel. Other aspects of the book include material developed for a chapter in Hutchings and Lee's anthology *Decolonising Education* (forthcoming from NZCER Press) and previously published material from 'Māori Television's Service to its Publics in an Era of Digital Plenty', *International Journal of Digital Television*, vol. 6, issue 2, 2015, pp. 185–202.

Introduction

Five Frameworks for Understanding Māori Television

Since its launch in 2004, Māori Television has become part of a global Indigenous television movement, including, among others, APTN in Canada, NITV in Australia, TITV in Taiwan and Ōiwi TV in Hawaii. These media providers give voice to the diverse perspectives of the First Peoples of Canada, Australia, Taiwan, Hawaii and New Zealand within wider societies where such points of view have been historically marginalised. Māori Television is a particularly interesting example of Indigenous media making in that it has been favourably received by a non-Māori majority culture. In its first ten years, Māori Television established itself within New Zealand's wider media culture to such an extent that local politicians and non-Māori media commentators described it as one of the best examples of public broadcasting in the country (Norris and Pauling, 2008; New Zealand House of Representatives, 2013a). In a media landscape dominated by commercially driven free-to-air media, Māori Television continues to provide its niche audience with programming that many non-Māori recognise as public-service content.

State funded to the level of approximately $48 million per year, Māori Television's founding legislation instructed it to promote Māori language and culture by providing media content that, among other functions, 'informs, educates and entertains a broad viewing audience' (Māori Television, 2012, p. 5).* Since its emergence, Māori Television has built a reputation for itself by

---

* Māori Television recieves $16.6 million in direct funding from Vote Māori Affairs to support broadcasting operations, $16.1 million in direct funding from Te Māngai Pāho to produce in-house programming, and approximately $16 million per annum in indirect funding from the contestable fund administered by Te Māngai Pāho (Māori Television, 2014a). Advertising revenue was reported as $1,002,000 in 2014 (Māori Television, 2014b).

offering substantial Māori-language programming, Māori news and current affairs, lifestyle television, all-day coverage of national events, and international art-house films and documentaries that have a broad appeal.

This book examines Māori Television's unique contribution to the media cultures of Aotearoa New Zealand in its first ten years on screen. Research for this project was undertaken between 2012 and 2015, and focused on the way in which the original legislation that established Māori Television (since amended in 2013) required it to protect and promote Māori language and cultural practices ('te reo Māori me ngā tikanga Māori'), at the same time as inform, educate and entertain 'a broad viewing audience', and to thus 'enrich New Zealand society, culture and heritage' (Māori Television Service Act 2003). These multiple demands give rise to a set of intriguing questions as to how one makes popular and appealing television that can also assist in language and cultural outcomes, at a time of great change in the way that television is produced, distributed and consumed. The legislation also raises questions as to how an Indigenous media provider might contribute to the enrichment of 'New Zealand society, culture and heritage'. In 2013 when the legislation was amended, the appeal to a 'broad viewing audience' was withdrawn and 'te reo Māori me ngā tikanga' changed to 'te reo Māori me ōna tikanga'. This book provides five frameworks for understanding the diverse demands made of Māori Television, the wider forces conditioning the organisation's efforts in its first ten years, and the network's innovation in New Zealand media production.

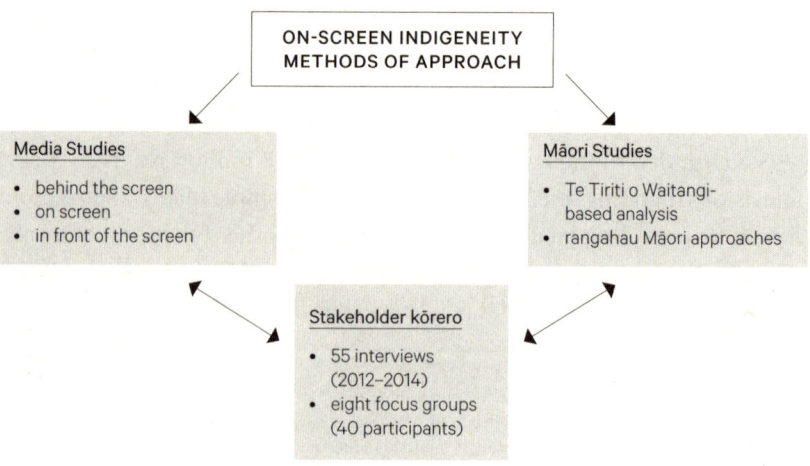

FIGURE 1.1 **METHOD OF APPROACH**

The concept of on-screen Indigeneity helped shape the thinking behind the project, and drew on Media Studies and Māori Studies methods to consider how what we see on screen on Māori Television is the result of a complex set of relations going on behind the screen, and in front of the screen. That is to say, to understand how Māori Television has negotiated its competing mandates in its first ten years, one must understand the larger forces that help shape the organisation's practices, and the audiences who watch Māori Television programming, as well as the climate in which such media is received. Behind-the-screen conditions include the long history of non-Māori media representing Māori issues, and the role played by Te Tiriti o Waitangi in Māori Television's 2004 launch. Other factors include Māori Television's governing legislation, the larger New Zealand media environment that helps shape its practices, and shifts within the Māori-language sector that impact on Māori Television as a language entity. Elements in front of the screen include the meanings made of Māori Television programming by audiences, media commentators, politicians and other media providers.

Insights from Māori Television stakeholders grounded the research agenda. These stakeholders included Māori Television staff, board directors, Te Pūtahi Pāoho Electoral College members, independent media producers, funders, language advocates, politicians, media commentators and academics. All interviewees were asked to reflect on Māori Television's major achievements to date, as well as the challenges facing this media provider. The insights of audience focus groups also played a vital role in shaping the arc of the book. In line with a rangahau Māori research approach, the book privileges the voices of those working in the Māori media sector, and those Māori audiences who engage with Māori Television. This kōrero was seen in the context of language revitalisation literature, policies from media institutions, legislation, and existing research on New Zealand media. Five frameworks for throwing light on the significance and impact of Māori Television in its first ten years emerged in the course of engaging with these diverse sources. These frameworks highlight the importance of history, tikanga, programming, audiences and politics when attempting to understand Māori Television's significance. The five-way approach developed as a tool to understand the many competing expectations facing Māori Television, including how it contributes to protecting and promoting te reo and tikanga Māori, its alleged role as a public-service media provider, and its capacity to be shaped by Māori ways of thinking and doing. The five frameworks do not

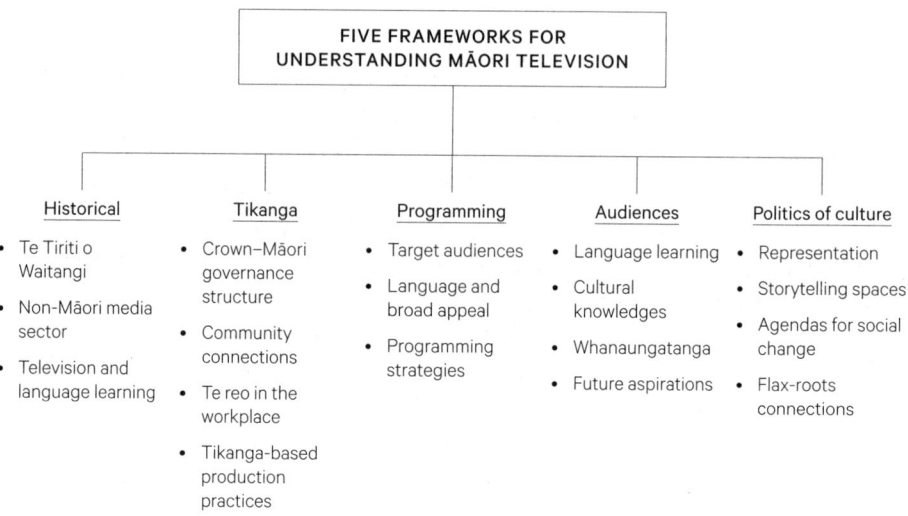

FIGURE 1.2 **A FIVE-FRAMEWORK APPROACH**

attempt to be definitive, but simply lay some provisional groundwork that may be useful for future research to do with the Māori media sector. Indeed, these frameworks would ideally be developed and expressed using the language, concepts and world views uniquely encapsulated in te reo Māori.

To understand how Māori Television has addressed the challenges of its governing legislation, we need to situate the network within the long history of Māori exclusion from New Zealand's mediated public sphere, and in relation to Māori aspirations for what television can do to enhance, rejuvenate and affirm Māori language and cultural practices. While attention is paid to the activist roots underpinning Māori Television's launch,* the book also explores the wider media culture that helps shape the organisation's practices, and the demands facing Māori media makers who must deliver quality programming that might contribute to language and cultural outcomes. Aspects of this wider media culture include a pervasively English-speaking society with a long-standing desire for global media content, the technological shifts facing television providers in an era of digital plenty, and the ongoing political and cultural aspirations of diverse Māori communities.

---

* One could also say that 2004 marked a watershed moment in te ao Māori with the passing of the Foreshore and Seabed Act and the launch of the Māori Party. See Smith, 2013.

Chapter one offers a historical framework that considers Māori Television's emergence and subsequent practices in light of a monolingual media culture dominated by the interests of non-Māori. It argues that understanding the longer and larger struggle for tino rangatiratanga that informs Māori Television's eventual emergence is important when considering the legacy that Māori Television programming will leave for future generations. While the struggle to gain better access to technologies of representation may have been won with the emergence of Māori Television, kōrero from stakeholders suggest that a struggle still remains for television programming that reflects and appeals to the full spectrum of Māori perspectives and practices.

The issue of what is a properly Māori perspective or practice when creating television is the topic of chapter two, which discusses a te reo and tikanga Māori framework for thinking about Māori Television's efforts to incorporate language and Māori cultural knowledge into its television practices. This framework takes into account Māori Television's aspirations to be a Māori media organisation in the face of certain institutional and economic pressures that condition the expression of its guiding kaupapa. Yet what does it mean to be a Māori media organisation, or to simply be 'Māori', under contemporary conditions? As the then general manager of programming Haunui Royal pointed out, the meaning of the word Māori encompasses a broad spectrum of experiences and understandings, so much so that 'it's becoming more and more difficult to say what you mean by that word now' (H. Royal, interview, 2012). It is a contention of this book that Māori Television has made an important contribution to diversifying ideas about what or who gets to count as 'Māori' under contemporary conditions. The network's presence in the media landscape of Aotearoa New Zealand has generated a greater understanding of the differences within the category Māori for those who have affiliations with the diverse worlds that constitute te ao Māori, and for some non-Māori. The term Māori is used in a range of different ways by interviewees and focus group participants, which demonstrates the complexities and diverse realities encapsulated within the term. So, too, the term 'Pākehā', is used by some interviewees and focus group participants to describe the non-Māori and English-speaking majority culture of Aotearoa New Zealand. Non-Māori describes those cultures and communities different from the diverse whānau and hapū that make up te ao Māori. Identity categories discussed remain mindful of what Te Ahukaramū Charles Royal has called the falsely unifying categories of 'Māori' and 'Pākehā' that have been naturalised in debates around Te Tiriti o Waitangi claims processes (Royal, 2007). In the wake of such categorical complexities, chapter two offers a discussion of the relationship between the diverse and contested cultural protocols and practices (tikanga) that make up te ao Māori, and the challenges of developing media-based tikanga practices within an industry and social context where non-Māori values, viewpoints and practices have long prevailed.

Chapter three deploys a programming framework to consider how Māori Television achieves its legislative obligations. According to the 2003 Māori Television Service Act, Māori Television must provide language-learning content that can grab the attention of both young and old television viewers, who are on a spectrum spanning both fluent and non-fluent speakers. This television content must be of a certain 'quality' that can appeal to a broad audience, as well as educate and entertain. It must be generated on time within a funding context where budgets have been frozen since 2008. Under such conditions Māori Television has provided much innovative, challenging and informative television content in its first ten years, and has helped to generate public debate about Māori matters. Chapter three offers insights into the programming practices of Māori Television, and how these practices have changed over the years in response to wider social, political and cultural forces.

Chapter four develops an audience framework to provide partial insights into the ways in which some viewers watch Māori Television, the meanings they make of Māori Television programming, and the ideas that some have as to what Māori Television could do differently. Based on eight focus groups from around the country conducted between 2012 and 2013 and involving participants who mostly self-identified as Māori, it offers insights and stories from some of those who access Māori Television content on a range of screens.

A significant recurring theme emerging from interviewee and focus group kōrero was the role of media in strengthening Indigenous political and cultural representations, and television's capacity to affirm and contribute to Māori ways of being and doing. In light of this kōrero, chapter five offers a politics of culture framework for understanding Māori Television, which is an overtly political framing derived from aspects of kōrero given by Māori Television stakeholders, including Māori Television staff, board and governance members, funders and media producers, as well as audiences. This final framework is designed to reveal the political and cultural aspirations tied to television, and the utopian dimensions embedded in such aspirations. Focusing on the politics surrounding cultural production, as well as on television's storytelling role in affirming the diverse worlds of Māori, it considers Māori Television's contribution to, and challenges in the face of, an overtly ideological way of looking at television. By offering this framework it gives voice to the aspirations that some have for Māori Television as an ideal, while also underscoring the challenging and constraining conditions under which television is made.

To demonstrate the utility of a five-framework approach to matters of Māori media, chapter six provides a brief glimpse of how these frameworks might work in relation to the 2013 events surrounding the current affairs programme *Native Affairs,* and its coverage of financial matters to do with Te Kōhanga Reo National Trust and its subsidiary arm Te Pātaka Ōhanga. This media event generated public debate about the role of a Māori news media programme, and the wider function of an Indigenous television provider, in an era when public-service media values are in decline. While coverage of Te Kōhanga Reo National Trust polarised many Māori communities, this chapter argues that the issues raised by the *Native Affairs* and Te Kōhanga Reo National Trust media event demonstrate Māori Television's capacity to stimulate debate, to raise matters of concern for te ao Māori, and to incite discourses about Māori cultural practices, world views and concerns, within a media environment historically hostile to such perspectives.

In sum, this book provides ways of thinking about the complex set of conditions underpinning those who work in the Māori media sector, and those who have laboured to realise a Māori television provider. In a world where viewers increasingly access media content on multiple platforms, from both local and global sources, and where commercialism prevails, the challenges facing any free-to-air media provider are complex. Indigenous media organisations such as Māori Television have the added challenge of protecting and promoting a minority language in a society where English speakers dominate, and providing a media platform flexible enough to give space to the many diverse voices from te ao Māori. The organisation must also conduct itself in a Māori way, and, as noted earlier, what constitutes a Māori way of being and doing is an increasingly vexed question. This book draws on kōrero from those who have a stake in Māori Television, to provide frameworks for understanding the complex ideals and expectations facing this Indigenous media provider.

Chapter One

The Long Struggle for Māori Television

> In 1972, Hana Jackson organised a petition to Parliament and it was an obvious place for us to go, to support Māori Language Day and Māori Language Week. As part of that activity, we had lots of discussion about the power of the media and how Māori were not valued, not only Māori language, but Māori people and Māori tikanga. So lots of discussion about the power of the media, and in 1978 we took another petition to Parliament, requesting that a Māori television production unit be established and that it should start producing a twenty-minute *Country Calendar* type programme, which became *Koha*. (C. Dewes, interview, 2012)

One cannot understand the impact and significance of Māori Television without understanding the longer history of Indigenous struggle in this country. Māori have been at the forefront of media activism in Aotearoa New Zealand for more than four decades, with the 1840 Te Tiriti o Waitangi (Treaty of Waitangi) the mobilising force. Article II of the Treaty guarantees that the New Zealand government, as one of the two Treaty partners, is responsible for protecting and promoting all things held dear to Māori: 'taonga'. Media activists have argued that te reo and tikanga Māori constitute important taonga of Māori society and thus are protected under Te Tiriti o Waitangi.

Given these roots, Māori broadcasting is directly linked to strategies of language and cultural revitalisation, and to issues of equitable Māori representation as a partner to Te Tiriti. As long-standing Māori educator Cathy Dewes (Te Arawa, Ngāti Porou)* suggests in the quotation above, the power

---

* This book includes iwi affiliations only for those who participated in the research and who agreed to having this information included.

of the media plays a crucial role in shoring up a sense of self and collective identity. If language is the cornerstone of a people's way of being, and if that language is not heard on a daily basis through media outlets and in everyday conversation, how can a people thrive? If the perspectives shown on television, heard on radio and filtered through feature films are resoundingly non-Māori, what does this do to the status of te reo and the many different values, norms and practices embedded in the language that help constitute diverse Māori worlds? Joris de Bres of the Human Rights Commission has argued that 'the right to language is a vital human right, because it goes to the very heart of a person's identity and culture. It is vital for the realisation of people's cultural, civil, political, social and economic rights' (Te Puni Kōkiri, 2011a, p. 21). Many generations of Māori have struggled to make the Crown fulfil its obligations under Te Tiriti o Waitangi. These struggles have come at personal and financial cost to Māori, and the struggles continue today.

Cathy Dewes's reflections on political strategies in the 1970s relate to present-day circumstances. According to Dewes, *Koha* (a 30-minute Māori magazine programme that emerged in 1980) was initially devised as a style of television that might appeal to 'heartland New Zealand', in the same way as the long-running television series *Country Calendar*, which covers rural life in Aotearoa. One tactic at the time was to think of how Māori perspectives and language might infiltrate the 'white man's house' and become a normalised and everyday part of the life of the nation. In a single-channel era where channel surfing was not yet an established norm, Dewes describes an incident associated with Māori Language Week activities:

> On television, a Pākehā student of Māori language was engaged to provide continuity in Māori during Māori Language Week. We knew that there would be a huge backlash from the Pākehā rednecks so we consciously, deliberately chose a Pākehā in order to show them that this was not just a Māori thing, that Pākehā were convinced of the value of te reo Māori as well. Because that was a huge invasion into their homes, a Māori-speaking person in their sitting rooms. They had nowhere else to go unless they switched it off or muted her, even though she was on for such a short time. (C. Dewes, interview, 2012)

Dewes's comments suggest that stealth tactics were a necessary feature of political strategies at the time, and that dealing with a large non-Māori majority was a crucial factor in attempts to advance Māori causes. Accordingly, getting non-Māori to engage with the language was an important part of language survival strategies.

Although New Zealand television culture has experienced significant shifts in attitudes towards te reo Māori since the 1970s, as well as technological shifts from a single-channel era to an era of digital plenty, there are interesting parallels between the 1970s strategies suggested by Dewes and the way in which former CEO of Māori Television Jim Mather (Ngāti Awa, Ngāi Tūhoe; CEO from 2005–2013) described Māori Television in 2013.

In an article titled 'From Political Football to Part of the Furniture', Mather noted that two-thirds of the viewers who watch Māori Television are not Māori (Hubbard, 2013, p. A6).* Mather acknowledged that he was pleased about the broad appeal the broadcaster had garnered. For him, te reo 'is a treasure belonging to all New Zealanders' and Māori Television is 'much more than a language revitalisation channel'. Mather argues for the importance of a large non-Māori majority in advancing the aspirations of Māori, and that by having all New Zealanders value te reo, Māori language and culture might become an everyday factor in the life of the nation, or 'part of the furniture'. Yet, one could ask, whose house is this furniture in?

When Moana Jackson and Atareta Poananga developed their Ngā Whare Rua or 'two-house' model for understanding the struggle for Māori self-determination, they drew on examples from Māori television programming found on national broadcaster TVNZ. This model has become a popular reference point for Māori media scholars:

> The TV One programmes *Marae* and *Te Karere* are contained within the mainstream house.... Both programmes attempt to portray values, language and issues related to the Māori house.... Within the mainstream house they occupy a 'room', but the 'house' is not Māori. They are still a minority within the whole industry and have to conform to the policies and practices of the mainstream house. They are probably fortunate that they are there at all, given that many ethnic minorities do not have a presence in the mainstream house. (Te Kawa a Māui Media Research Team, 2005, p. 23 cited in Hokowhitu and Devadas, 2013, p. xxix)

---

* These figures are based on a telephone survey conducted by Research New Zealand on behalf of Māori Television on 2–25 November 2011 and including a sample range of n=1004 respondents aged 15+. In 2014 a Colmar Brunton survey conducted on behalf of NZ On Air found that 50 per cent of Māori Television viewers were Māori. This figure was based on N=1000 telephone and N=400 online interviews conducted on 4 April–4 May 2014 (excluding Easter and Anzac Day) and involving respondents aged 15+.

In the wake of the 2004 launch of Māori Television, the possibilities for Māori control over media have improved. Following Jackson and Poananga's model, Māori Television has significantly increased the amount of Māori media content available when compared to the offerings on other free-to-air networks such as TVNZ and MediaWorks. But does Māori Television constitute a house of its own, run by Māori, for Māori and about Māori? Māori Television constituted a significant shift in terms of offering a greater range of Māori media, on multiple screens, nationally and internationally – and in prime time – and this shift has been achieved by deftly negotiating a range of cultural, technological, institutional and historical factors. Aspects of government policy, the funding climate, and the institutional norms of television have helped to shape Māori Television practices. Yet these policies, funding regimes and television industry norms (how programming should look and sound, as well as the focus on audience share) are practices long embedded in non-Māori ways of doing things. As such, Māori Television offers intriguing insights into how a media entity can contribute to te reo and tikanga Māori, and thus to the betterment of te ao Māori, while working within these existing constraints.

A historical framework for understanding the struggle to establish Māori Television and the diverse expectations placed upon it provides insights. This framework allows us to see how the Māori media sector is connected to larger efforts to have the Crown recognise its obligations under Te Tiriti o Waitangi. Māori Television is tied to a larger Tiriti-based politics, at the same time as it is part of a broader media culture dominated by an English-speaking non-Māori majority.

Its history also draws attention to Māori Television's educational role in revitalising a minority language, using a popular form of entertainment media. Educational imperatives bump up against entertainment imperatives, in ways that give rise to persisting tensions between those who think that a Māori media provider should appeal to a broad audience, and those who think the network should be more strictly by Māori, for Māori and about Māori. When Dewes describes the stealth tactics of the 1970s (to infiltrate the 'white man's house' with te reo), her approach resonates with the inclusive strategy championed by Mather in 2013. Both Dewes and Mather underscore the importance of a large non-Māori majority to Māori media initiatives. Yet other Māori Television stakeholders have consistently argued for a more Māori-focused approach to Māori media.

Te Tiriti, te reo and the fight for broadcasting

Ko te reo te mauri o te mana Maori.
James Henare, 1985 (cited in Waitangi Tribunal, 1986, p. 43)

James Henare's often-cited whakataukī states that the Māori language is the essence of Māori identity, and it is this viewpoint that has grounded Māori efforts for greater access to media technologies. Prior to Māori Television's emergence, the wider television culture of Aotearoa New Zealand had been dominated by the English language and by non-Māori perspectives. Everyday linguistic dominance places in peril the possibility of thinking from a perspective other than English. Ngāti Porou director and writer Kath Akuhata-Brown suggests that te reo has the power and potential 'to change the internal thinking process of those who are able to speak it'. Discussing the impact that understanding te reo can have on personal identity, Akuhata-Brown stated:

> I know what it means to have another language. You know, the sort of person you can be with your own language. Especially te reo, it is so beautiful. I think you look at statistics affecting Māori right now – they are dreadful. Our language is the language of poetry. Imagine, a nation of poets. (K. Akuhata-Brown, interview, 2012)

Akuhata-Brown's kōrero underscores the vital role that language plays in expressing the internal life of an individual and, by extension, the internal life of cultural groups and of a nation. The capacity to think, do and be through the medium of te reo Māori has been denied to many generations of Māori due to historical and contemporary forces. Linguist Joshua Fishman has argued that it takes one generation to lose a language but at least three generations to revive it (Fishman, 1991). Under Te Tiriti o Waitangi, the Crown, as well as Māori, has a responsibility to protect and promote Māori language and culture. As Akuhata-Brown's comments suggest, the renewal of te reo Māori has benefits for all citizens of Aotearoa.

Aotearoa's predominantly monolingual culture is due to settler government practices in the early colonial era, and ongoing assimilationist policies. While colonial government agents and church representatives in the early days of settlement made efforts to gain proficiency in te reo Māori, these attempts were often used to progress colonial and religious projects. *Te Reo*

Mauriora, the 2011 review of state spending in the Māori-language sector and on the Māori Language Strategy, provided the following perspective:

> From the intended and forced break up of Māori communities, the alienation of Māori from their land and territories to the specific laws that attacked the status and use of te reo by Māori children and their families, the Crown and its agents led, resourced and supported various campaigns that eroded the position of te reo in this country. (Te Puni Kōkiri, 2011a, p. 31)

Government edicts, such as Governor George Grey's Ordinance of 1847, ensured funding for English-language learners only. Acts of Parliament, such as the 1867 Native Schools Act, made sure that schools were English-speaking only, and those who spoke te reo were often violently punished (Te Taura Whiri i te Reo Māori, Te Puni Kōkiri, Statistics New Zealand, 1995). In the 1930s te reo remained the dominant language for Māori homes and communities, but the use of English increased in other sections of society. After the Second World War and during the 1950s and 1960s, the increase in urban migration saw a decline in the use of te reo. Over the next few decades the percentage of Māori school children able to speak Māori went from 90 per cent in 1913, to 26 per cent in 1953.* Out of this newly urbanised Indigenous population arose new forms of Māori political agency hitherto unseen (Hill, 2012).

In the same year that New Zealand's first television broadcast took place (1960), Jack Hunn was commissioned to provide a report on the Maori Affairs department. His report, known as 'The Hunn Report', ranged wider than just the department to include commentary on the state of Māori culture more generally. Hunn recommended that New Zealand move beyond 'assimilation' to 'integration' in order to become one people through the mixing of two cultures. Hunn found that while 'the fittest elements' of Māori culture had survived, 'language, arts and crafts, and the institutions of the marae are the chief relics' (Hunn, 1961, p. 15).

Not all agreed with this report. In contrast to Hunn's perspective, the 1960s saw a range of different discussions by Māori occurring on marae, at universities and in homes about the decline in the use of te reo Māori, and the need for educational and broadcast institutions to take seriously

---

* http://www.parliament.nz/timeline, 2013.

the Crown's obligations to Te Tiriti o Waitangi. Māori advocacy groups Ngā Tamatoa and Te Reo Māori Society were significant drivers of change in this period. In 1972 representatives from these groups, led by Hana Jackson (née Te Hemara) and Lee Smith, formally submitted a petition to the government with over 30,000 signatories calling for Māori language to be offered in schools. This petition called for the Crown to deliver on its responsibilities to te reo Māori as guaranteed under Te Tiriti o Waitangi. According to Joan Metge, the petition stated:

> That courses in Maori language and aspects of Maori culture be offered in ALL those schools with large Maori rolls and that these same courses be offered, as a gift to the Pakeha from the Maori, in ALL other New Zealand schools as a positive effort to promote a more meaningful concept of Integration. (Metge, 1976, p. 99)

This petition led to the inauguration of the first Māori Language Day in 1972, and then the first Māori Language Week in 1975.

Also in 1975 the historically significant Māori Land March led by Dame Whina Cooper occurred, which highlighted Māori land loss. In that same year the Waitangi Tribunal was established to address Te Tiriti infringements. In 1979 Kāterina Te Heikōkō Mataira and Te Kumeroa Ngoingoi Pēwhairangi established the community-based language-learning movement Te Ataarangi, which sought to restore Māori-language knowledge to Māori adults within the community (Te Taura Whiri i te Reo, Te Puni Kōkiri, Statistics New Zealand, 1995). Three years later Te Kōhanga Reo movement emerged to foster the growth of te reo among preschoolers.

Many of the claims to the Waitangi Tribunal positioned the broadcasting sector as second only to the education sector in helping to support the revival of a language. Yet the struggles to make the Crown accountable for its obligations under Te Tiriti were long, costly and waged on multiple fronts. In 1976 the New Zealand Māori Council (chaired by Graham Latimer) made submissions on the Broadcasting Bill (under review at the time) calling for a weekly television programme addressing Māori and Polynesian affairs, educational programming for Māori, and a Māori radio station (Boyd-Bell, 1985).

Te Reo Māori Society presented a second petition in 1978 calling for the establishment of a Māori television production unit within the New Zealand Broadcasting Corporation, to 'add a Māori dimension to regular viewing'

(Middleton, 2010, p. 149). While significant works such as Barry Barclay and Michael King's *Tangata Whenua* documentary series had emerged in 1974, veteran broadcaster Tainui Stephens argues that:

> Māori people were rarely seen on television... the Māori language was almost never heard on the airwaves, and the whole spectrum of social and political issues important to Māori people were largely ignored both by radio and TV. (Middleton, 2010, p. 149)

In 1980 Ray Waru established the Māori Production Unit at TVNZ which featured the first regular Māori programme, a 30-minute magazine show (in English) called *Koha*, screened in prime time and featuring the talents of Merata Mita, Derek Fox, Wena Harawira, Tainui Stephens and Debra Reweti, among others. Ernie Leonard, a producer for *Koha*, would go on to become the first head of TVNZ's Māori Programmes Department in 1986. Aimed at a broad audience and with limited Māori-language content, Fox described *Koha* as 'a soft, cute window on Māori society through which Pākehā people could peer' (Stephens, 2004, p. 262).

During the 1982 Māori Language Week, Derek Fox (then a *Close Up* reporter and charged with providing a two-minute translation of the general news) used his brief to assemble a bulletin of Māori-focused news in te reo Māori. This eventually led to the emergence of *Te Karere*, the country's first regular Māori-language news programme.

While *Koha* and *Te Karere* were clear signs of progress, Debra Reweti describes the hostility of the workplace at the time:

> I can recall a respected Pākehā news reporter spinning on his heels angry that he had to wait for a *Te Karere* item to be edited, saying loud and clear, 'F_kin jungle bunnies' – the general attitude was that Māori programmes were of high nuisance value and minimal importance. (Middleton, 2010, p. 152)

Wena Harawira has suggested that the negative environment at TVNZ at that time was an inspiration to persist:

> So the nasty remarks from camera crews who referred to it as the 'coon round', the grumpy reporters who resented our work with the nasty camera crews, and the complaints of viewers who took offence at having 5-minutes of their TV time taken over by 'Māoris', provided even more incentive for *Te Karere* to endure. (Harawira, 2008)

More recently, Mihingarangi Forbes (Ngāti Paoa, Ngāti Maniapoto), former current affairs journalist and *Native Affairs* presenter for Māori Television, described her time at TVNZ in the following way:

> I was keen to go over to mainstream because I felt like I'd done *Te Karere*. I was young and probably had a huge ego and was really ambitious and thought, I can do that. I think the thing was I was just sick of being treated as the last cab off the rank, and that's often how you feel at *Te Karere* and within Māori programmes, because TVNZ, the institution, treats you like that. (M. Forbes, interview, 2013)

The 1980s saw a range of skilfully argued Waitangi Tribunal claims, and court proceedings by Māori against the Crown, including the BCNZ Assets Case, the Frequencies Cases and the Sale of Commercial Radio Cases. These actions were taken in response to the neoliberal reforms of the 1984 Labour government, including its decisions to turn broadcasting assets into state-owned enterprises and to auction off radio frequencies. When the government invited applications for a third television channel in 1985, the New Zealand Māori Council made a pitch under the name Aotearoa Broadcasting Systems. According to kaupapa Māori scholar Leonie Pihama the government and BCNZ withdrew support for Aotearoa Broadcasting Systems' bid at a crucial stage in the process, and the subsequent failure to secure the third channel warrant constituted a lost opportunity for the development of a Māori television channel (Pihama, 1996).

In 1985 Te Huirangi Waikerepuru and Ngā Kaiwhakapūmau i te Reo (Guardians of the Language) submitted the Te Reo Claim (WAI 11) to the Waitangi Tribunal, asking the tribunal to recommend 'that Te Reo Māori (The Māori Language) should be recognised as an official language throughout New Zealand, and for all purposes' (Waitangi Tribunal, 1986, p. 7). They argued that the Crown had breached the Treaty of Waitangi in failing to protect the Māori language as a taonga. A wide range of individuals and groups appeared before the tribunal as claimants, including the New Zealand Māori Council, the Māori Women's Welfare League, the Māori Economic Development Commission and Pakehas against Racism. Claimants told the tribunal that, 'Ka ngaro te reo, ka ngaro taua, pera i te ngaro o te Moa' (if the language be lost, people will be lost, as dead as the moa) (Waitangi Tribunal, 1986, p. 7).

At this time Dr Richard Benton produced the results of an extensive survey carried out by the Māori Unit of the New Zealand Council for Educational

Research, which identified a rapid decline in the number of Māori speakers. Noting that a major contribution to this decline was the lack of reo spoken in the home, Benton's report also noted adverse effects due to the media:

> For children especially, the massive influence of English at school, and in the neighbourhood through radio, television and the movies has had the same effect where the Maori language is concerned as pollutants have on the health of oysters in an oyster bed; when the environment becomes polluted beyond a critical point neither the oysters nor their linguistic counterpart can survive. (Benton, 1985, p. 4)

The claimants sought many specific recommendations, with the body of evidence before the tribunal relating to broadcasting being second only to that relating to education. Claimants urged the tribunal to recommend that particular radio stations be used for Māori-language transmission, and that one of the existing television channels be required to broadcast a minimum number of hours per day, or weekly, focused entirely on Māori language and culture. In the subsequent *Report of the Waitangi Tribunal on the Te Reo Maori Claim (Wai 11)* (Waitangi Tribunal, 1986), the tribunal established that the Māori language is a taonga under the Treaty of Waitangi and is the 'embodiment of the particular spiritual and mental concepts of the Maori' (Waitangi Tribunal, 1986, p. 17). The tribunal wrote in their report:

> We are quite clear in our view that Article II of the Treaty guarantees protection to the Maori language as we have said, and we are also quite clear in our view that the predominance of English in the media has had an adverse effect upon it. (p. 41)

This report resulted in the passing of the 1987 Māori Language Act, which made te reo Māori an official language of New Zealand. Te Taura Whiri i te Reo Māori (the Māori Language Commission) was established in this same year to promote and provide support for the language. While Māori were agitating for greater access to broadcast technologies at this time, the 1986 Royal Commission on Broadcasting undertook to examine the role of Māori language and culture in New Zealand's broadcasting environment. According to Rangi Matamua the commission made the following recommendations:

> [T]he establishment of a Māori Advisory Board, the independent production of Māori programmes, implementation of training programmes for Māori broadcasters and

journalists, and the immediate implementation of the Māori Radio Network proposal by Radio New Zealand. (Matamua, 2014, p. 337)

In 1988 Māori took court action against the government in relation to the BCNZ Restructuring Act, which was part of the government's strategy to transfer broadcasting assets into new state-owned enterprises. According to Trisha Dunleavy and Hester Joyce:

> Because the 1988–89 transfer process placed BCNZ assets momentarily in Crown hands, it was possible for an appeal to be lodged with the High Court by Māori authorities wanting to protect Māori language on television and radio... This intervention was important because, under pressure to secure a successful assets transfer process, the Crown made a legally binding commitment to provide for Māori broadcasting at a later date. (Dunleavy and Joyce, 2011, pp. 110–11)

Efforts by the New Zealand Māori Council and Ngā Kaiwhakapūmau i te Reo (via WAI 150 and WAI 26) eventually led to the 1993 Privy Council case which upheld the 1991 High Court findings in favour of the Crown, yet found that the Crown had an obligation to follow through on promises made to Māori relating to protecting and preserving te reo Māori via broadcasting technologies (Matamua, 2014). Parekura Horomia, the Labour Minister of Māori Affairs from 2000 to 2008, described the Privy Council decision in the following manner:

> A Māori television service was given impetus as a result of the 1993 Privy Council decision in the broadcasting assets case. The Privy Council noted, amongst other things, that the Government had made a commitment, by Cabinet agreement in 1991, to set aside funding for the purpose of promoting Māori language and culture in broadcasting, part or all of which could be used to assist in the development of special-purpose television. (Horomia, 2003, p. 4908)

As film and media scholar Roger Horrocks has argued, Treaty-based arguments in the late 1980s and in early 1990 slowed down attempts by the incumbent Labour government to sell off TVNZ (Horrocks, 2004). Based on tribunal recommendations in 1986 and 1990, a range of iwi radio stations emerged throughout the country, and Māori programme funding agency Te Reo Whakapuaki Irirangi, later known as Te Māngai Pāho (TMP), was established in 1993 and began operations in 1995. Under the legislative framework of the 1993 Broadcasting Amendment Act TMP was charged with the task of promoting Māori language and Māori culture, and 13.5 per cent of the broadcasting licence fee revenue received by NZ On Air was diverted to fund the initiative (Horrocks, 2004). While TMP was to provide specific funding for Māori programming, under broadcasting legislation, its sister funding agency, NZ On Air, also had an obligation to promote Māori language and culture. Between 2002 and 2008 NZ On Air's Rautaki Māori content strategy guided the assessment of their Māori programming funding, shifting in 2008 to a new title of Māori Programmes Innovation Fund (NZ On Air, 2010). In a 2010 report to NZ On Air, the research team Ngā Matakiirea discussed how NZ On Air had contributed to Māori programming:

> Initially, NZ On Air defined mainstream Māori programming as programmes with a high content of te reo and tikanga Māori. With Te Māngai Pāho taking on the role of funding these programmes in 1993 and receiving a proportion of NZ On Air funding to do so, the definition changed to 'mainstream programming, primarily in English, that features Māori and Māori perspectives intended for a general audience including Māori'. The definition has included (not always consistently) the requirement that 'to ensure an authentic Māori perspective . . . at least two of the three key roles of producer, director and writer/researcher must be Māori'. (NZ On Air, 2010, p. 4)

During the early 1990s the Minister of Communications, Maurice Williamson, under the incumbent National government, hosted a range of hui to discuss Māori views on broadcasting policy which eventually led to the 1991 report *Māori Broadcasting: Principles for the Future*. In 1996 a joint Māori–Crown Working Group on Broadcasting Policy was established, and in the same year the pilot Māori television initiative, Aotearoa Television Network (ATN), emerged for a brief period (thirteen weeks) in the Auckland region.

As Dunleavy and Joyce (2011) argue:

> Whilst the creation of ATN after decades of lobbying for a separate Māori TV channel was an important step forward, the trial was characterised by insufficient planning and a paucity of government funding, both of which led to the channel's collapse in 1997. (p. 177)

Some commentators at the time suggested that the venture was 'set up to fail' by insufficient resourcing and untenable time constraints. According to former employee Derek Burns:

> The most poignant fact in this whole saga is that, measured according to its delivery of quality television programmes, Aotearoa Television did not fail the Māori people ... the Government, and even more so, the [Opposition] Labour party, killed Aotearoa Television, and the television and print media put the nails in the coffin and buried it. (Burns, 1997, p. 7)

ATN's closure also received hostile media coverage that framed Māori broadcasting as a 'waste of tax payers' money' and that called into question the fiscal responsibilities of Māori organisations (Bell and Guyan, 1997).

Piripi Walker (Ngāti Raukawa), secretary for Ngā Kaiwhakapūmau i te Reo between 1984 and 1996, describes the political climate of these times:

> The agenda of the political parties was to absolutely stonewall the arrival of Māori Television. The cost was unconscionable and totally unpalatable to them politically and they sabotaged it year by year by year. All of the wherewithal had to be cantilevered into place over that sixteen continuous years of litigation. Nine big court cases, tribunal cases – which Māori had to fund. The language claim was lodged in 1985, and then through to 1997 with the end of the sale of the radio networks cases. Each of the large blocks, Māori had to conceive it, design it and cantilever it into place with wins in some cases, and with the Crown unable to resist it. The political parties, essentially neither of the two major parties allowed it into their manifesto. (P. Walker, interview, 2013)

In 1998 the National-led government supported the establishment of Te Reo Māori Television Trust (Te Awhiorangi), which presented a business case to the Minister on Māori broadcasting. In 2000 the ministry responsible for Māori broadcasting changed from the Ministry of Commerce to Te Puni Kōkiri. In this same year a Māori Broadcasting Advisory Committee (MBAC) was established, chaired by Derek Fox and including committee members Joanna Paul, Hone Harawira, Hone Edwards, Tainui Stephens, Hemana Waka, Robert Pouwhare and Te Maumoko August (Te Puni Kōkiri, 2000). MBAC were given just six weeks to make recommendations on Māori broadcasting policy based on the following vision:

Our vision is for a time when the Maori language can be seen and heard, and cherished by all New Zealanders. Our vision is for a time when hearing the Maori language on mainstream radio and seeing it on prime time TV is commonplace. Our vision is for a broadcasting service in this country through which Kaupapa Maori can be presented and debated in both English and Maori. Our vision is for a secure, comprehensive and widespread Maori media presence that has become a normal part of New Zealand life. (Te Puni Kōkiri Report, 2000, p. 3)

The efforts of MBAC and Te Awhiorangi eventually led to the Māori Television Establishment Board, and as former chair of the Māori Television Board Derek Fox stated, 'the process to breathe life into MTS began' (Fox, 2009, p. 14). Board members undertook the hard task of lobbying for better funding for the service, and conducted searches for premises that would suit their needs. Māori Television eventually came on air on 28 March 2004.

The period leading up to the launch saw non-Māori media outlets return to the alleged failings of ATN rather than the aspirations and intentions of the new channel (Kiriona, 2004). There was also controversy surrounding the 2002 appointment of the Canadian CEO, John Davy. Hired as the first CEO for Māori Television, and then fired six weeks later once it was discovered that his qualifications were false, Davy was sentenced to jail for eight months and subsequently deported.

In the wake of Davy's departure, Derek Fox was appointed as acting CEO for six months. When Fox subsequently resigned from this position in 2003 after a human resource issue, negative media coverage was prevalent again. ACT MP Rodney Hide told Members of Parliament that the Māori Television Service was wasting taxpayers' money and 'embarrassing Māori'. Addressing the Labour government's Māori Affairs Minister, Parekura Horomia, Hide stated: 'The minister needs to do some real fast explaining, and we need the Auditor-General to get inside and find out just where all these millions of dollars have gone.' Hide also asked: 'How much money are they going to pour into what is an obvious failure?' (*New Zealand Herald*, 22 August 2003). Despite these criticisms deputy chair of the Māori Television Establishment Board Ani Waaka took over as acting chief executive (with Wayne Walden as chair) and in February 2005 ex-accountant and former officer in the New Zealand Army Jim Mather became CEO of Māori Television, remaining a high-profile face of the network until his departure in October 2013. In May 2014 former chair of Ngā Aho Whakaari (a group that represents and advocates for the Māori screen production industry) and previous general manager of TVNZ's Māori and Pacific Programmes Department Paora Maxwell took up the position of CEO.

Describing the process of getting to air from the perspective of the Māori production sector, long-time language and culture consultant and media producer Chris Winitana throws light on the efforts involved to realise the vision for a Māori television network:

> Since 2002, independent producers have been pitching programme ideas at Māori television bosses. By mid-2002, scores of programmes have been given a broadcast convenant from the Māori Televison Service and have secured funding from the trove of Te Māngai Pāho. The Māori independent production community nationwide is going ten to the dozen. Camera and sound operators are busy to the max. Studios are booked out. Mini home studios, one reportedly in a barn, crop up to cope with the amount of work to be completed. Once the Māori Television Service starts, it will broadcast an average eight hours a day, seven days a week. By the end of 2004, it will have acquired 2,020 hours of programmes – 1,122 hours of which are original homemades. Māori language across its programme schedule will run between 60 and 70 percent of the time. That's a heck of a lot of language, when you are not used to any. (Winitana, 2011, p. 272)

Ten years after its launch, many politicians claim that Māori Television is 'the best public broadcaster' and 'the best of the free-to-air channels' in this country. Trevor Mallard has even suggested that if 'we put the management of the Māori Television Service [into TVNZ], maybe that might make a difference and we would have good television, rather than a bloated bureaucracy' (Mallard, 2013, p. 8792). From the earlier days of political ill will, legislative inertia and negative media coverage, those involved in the Māori media production sector proved that a Māori television service could provide quality broadcast content for a broad audience.

While there is no doubt that popularity and political favour are positive things for Māori Television, and for te ao Māori overall, the very language used to describe the broadcaster by politicians such as Mallard is the language of public-service television. Media scholar, practitioner and founding member of Ngā Aho Whakaari Ella Henry (Ngātikahu ki Whangaroa, Ngāti Kuri, Te Rārawa) expressed this concern when she stated:

> [W]e have ministers now talking about Māori Television in the same language they use to describe state broadcasters. That, to me, is hugely problematic. If Māori Television is ever to really deliver, not just language and cultural revitalisation, but self-determination, which was always, always the primary goal: that by revitalising our language and culture, we would strengthen our identity, and our resolve for sovereignty, for self-determination, for tino rangatiratanga. And the fact that that has not happened is a direct consequence of the creation of the Māori Television Service. (E. Henry, interview, 2012)

Henry's comments remind us of the activist roots of Māori Television, roots embedded in larger questions of Te Tiriti o Waitangi rights, and tino rangatiratanga. However, former CEO Jim Mather has stated that the broadcaster is 'much more than a language revitalisation channel' and has refuted the idea that Māori Television is about Māori self-determination:

> I don't think it's probably one of the objectives of Māori Television to be promoting Māori self-determination. I think I'd probably phrase it differently – that we're a flagship Māori organisation that promotes Māori language and culture, but more widely Māori success and, although respectful of the history of the organisation and the challenges to get it established, our focus is more firmly fixed on the future and what we can do there. We don't have any aspirations around promoting Māori self-determination, but I suppose the term 'tino rangatiratanga' is important to us. Having the independence to make the decisions that we think are going to be in the best interests of Māori viewers is really important to us. (J. Mather, interview, 2012)

These divergent viewpoints as to the primary role of Māori Television demonstrate the many different investments and agendas that are attached to this state-funded Indigenous broadcaster – as an existing institution, and as an ideal yet to be realised. While the argument for greater access to media institutions and technologies focused on language rights, and the Crown's obligation to protect and promote te reo, the activist roots of Māori media have always included a larger argument about the representational rights of Māori more generally.

So what do we make of the popularity of Māori Television among politicians and non-Māori audiences, in the wake of long-term historical resistance to Māori broadcasting rights? To answer this question we need to understand New Zealand's broader broadcast culture.

A brief overview of New Zealand television

> You can't see what's happening with Māori Television in isolation from a withdrawal of the concept of public. (L.T. Smith, interview, 2013)

Although Māori broadcasting has become an everyday household presence for many New Zealanders, this was not always the case. New Zealand's first regular television broadcast occurred in 1960, originally under the banner of the New Zealand Broadcasting Service and then the New Zealand Broadcasting Corporation (NZBC) in 1961. The NZBC was replaced by the Broadcasting Council of New Zealand (BCNZ) and finally by TVNZ from 1980 (Horrocks, 2004). Roger Horrocks suggests five phases in the history of regular New Zealand television:

a. government broadcasting (1960–61)
b. public service diluted by commercialism (1961–88)
c. TVNZ as a commercial broadcaster, counter-balanced by NZ On Air (1989–95)
d. dominant commercialism (1995–99)
e. attempts to revive public-service broadcasting (since 1999). (p. 26)

Media historian Trisha Dunleavy argues that the early days of television introduced cultural characteristics that still endure today. These include viewers being highly receptive to imported television content from the United States, Britain and Australia, and a small local population size that limited funds for locally produced material.

From 1975 to 1979 New Zealand television had two national channels: TV One, based in Wellington, and the Auckland-based channel TV Two, later renamed South Pacific Television (SPTV). From 1980 to 1988 these two channels were restructured under the name TVNZ and were characterised by a 'complementary scheduling' strategy, whereby one channel would not replicate offerings screened at the same time by the other channel (Dunleavy and Joyce, 2011, p. 44). In 1980 Ray Waru established TVNZ's Māori Production Unit, and in 1986 Ernie Leonard became the first head of the Māori Programmes Department. Programming included *Koha* (1980–89), *Te Karere* (1982–) and *Waka Huia* (1987–), the latter created by Whai Ngata, who also worked with Leonard to set up TVNZ's Māori Programmes Department.

In 1986 Te Manu Aute (with membership links to present-day Ngā Aho Whakaari) emerged as a significant Māori broadcasting lobby group, focused on promoting Māori perspectives on broadcasting. It included key industry personalities such as Barry Barclay, Merata Mita, Wi Kuki Kaa and Tama Poata. Te Manu Aute's manifesto stated:

> Every culture has a right and a responsibility to present its own culture to its own people. That responsibility is so fundamental it cannot be left in the hands of outsiders, nor usurped by them. (Barclay, 1996, p. 127)

Barclay relates how this period saw the emergence of Māori-run training workshops for the broadcast sector, including the Department of Māori Affairs-funded TVNZ training scheme Kimihia, designed to foster Māori into the industry.

Between February 1988 and March 1989 Kimihia provided training for Māori media practitioners such as John Miller, Rangimoana Taylor, Paora Maxwell, Tainui Stephens, Haunui Royal, Gabrielle Huria and Whetu Fala, among others. According to John Miller two positive outcomes came of the Kimihia programme. Writing in 1989 Rangimoana Taylor and Miller argued that due to the scheme:

> There are now more Maori people around who know something about how television stations are run – and, more importantly, have a much sharper perception and understanding as to the total necessity for Maori people to some day control and operate their own TV stations producing programmes of direct interest and relevance to the Maori people, *and* screened at a time of day when the people will actually see them! (Taylor and Miller, 1989, p. 13)

This period also saw the release of the first Māori feature films, *Ngati* (1987), by Barclay, and *Mauri* (1988), by Merata Mita. It also saw the failed bid by the New Zealand Māori Council to launch a third channel (discussed earlier), a bid won by TV3, the first privately owned channel. TV3 emerged in 1989 but went into receivership after only six months.

By the late 1980s the once heavily regulated television sector had undergone extensive deregulation. The 1989 Broadcasting Act restructured TVNZ as a state-owned enterprise (SOE), a move that was considered by many to be a bid to make TVNZ attractive to potential buyers (Horrocks, 2004). This prompted Māori to take the legal actions described earlier. In this period television was treated as a business, and networks and transmission frequencies as assets to be exploited for profit (Easton, 1997). According to Horrocks, this new model included:

> increased advertising and sponsorship, more 'populist' programmes (with an emphasis on brisk pacing and emotional impact), a rejection of slow and complex modes of presentation, an increased interest in strategic scheduling and the 'branding' of channels, and a huge expansion in ratings, market research, and financial scrutiny of every area of the schedule and every series. (Horrocks, 2004, p. 30)

By 1999 the government had abolished the Public Broadcasting Fee, a key feature of the funding of NZ On Air (the institution developed to support public-service programming), and TVNZ sold its shares in the pay television service Sky, a service that 'started in 1990 but became a major player in 1996 when it purchased major rugby union and league games' (Horrocks, 2004, p. 34). In 2003, through the TVNZ Act, the Labour-led government changed the status of TVNZ from an SOE to a Crown-owned company (CROC) and devised a charter for the broadcaster, which included a dual mandate to deliver public-service content at the same time as remaining commercially viable. NZ On Air were put in charge of TVNZ's charter funds to ensure transparency and accountability. When the National-led government came to power in 2008, these charter funds became part of a contestable pool of monies called the Platinum Fund. By 2011 the charter era was over.

Between 2004 and 2007 the Labour-led government devised a range of initiatives to address technological change in the media sector, while maintaining some form of commitment to public-service television and Te Tiriti o Waitangi-protected media obligations. The government established the digital platform Freeview, and as a strategy to encourage viewers over to digital before the 2013 digital switch over, the government launched TVNZ6, and in the following year TVNZ7, both publicly funded digital channels. TVNZ6 provided education and entertainment programming primarily for preschoolers and families, while TVNZ7 offered news, factual and arts programming.

TVNZ6 ceased broadcasting in February 2011 and was replaced in March 2011 by TVNZ U, targeted at a youth audience (15 to 24). TVNZ7 was closed down in July 2012 by the National-led government and replaced by the timeshift channel TVOne Plus 1. TVNZ6 and TVNZ7's popular public-service content, such as *Kidzone* and *Heartland* (the latter including archival programming from TVNZ funded by taxes), was now locked behind Sky's pay wall (Norris, 2010). Freeview became firmly embedded in New Zealand's television environment, making up approximately 61.7 per cent of the digital television share in 2014. In 2013 New Zealand's digital switch over was completed, meaning all New Zealanders now needed Freeview, Sky, IGLOO (2012–2016) or Vodafone to watch any kind of free-to-air television. As a consequence of the digital switch over, New Zealand audiences lost free-to-air access to community television provider Triangle TV, which also operated Stratos Television between 2007 and 2011. In 2013 Triangle TV reappeared on Sky as FACE TV.

In 2014 the broadcasting environment surrounding Māori Television included two major free-to-air broadcasters: TVNZ (TV One and TV2) and MediaWorks (TV3 and C4). Other free-to-air broadcasters included Sky's channel Prime. Sky also offered a pay television service (NZ On Air, 2014a).

From 2001 all major free-to-air channels were available on Sky's digital satellite service, including Māori Television from 2004. Unlike some other countries, New Zealand has no restrictions on cross-media ownership, and it does not require Sky to pay a levy on its profits to subsidise public-service television. Sky also has no imperative to share access to sporting coverage. In 2009 the new National government shut down the Labour-proposed review of the policy and regulation governing the digital broadcast market, which would have raised some significant questions about Sky's dominance in New Zealand's media culture (P. Thompson, 2011).

Given this larger broadcasting context, one must understand Māori Television in relation to a pervasive commercial climate, with television audiences still highly receptive to imported television content from the United States, Britain and Australia. The National government gave no priority to public-service television, and indeed, as Peter Thompson argues, 'the government will have us believe that public service television is merely a "nice-to-have" and that in the current financial climate we simply can't afford it' (cited in Barton, 2011). Ella Henry described the media climate in 2012:

> If you look at TV One, TV2 and TV3 it's just a shambles what they deliver to New Zealand audiences. So what Māori Television delivers to Māori audiences and New Zealand audiences is interesting, exciting, innovative, informative entertainment and for that they deserve to be praised. (E. Henry, interview, 2012)

But to return to Henry's concerns about Māori Television being seen as a state broadcaster, how might we better understand Māori Television outside of the frame of public-service television? For this we need to consider television's contribution to language and cultural rejuvenation.

Television's role in language and cultural revitalisation

> I've always said that the Māori Television channel is worth 25 MPs to Māori; that's my equation on the matter. (P. Walker, interview, 2013)

Māori struggles to have the Crown uphold obligations to te reo have been closely related to the larger issue of minority rights in a country where Māori constitute 14.9 per cent of the general population (Statistics New Zealand, 2013). For many, the fight for te reo involves a larger fight for the voice of Māori to be heard in public forums, and for recognition of te reo through legislation and policies. As Piripi Walker's statement suggests, Māori Television's representational role goes beyond simply offering te reo Māori language provision – it is considered by some to have a significant political function.

Given that 'the current reality is that 23 per cent of the Māori population identify themselves as being able to speak te reo to some degree' (Te Puni Kōkiri, 2011a, p. 27), offering content that appeals to non-te reo speaking Māori is important. This explains Māori Television's approach to programming in the early days. As former Māori Television executive member Joanna Paul (Ngāi Te Rangi) notes:

> When you look at the stage that we were at, the stats were something like 4 per cent of Māori were native language speakers, and of those the majority were over 65 years old. Then you had a 60-something percentage who were learning, but they were learning at about [language] level one. The rest of them either didn't give a damn or spoke English. What we needed to do was encourage them to come over to Māori Television, and talk to them in a language that they understood. I disagreed with some of the more, what I term the extreme, both board members, and, subsequently, independent industry people, who believed that we should only be making te reo programmes. The reason I did so was because we had the chance to have a public-service television broadcast system for Māori by Māori. (J. Paul, interview, 2012)

This approach continues today and involves a recurring demand to find a balance of content that appeals to three kinds of viewers: fluent speakers, second-language learners, and a receptive audience who have little or no te reo capacity. As the 2008 to 2014 general manager of programming Haunui Royal (Ngāti Raukawa, Parehauraki, Ngāpuhi) argues:

> There is te reo which is the language, and te reo which is the voice, and that we are the voice of Māori people. It was the driver. I think language was the political leverage that got us there because by using the Waitangi Tribunal – the language case, so Article II [of the Treaty] and te reo [being seen as a taonga] – that was our leverage to get resourced to be a broadcaster. But it was always broader to the broadcasters and the whole argument, it wasn't just about the language, it was about 'we're invisible over here, let's get our own channel in and have some sense of independence, and put in prime time those things we think are important'. And language, of course, was really significant within it, but not the only thing.* (H. Royal, interview, 2012)

Implicit in this statement are assumptions about television's capacity to provide uplift and support for language and for cultural perspectives. But how exactly does a television broadcaster help shape greater literacies in te reo and tikanga Māori?

Research on language and media demonstrates that there is no way to identify a definitive link between broadcasting practices and increases in the health of a language (Bell, 2010; Hollings, 2005; Te Puni Kōkiri, 2011c). Indeed, Māori language and broadcasting scholar Rangi Matamua argued in 2014:

> With more than twenty years of Māori-controlled radio and nearly a decade of Māori television, it would be logical to conclude that the te reo Māori situation has improved considerably. Yet this is not the case, and recent research suggests that the position of te reo Māori has, in fact, deteriorated in the past twenty years. (Matamua, 2014, p. 343)

The recent research alluded to by Matamua could be the 2013 census, which found that 125,352 Māori (21.3 per cent) could hold a conversation about a lot of everyday things in te reo Māori, a 4.8 per cent decrease from the

---

* Royal held the position of general manager of programming from 2008 to 2014. In 2015 his title was changed to head of programming.

2006 census (Statistics New Zealand, 2013). Matamua went on to acknowledge how the founding argument for the development of Māori radio and television (based on their role in supporting language and culture) placed too much responsibility for language acquisition on media providers. Matamua noted that media entities such as Māori Television had provided valuable resources for language uplift, including language-acquisition programming, and te reo Māori role models such as Julian Wilcox, Pānia Papa and Scotty Morrison, and yet Māori did not appear to be taking up the opportunities provided by such resources. Placing emphasis on the importance of Māori participation in such media opportunities, Matamua concluded:

> Without the support of the people, these mediums [radio and television] will become lost amidst the numerous languages and voices that invade the airwaves every day, and this vitally important resource will never realise its full potential. (Matamua, 2014, p. 347)

In the wake of disconcerting reports on the health of te reo Māori, the onus is not just on Māori to participate more fully in Māori-language media, but also on the Crown, which has a role to play. There is a pressing imperative to develop frameworks of analysis that can account for the more intangible and longitudinal impacts of broadcasting, and its role in language wellbeing. The census only measures language use, and not the role that Māori media organisations might play in enhancing the voice and representational powers of minority communities.

Many media scholars and media practitioners agree that Māori broadcasting has the ability to support this minority language and culture in ways that may effect longitudinal change. According to Allan Bell, a language and media scholar called as expert witness in claims to the Waitangi Tribunal from the late 1980s to the late 1990s, Māori broadcasting has the power to transmit and teach the language to new generations of speakers, and by using broadcast technologies the prestige (or mana) of the language is promoted and uplifted. Ruth Lysaght, a scholar who conducted a comparative analysis of Māori Television and Irish broadcaster Teilifís na Gaeilge (TG4), argues that the visibility of a minority language across a broader audience encourages non-speakers, and reassures fluent speakers that the language is viable and vibrant (Lysaght, 2010). Mike Cormack, a scholar studying Gaelic media in Scotland, argues that by enabling minority languages to be heard in public domains, the language is affirmed in a modern and contemporary sense and that can help shape prevailing notions of national identity (Cormack, 2007).

Not only do we need more research and expanded research paradigms on the media's relationship to te reo Māori and tikanga Māori, we need the labour of Māori Television practitioners to be seen in the light of initiatives and institutions in the larger Māori-language sector. Jo Mane, an expert in Māori radio, argues (along with many others) that broadcasting needs to be part of a co-ordinated approach to language uplift including the education and public sectors (Mane, 2009). This is also the viewpoint of former Māori Television programming commissioner Annie Murray (Te Arawa), who said of Māori Television in 2013:

> We are just one waka in the fleet and there needs to be an overarching strategy from the government to guide us, and that hasn't happened, and it doesn't appear to be coming anytime soon, so we need to work it out for ourselves for now. (A. Murray, interview, 2013)

While the 2014 review of the Māori Language Bill promised significant shifts in the Māori-language sector in the near future, Murray's point of view chimes with Mike Cormack's argument that an inclusive approach needs to be taken to address how the media can contribute to the maintenance of a minority language. This is because media institutions and texts are not primarily designed to have a direct and practical effect on language revitalisation. As Cormack argues, '[a]sking the media to help in language maintenance is a bit like using an axe to dig a hole – it may be possible but it is certainly not what it was intended for' (2007, p. 62). Former teacher and producer of the popular bilingual programme *Hunting Aotearoa* Piripi Curtis (Te Arawa) expresses a similar view about the limits of television as a teaching tool:

> Sometimes I think people confuse MTS's role to revitalise te reo with teaching te reo. Televison is not a stand-alone teaching tool. Teaching and learning is a two-way process between the teacher and the learner. Assessment and evaluation are teaching tools that can only be used (effectively) through human interaction. While we can broadcast some amazing and inspirational teachers of te reo, at the end of the day, television is a one-way process. It is a tool to support the teaching and learning that happens at our kōhanga, kura and whare wānanga et cetera. Televison's greatest impact

is to help shape societal attitudes and promote te reo and tikanga in a positive way, and thus set a positive platform needed for those learning te reo and understanding our tikanga in this country. (P. Curtis, interview, 2014)

One emerging research paradigm making an impact on the Māori media sector is the ZePA model of language revitalisation developed by Rawinia Higgins and Poia Rewi. Their book, *The Value of the Māori Language: Te Hua o te Reo Māori* (2014), acknowledges the lack of research on Māori language, and offers the first sustained examination of the perceived value of te reo Māori since the language became official in 1987. In their book the editors provide a provocative critique of existing language strategies, as well as offering a model for thinking about the attitudinal and psychological positions accompanying language-use practices. Higgins and Rewi pose a challenge to existing approaches to language revitalisation (particularly to the 2003 Te Puni Kōkiri and Te Taura Whiri i te Reo Māori language strategy), which are founded on arguments to do with the language's status as a taonga under Article II of Te Tiriti o Waitangi, approaches that focus on increasing the number of te reo speakers and enhancing proficiency levels. Such approaches, they argue, run the risk of confining te reo Māori to particular domains of New Zealand society, with Māori the privileged stakeholders in language acquisition.

Higgins and Rewi argue for a co-ordinated and inclusive model of language normalisation that treats te reo Māori as a living language, relevant to a dynamic and modern society. They offer a framework for thinking about the attitudes underpinning language use, and have devised the acronym ZePA to describe these attitudes in relation to the following zones:

- Zero (kore), which reflects individuals positioned in a dismissive or resistant attitude to the Māori language
- Passive (pō), which reflects a cohort that is relatively inert in relation to te reo Māori use, but with a receptive and accommodating approach to Māori-language acquisition
- Active (awatea), which describes those individuals who 'operationalise' the language and who 'actively strive to advance the Māori language in all arenas' (Higgins and Rewi, 2014, p. 23).

The ZePA model departs from earlier strategies that sought to measure, scale or grade language proficiency. Instead, the zones express attitudes and capacities that enable reflection on how individuals or entities might be shifted, either left or right, along the ZePA continuum. Thus 'right-shifting' encapsulates this alternative model of language normalisation:

> Right-shifting demonstrates a transition across the three stages, from a state of Zero thinking or acting to a Passive position, which means a shift is at least made at a conscious level. We use 'conscious' here, as opposed to subconscious, because in terms of considering the existence of the Māori language, an individual or entity has moved from a point of zero-consideration and possibly zero knowledge, to entertaining a thought regarding it. The shift from Passive to Active means a commitment to operationalising the conscious: transferring the thought to action. (Higgins and Rewi, 2014, p. 28)

Higgins and Rewi argue for a more inclusive approach to te reo Māori, whereby all sections of society have a relationship with the language, and where a Zero positioning still affirms a link with te reo – albeit a resistant one. Instead of confining te reo initiatives to Māori communities, households and marae, Higgins and Rewi argue that responsibility for te reo needs to be taken on by non-Māori as well. One of the most crucial sites of activity the ZePA model identifies is the breaking down of negative attitudes towards te reo, and the development of an overarching strategy 'that is developed with Māori that is equally inclusive of non-Māori' (p. 29). Rather than Article II of Te Tiriti as the founding principle of language strategies, 'that speaks of the language as an archaic taonga to be preserved', the editors recommend that Article III be the founding principle, which promotes te reo Māori 'as part of the citizenship of this country' for all New Zealanders (p. 31).

The argument for Māori Television's existence was based on Article II of Te Tiriti; yet Higgins and Rewi's focus on citizenship as the basis for language strategies complements existing scholarship on the socialising role played by television, and its potential impact on language use. For Bell, the technologies of television can enhance the mana of te reo Māori; for Lysaght, greater visibility of te reo reassures fluent speakers; while Cormack argues that greater public presence of a minority language can enhance its relevance and contemporary nature.

Higgins and Rewi's emphasis on an inclusive and co-ordinated approach to language normalisation fits with the broad audience appeal that is such a hallmark of Māori Television's programming strategies, as we shall see in chapter three. When asked about the significance of non-Māori viewers of Māori Television, Higgins noted:

> Public engagement in Māori Television is moving non-Māori, and Māori with little or no language proficiency, viewers who were potentially in the Zero zone, into a Passive zone. For us ZePA was never developed to measure proficiency, it was about understanding what shifts people to change their attitudes and behaviours when it comes to the language. Within that zone there might be varying levels of what Passive and Active means. We view Māori Television as having the ability to shift people who choose to engage with it. They are at least passively engaged and don't have a bad attitude [to te reo] because if they did they'd just change the channel. (R. Higgins, interview, 2014)

As language specialists, these researchers concentrate on te reo as language rather than as voice. A media studies perspective can help shed light on ways of understanding Māori Television's potential contribution to enhancing the representational powers (both cultural and political) of this Indigenous broadcaster. A key concept from media studies relevant to this discussion is the agenda-setting function of the media, which posits that the media may not tell us what to think, but certainly tells us what to think about (McCombs and Shaw, 1972).

If te reo and Māori representations are now more prominent in the public domain due to the emergence of Māori Television, perhaps the broadcaster has the potential to shape emerging and ongoing narratives of what it means to live and be in Aotearoa. An agenda-setting function is reflected in comments made by interviewees about the possible progressive effects of seeing and hearing more Māori programming on screen.

Many of those interviewed noted how Māori Television's coverage of news events from the viewpoint of Māori could help foster an increase in non-Māori support, and enhance understanding of Māori issues. Such perspectives suggest that the more people are exposed to te reo and Māori ways of thinking, the more likely it is they will understand the wider issues facing Māori. Political commentator and academic Maria Bargh (Te Arawa, Ngāti Awa) demonstrates such a perspective when she discusses Māori Television's non-Māori audience:

Knowing that lots of non-Māori watch Māori TV is important, because it supports and encourages the existence of Māori TV and encourages Pākehā to have more positive ideas about Māori generally, and I think that assists us when we seek constitutional change or rights regarding say water, or whatever it might be. Perhaps these slightly more positive images of Māori just sit at the back of people's minds, but hopefully those lingering images might come to the fore when they come across say some nasty comments about Māori in the paper. Hopefully those lingering images of Māori might at the very least make them puzzle over the nasty comments about Māori, and at best might make them do something to stick up for Māori. (M. Bargh, interview, 2012)

Minister of Māori Development Te Ururoa Flavell (Ngāpuhi, Ngāti Rangiwewehi, Te Arawa) made a similar argument in 2013 when he talked of the importance of having a mainstream audience for Māori Television:

It's important that it brings a particular segment of New Zealand society across the line to have an understanding about how Māori feel, how we do things – tangi, all those things that are involved, the King movement, why do Māori believe in a King movement? What's it all about? Who are the key players? So now, many people are a lot wiser. If King Tuheitia calls a meeting, they actually know who he is, number one; where he lives, number two; and his place in terms of, and Tainui's place in terms of, the bigger Māori picture. So it was a positive move in terms of bridging the gap, in terms of race relations, I think, because it opened people's eyes up to a number of things. That's generally the call I understand from those who watch Māori Television – that it opens their eyes up to issues that they'd never ever thought about, simply because the mainstream provider doesn't do it. (T. U. Flavell, interview, 2013)

Piripi Walker makes a case for understanding the symbolic power of the broadcaster when he states:

It's there and it's both a practical presence in terms of the daily life of the country, but also a highly symbolic presence when you live in New Zealand or you grow up in New Zealand. Now you grow up with Television New Zealand, but you know that there is the Māori channel – Māori are being Māori and looking good while they're doing it. And the Māori universe is marching along, talking excitedly about itself in a positive way, and the Māori universe's best values are on show daily, they're there, people can drink from the cup. (P. Walker, interview, 2013)

While a non-Māori speaking majority may contribute to a greater valuing of te reo Māori over time, and while Māori Television might function as a window to te ao Māori for many non-Māori, television is still a technology at a distance from face-to-face encounters with people in the world. Primarily a form of entertainment, television can also function as a way of disengaging with the world. When asked to comment on Māori Television's capacity to decolonise non-Māori, Linda Tuhiwai Smith reflected on the potential for Māori Television to provide an exotic form of difference in the New Zealand media landscape:

> I think it informs things, definitely, and I'm not sure if it decolonises, but it opens up a different kind of world view. I'm not sure it does the work of forcing [non-Māori] to question, because there's the thing I guess you'd call privilege – you can always go back to the mainstream broadcasters. Because you've got how many more channels that you can flick between, whereas [for] Māori, that is the channel that we expect ... to do everything, in that timeframe and in that small opportunity really. Whereas for mainstream viewers it's probably, it is slightly exotic for them, it is different, but they can always choose the default, whereas we don't have a range of things on simultaneously. (L. T. Smith, interview, 2013)

So, while Māori Television is now part of the nation's 'furniture' (Hubbard, 2013, p. A6), and while non-Māori speaking audiences watch Māori Television content, the contribution that this broad appeal might make to greater language shifts will only be seen in the years to come.

∼

Māori Television's significance cannot be understood without a wider understanding of the social and political history underpinning the struggle for te reo Māori, the longer history of television culture in Aotearoa New Zealand, and the role played by media in revitalising minority languages. The struggles leading to Māori Television's 2004 emergence focused on understanding te reo Māori as a taonga that needs to be protected as guaranteed by Article II of Te Tiriti o Waitangi. Many Māori media practitioners have continually argued that te reo is as much about the voice of te ao Māori, and stories, sounds and images that express diverse Māori viewpoints, as it is about language. There has also been a long-standing recognition that non-Māori play an important role in the struggle to revitalise Māori language and culture. These wider political and cultural forces have helped shape the look and sound of Māori Television today.

Although statistics on the health of te reo Māori suggest that its use is in decline, Rawinia Higgins and Poia Rewi suggest that te reo Māori thrives in certain parts of society. They argue that Article III of Te Tiriti o Waitangi, with its focus on citizenship and nationhood, is the more appropriate article at this time to serve as a basis for devising ongoing te reo Māori revitalising strategies.

As we shall see in chapter three, Māori Television's initial broad appeal to audiences involved a nation-building agenda that chimes with the kinds of language strategies that Higgins and Rewi advocate. While Māori Television's impact on te reo Māori use cannot be measured using simple cause–effect measures, the intangible impact the broadcaster has on shaping public opinion, setting Māori-oriented political agendas, and contributing symbolic value to the mana and prestige of te reo Māori and things Māori forms the basis of the broadcaster's status as an agent of social change.

Chapter Two

Bringing Tikanga to Television

The roots of Māori Television lie in the larger and longer struggle to revitalise a language and culture damaged by Crown negligence and active suppression. According to the 2003 Māori Television Service Act, the network is required to address this history by offering media content that might revitalise te reo and tikanga Māori, as well as appeal to a broad audience.

Yet language reform and attendant tikanga practices are often incompatible with established media processes. On the one hand Māori Television must provide te reo Māori on screen, drawing on practices that align with tikanga; on the other hand the network must offer recognisable 'quality' content within a media environment dominated by non-Māori norms since the 1960s, including expectations about how television should look and sound. While marae-based tikanga derive from established histories related to people and place-based knowledges and practices, media-based tikanga practices are an emerging phenomenon led by figures such as Barry Barclay, Merata Mita, Don Selwyn, Whai Ngata and members of the independent Māori media sector (Barclay, 1990; Mita, 1992; Henry and Wikaire, 2013). This chapter focuses on how Māori Television negotiates these diverse agendas.

As well as attempting to reconcile the contradictory demands of te reo, tikanga and television, Māori Television operates in a deregulated media environment where media providers aggressively compete for audience share, and where international media often provide the preferred content. The prevailing conditions that raise challenges for Māori Television as a tikanga-based organisation include: its Crown–Māori governance structure; the loss of te reo over generations leading to difficulties in finding fluent te reo Māori media practitioners; the day-to-day demands of producing media content; and the diverse expectations of audiences.

The magnitude of these challenges was alluded to when Minister of Māori Development Te Ururoa Flavell argued that 'many people would suggest that the money that [Māori Television] get anyway is pretty minimal if you put it against the loss of the language over the many years, [loss] that transpired through the education system' (T. U. Flavell, interview, 2013). Under these conditions, Māori Television is required to bring te reo and tikanga Māori to a media industry shaped and honed by non-Māori practitioners, within a larger social context where English speakers, thinkers and doers remain the majority. The network must also support the health of te reo and tikanga using a tool (television) that has not been designed for the task.

This chapter discusses the challenges of tikanga-based television in both on- and off-screen ways. As a Māori-language organisation the network must 'walk the talk' laid down by the kaupapa of promoting and protecting te reo and tikanga, by developing processes and practices that reflect values and ideals from te ao Māori. Tikanga, in this framework, refers to the correct way of fulfilling the prevailing kaupapa of language and cultural wellbeing for Māori in ways that align with Māori principles and values. This requires a tikanga framework for understanding:

- the governance structure underlying Māori Television
- Māori Television workplace practices
- tikanga and the norms of media production
- community outreach
- the challenge of developing tikanga-based media practices.

Māori Television's efforts to align media industry practices with tikanga Māori must be considered in relation to broader issues, for example, the governance structure implemented by the Crown, multiple legislative imperatives, technological shifts, and production practices constrained by finance, time and expertise. Providing insights into the realities of being an independent Māori media producer, Chris Winitana offers the following reflection:

> The producer tag might sound flash but let me tell you it's not. It's a euphemism for hardcore, hard work, hard out – when your programme is wanted yesterday, on last decade's budget. When you're chasing the very best product you can possibly get, you do what you have to do. (Winitana, 2011, p. 279)

The nature of Māori Television has evolved as Māori media practitioners strive to align established media industry practices with the dynamic forces of te reo and tikanga Māori. As former Member of Parliament Hone Harawira has said:

> So the things that we would like [Māori Television] to do, it struggles to do. I think if it had enough money it could focus on developing a whole range of programmes, which it's unable to do because of [limited funds]. I think they're innovative in the way in which they do make programmes, and I think their recognition in television awards reflects that. They're a new Māori business, so I think they're still developing tikanga appropriate to those kinds of work situations. But still, for all of the ups and downs, they're working hard on it. (H. Harawira, interview, 2013)

Harawira's comments suggest that Māori Television's efforts to incorporate Indigenous values into television's organisational and production practices are restricted by the amount of funding it receives. According to a briefing to incoming ministers, Māori Television is also dependent on Te Māngai Pāho for 90 per cent of its programme funding (Māori Television, 2014). This reflects ongoing institutional and economic constraints facing those who labour in a media sector where te reo (understood in the broadest sense of te reo as voice) and tikanga Māori outcomes ground the majority of state-funded Māori media activities.

Māori Television's governance structures

Commenting on the steep learning curve faced by Māori Television as a cultural organisation, Jim Mather said:

> We're sort of like a person that really didn't have a childhood. We went straight to young adulthood and there was no opportunity at the beginning after the launch to go through extended periods of progress – we just had to get out there and deliver to the expectations of many. (J. Mather, interview, 2012)

These expectations included delivering on the language and cultural priorities of the organisation, as well as the imperative to be a fiscally responsible business and to deliver on funding expectations. Mather continued:

> And then on the cultural, language and programming side, there's obviously a whole range of expectations from different segments of viewers. Some have higher expectations in terms of language and culture, and at the other end of the spectrum some viewer segments see it as almost less relevant to them, and it's more about the entertainment to them, and local content, and different viewing options and the like. So there is that natural tension that exists in terms of trying to meet a whole range of demands, and then trying to do that within a funding base that's static, and in real terms is actually diminishing each year. (J. Mather, interview, 2012)

The static funding climate that Mather refers to is the 2008 National government's austerity measures across the public sector in response to the global financial crisis (P. Thompson, 2011) and the impact of inflation across the years. To assist in delivering on cultural expectations, Mather and his team have been supported by the Kaunihera Kaumātua, a council of elders established in 2005. The Kaunihera Kaumātua includes a range of iwi representatives, and its function is to provide advice on matters of tikanga, kaupapa and kawa (protocols).

The Kaunihera Kaumātua are considered the kaitiaki of the values of the organisation. Kaumātua who have sat on the council have included Kingi Ihaka, the late Apirana Mahuika, Te Huirangi Waikerepuru, the late Don Selwyn, Bill Wiki, Esther Davis, the late Merimeri Penfold, Te Ariki Morehu, Hauata Palmer, Timi Peri and Huata Holmes. Jim Mather describes the role of the Kaunihera Kaumātua:

> There are ten kaumātua, and basically these elders are like our cultural reviewers, they're the kaitiaki of the values of the organisation, and they maintain the cultural bearings, and make sure we have cultural checks and balances in place, and that we're heading in the right direction and not losing sight of where we're heading as a channel. And also they're very pragmatic people. They talk to us about what their dreams and hopes and aspirations for the channel were, and we're able to ask them are we achieving that, or are there areas we've not done so well where they might have felt let down. (J. Mather, interview, 2007)

The council offers advice on cultural protocols and helped develop the organisation's guiding kaupapa, framed in the following way:

> Kia tika – be professional and maintain high standards. Kia pono – be truthful, honest and act with integrity. Kia aroha – be respectful and demonstrate empathy. Kia Māori – maintain and uphold core Māori values. (Māori Television, 2008)

While there is kaumātua support at the CEO level, general Māori staff members do not have access to the counsel of kaumātua on a day-to-day basis to support the practices of tikanga and the overall culture of the organisation, although there is a general manager within the organisation who advises on te reo and tikanga in relation to programming practices. According to kōrero from stakeholders, one way of making Māori Television more 'Māori' could be to draw on the expertise, advice and talents of the Kaunihera Kaumātua in a more extensive and daily way, and to value the experiences of non-media professionals who nonetheless have cultural expertise. This is one of the aspirations of ex-Te Pūtahi Pāoho member and current Māori Television Board member Piripi Walker, when reflecting on the need for support from elders:

> I always thought that a functioning Māori operating unit that was really truly Māori would have kaumātua right there in the centre. And it's easy to operate without them in the modern world that the young professionals want to live in. (P. Walker, interview, 2013)

According to Walker, the daily presence of kaumātua within the organisation could be a step towards strengthening Māori Television's cultural integrity.

In its first ten years Māori Television has had two stakeholders that represent the Tiriti partnership agreement underpinning the broadcaster's emergence: the Crown (through the Minister of Māori Affairs and the Minister of Finance), and Te Pūtahi Pāoho (the Māori Electoral College). The make-up of the college was negotiated during the drafting of the Māori Television Service Act 2003, and consisted of representatives from eleven Māori organisations, all of whom have a role in promoting te reo Māori. These organisations included the National Māori Congress, Te Rūnanga Nui o ngā Kura Kaupapa Māori o Aotearoa, Te Whakaruruhau o ngā Reo Irirangi o Aotearoa, Te Tau Ihu o ngā Wānanga, Kawea te Rongo, Te Rūnanga o te Ataarangi, Te Kōhanga Reo National Trust, Māori Women's Welfare League, Ngā Aho Whakaari, and Ngā Kaiwhakapūmau i te Reo Māori.

As the Māori stakeholder, Te Pūtahi Pāoho (TPP) appoints board directors with the appropriate skills and experience to govern the strategic direction and operations of the organisation. The next level of governance is the Māori Television Board, made up of seven directors: four appointed by TPP and three appointed by the Crown, through the Minister of Māori Affairs and the Minister of Finance. In the 2009 review of Māori Television, carried out by Te Kāhui o Māhutonga (with panel members including Jane Huria, Hone Edwards and Tainui Stephens), TPP was a topic of discussion. The review raised questions about the partnering relationship between the Crown and TPP, as well as the membership of TPP, including concerns about a conflict of interest in relation to Ngā Aho Whakaari's representation, and the lack of iwi representation on the council. There were also questions over the appropriateness of the National Māori Congress (a body that, in the words of the report, 'scarcely exists') being a key member. The review included public submissions from stakeholders concerned that TPP was being overlooked by both Māori Television and the Crown.

Another submission raised issues over TPP's ability to fully reflect the diverse interests of te ao Māori:

> The current accountability provisions of the Act seem best suited to government accountabilities and reporting to appropriate ministries. The Māori partner needs to spend some time thinking how the Māori partner can be better accountable to Māori, which means Pūtahi Pāoho need to reflect on it in Te Ao Māori who they are accountable [to], and disseminate some information out to Māori about their decision-making and processes. (Te Kāhui o Māhutonga, 2009, p. 29)

Although Te Kāhui o Māhutonga expressed a desire for greater accountability to communities from TPP, at times the communication flow between TPP, the Māori Television Board and the Māori Television executive team has also been less than ideal. This was the case when Māori Television launched its second channel, Te Reo, in 2008, to the surprise of many in the industry – as well as the surprise of some TPP and board members. Independent Māori media producer Kay Ellmers (Ngāti Tamaterā, Ngāti Raukawa) captured the kinds of questions raised in the production sector at that time:

> The positioning of Māori Television in that mix got really confused as well because then it was like, so okay, does that mean Māori Television is less about the reo now and more about a Māori world view because we've got Te Reo? (K. Ellmers, interview, 2012)

Considered a 'rushed exercise' by some, the Te Reo channel has drawn criticism for its repeat programme screenings, its high placement on the electronic programming guide, which restricts its public visibility, and for the lack of new and innovative programming coming through for native or fluent speakers. As Te Kāhui o Māhutonga notes, Te Reo has been treated as the teina (younger sibling) to the main Māori Television channel when it should be seen as the tuakana (elder sibling):

> Those who criticise incorrect language are most concerned that a continued decline in standards will lead to a dilution of the 'Māoriness' of the language. This concern is expressed by many stakeholders who feel that the mana accorded the Te Reo channel is compromised by a lack of regard and resource. The tuakana tongue is being afforded junior sibling status. (Te Kāhui o Māhutonga, 2009, p. 13)

Chris Winitana offers another way of thinking about the relationship between the bilingual Māori Television channel and Te Reo when he writes:

> At another level, the separation of the two audiences might end up being the best thing since sliced bread. Let the Māori Television Service parent do what it has to do for our nationhood – the idea of a shared destiny, a shared heritage. Remember that? Reflect our country as it is, not as white eyes would have it be . . . . Let the Māori Television Service drag Aotearoa to a new level of self-analysis and self-correction. [. . .] Let it do what a parent does. Fight for its babies. The Te Reo channel is the baby. The Māori Television Service's first fight is to survive. No survival, no baby. (Winitana, 2011, p. 276)

Jim Mather's 2007 vision for Te Reo included offering stronger reo-Māori content for older audiences, which would increase the amount of te reo on the main channel (J. Mather, interview, 2007). However, in 2014 the third chair of TPP, Willie Jackson (Ngāti Porou, Ngāti Maniapoto), expressed the concern of many on TPP that Te Reo allows the broadcaster to fulfil its language responsibilities so that there is more space on the main channel for English-speaking programming. According to Jackson:

> [T]he Pūtahi Pāoho thrust is they want reo Māori treated with respect, and you can understand that. Don't just sideline it so you can fulfil your commercial means and your obligations. So there's been a frustration that some of the te reo Māori obligations

are being sidelined a bit and the reo Māori channel has been put up as a front. But that channel doesn't cater, and I know for a fact, for a lot of the traditionalists who just see repeats of programmes, not enough new programming coming through. And so Te Pūtahi Pāoho has got some real negotiation power, there's no doubt about it. I don't mind carrying that take [*issue*] to Māori TV management and saying, 'You need to put on more quality stuff.' (W. Jackson, interview, 2013)

During 2013 and 2014 non-Māori media reported tensions between TPP and the Māori Television Board regarding the search for a new CEO to replace Jim Mather. According to Willie Jackson, TPP's chair at the time, the Māori Television Board could have drawn on TPP's broad expertise to better manage the issue, and Jackson said publicly that he was disappointed they did not do so.[*] In a later interview, and in the wake of Paora Maxwell's appointment as the new CEO, Jackson reflected on TPP's relationship with the board in the following manner:

We are asking if we can work closer together. They agree that they need what we call a tuarā, a good backing behind them, because the Electoral College is very strong in terms of Māori-language skills, in terms of representation, in terms of Māori broadcasting. It comes from all the different areas. (W. Jackson, interview, 2013)

Hone Harawira has suggested that Māori Television is an emerging Indigenous media entity that is working hard to balance out media industry norms and the guiding kaupapa of tika, pono, aroha and Māori. The various community representatives on the Kaunihera Kaumātua, TPP and Māori Television Board all play a role in addressing this balance, and sometimes these groups come into conflict with Māori Television decision-making processes.

Māori Television has acknowledged the tensions between cultural values and industry norms in an internal report on the Māori Television draft 'Rautaki Reo' plan, which explicitly refers to the difficulty of maintaining a Māori 'culture and atmosphere' within the television industry (Edwards and Stephens cited in Lysaght, 2010, p. 112). According to this plan, Māori Television's 2014 goal was to encourage in Māori Television a corporate culture that was 'a fusion of professional requirements and cultural authenticity'. While the Kaunihera Kaumātua and TPP may help support Māori Television's

---

[*] *Te Manu Kōrihi*, Radio New Zealand, 7.02 pm, 5 September 2013.

various kaupapa, and while Māori Television makes efforts to engage with its audiences and communities through a range of activities, a recurring theme from stakeholder kōrero was the desire to see the broadcaster do more to be accessible to its communities.

Māori Television's engagement with communities

> I have always thought that relevance is important. Relevance and accessibility are a big challenge for [Māori Television]. Are they accessible by Māori people? Do [Māori] people actually 'own' Māori Television? Do they actually feel like their communities are reflected in Māori Television? I don't think so. I think the Māori Television model is based upon a strict Pākehā model. They should be investing in regional offices, in getting out there and having a presence among the communities. Because that's really how Māori culture works, it's reflected in the communities. (P. Curtis, interview, 2014)

For Māori Television to reflect the kaupapa of 'kia Māori', many stakeholders expect the network to engage with te ao Māori in sustained and meaningful ways. As producer of *Hunting Aotearoa* Piripi Curtis asks in the quote above, do people actually feel their communities are reflected in Māori Television? While many programming strategies attempt to reflect the diverse groups that make up te ao Māori (as discussed in chapter five), the network has developed specific strategies to remain accessible to its audiences at the same time as deliver content to the screen. These strategies include a range of practices, such as having an open-door policy at its Newmarket offices, and developing more regional coverage in its news and coverage of iwi events.

Rotorua-based Piripi Curtis's regional vision for Māori Television clashes with the existing location of Māori Television in the fashionable shopping area of Newmarket in downtown Auckland. According to media scholar Ruth Lysaght, Newmarket was originally selected for its critical mass of media professionals and proximity to public transport (Lysaght, 2010). This location has drawn criticism from some, who see Newmarket as a non-Māori space, while others argue that the design of the Newmarket offices, particularly the glass doors of the main studio, function as a gesture of openness to the public. With the lease on these offices up for renewal in 2017, Māori Television entered into discussion in 2014 with a range of potential landlords at locations such as Rotorua, Hamilton, or another site in Auckland.

Engaging with the public was always the vision for Māori Television's studio and office spaces, with the hope that the architectural features might encourage people to come in and out of the studio and be part of an audience (K. Graham, interview, 2012). Reflecting on the start-up phase of Māori Television, Joanna Paul recalls being inspired by a television studio based in Canada:

> I went to Canada to buy some programmes and one of the things I saw was a place called City TV ... at City TV the doors are always open and the studio has always got something happening in it, and instead of having ... a locked away little unit where all of the important people sit – like the director, and the vision switcher, and the sound guy, and the other guy, the producer – they're all on the floor at City TV, and so they can walk over and interact.... And they also have these doors open ... so that when people came in they could see television being made, and if they wanted to, at City TV they've got these bleachers ... and you could sit down, and just be part of the audience for an hour, for half an hour, it didn't matter, [there] was always something happening. (J. Paul, interview, 2012)

Attempts were made in the early days to draw the public in to Māori Television, most directly with Te Kokonga Kōrero (Speaker's Corner), a mini-studio the public could access in order to record brief messages for broadcast on Māori Television. An ongoing open-door policy has enabled the public to tour the Newmarket premises, whenever possible. Independent producer Kim Muriwai recalls her time at the Newmarket offices on the set of the popular and pioneering studio-based agony aunt show *Ask Your Auntie* (2005–2007):

> At that stage it was interesting developing the tikanga when it came to [welcoming] manuhiri to the building, and balancing that with the demands of trying to record five and sometimes six half-hour shows within a ten-hour period. There was an expectation that if manuhiri came during the lunch break that they would get a tour. Especially when [the aunties] became very popular – school groups, people, kaumātua all wanted to meet and interact with the aunties and talk. (K. Muriwai, interview, 2014)

As Muriwai describes it, the demands of a restrictive production schedule, as well as limited access to the in-house production crew responsible for shooting *Auntie*, had an impact on the manaakitanga able to be offered to visitors to the set. Yet studio tours remain a continuing feature of Māori Television's commitment to accessibility. According to recent policy documents, Māori Television continues to offer tours to kōhanga reo, puna reo and kura kaupapa Māori as part of its community engagement strategy (Māori Television, 2014, p. 23). In addition to these tours, community engagement was also fostered by the popular live Friday-night karaoke show *Hōmai te Pakipaki* (2007–2015) which drew record crowds on Friday evenings, as potential contestants and their whānau and friends gathered to enter the studio (Lysaght, 2010, p. 122).

Many of those interviewed for this project considered the talent show *Hōmai Te Pakipaki* to be an excellent example of the kind of community-based television that Māori Television could do more of. Board member Cathy Dewes is also of the opinion that more could be made of getting into communities, but that this kind of television requires higher rates of funding than are currently available:

> Rikirangi Gage calls it consumer sovereignty, which is absolutely koia te tikanga [*correct indeed*]. We want consumer sovereignty and all of our people to be raving fans, that's all of our Māori people to be raving fans. Currently they're not: we're getting feedback from fluent speakers of Māori, native speakers of Māori, they're giving us ideas on how we can improve our service. So that's a goal for me, raving fans. Be there wherever our people are being themselves and being well, and healthy and happy. And all the tribal papa tākaro or tribal sports competitions that go on, you know, it doesn't have to be a long programme but we should be there at the Māori tennis, and the Māori touch, and the Māori hockey. But we're getting there, again, I say, the constraint is the funding resource. (C. Dewes, interview, 2012)

The idea of consumer sovereignty in relation to Māori Television is a provocative one and requires a rethinking of how television is currently made, and what expectations audiences might have of television. Consumer sovereignty over Māori Television might mean that audiences and members of Māori communities see themselves better reflected in – and as active agents of – the television programming offered by the broadcaster. This form of television would no doubt challenge existing theories about what constitutes 'quality' television (which Māori Television must provide as part of its 2003 statutory requirements). There would also be a shift in the expectations placed on Māori media professionals.

For independent producer and Ngāpuhi language expert Quinton Hita, a more 'Māori' form of Māori Television would be one that allowed for programming that reflected the rhythm, timing and pace of te ao Māori, a form of television that did not interrupt the immersive environment of te reo with English-speaking adverts, and a structure that connected to whānau in a way similar to the Kōhanga Reo movement. This is how Hita expresses his vision:

> The Kōhanga movement became more than just a vehicle to teach our kids, it became a way of bringing us together as a community, enhancing us as a people. Māori Television does not achieve that in my opinion, because it's centralised. They asked at the Rotorua meeting – that hui we had – if you could reimagine Māori Television, what would it look like. To me it would look something like that, devolving out to our communities, and then you would end up with something far more meaningful. Devolve it to our communities and then the broadcaster becomes a portal that distributes that [content] to the country. (Q. Hita, interview, 2014)

While acknowledging that such a devolved structure would include demanding learning curves over a long period of time, Hita's vision for Māori Television perhaps anticipates the technological shifts now affecting the broadcasting industry.

If Māori Television were to become a 'portal' for the dissemination of community-based media content, its role as a curator of content would expand and enable the wider dissemination of stories told from the flax roots of Māori society. Hita's comments also underscore the importance of a long-term vision, one based on getting things correct at the start:

> So going back to what I said before about when we start these ventures, we pick Pākehā structures because they give us credibility. But I think at some point Māori go, Okay, let's review this. I think we are going into that stage right now with the call for the [new] Māori Language [bill]. (Q. Hita, interview, 2014)

Hita's vision for Māori Television involves a substantial re-visioning of ideas about what constitutes good-quality Māori media. The focus is on imagining a form of television that is by Māori, for Māori and about Māori, and connecting to whānau and communities. As such, Hita argues for a form of Māori Television that challenges the aesthetic and production norms of conventional television. Following the logic of Hita's vision, if Māori Television were a portal for community-based Māori media initiatives, imagine how expansive the landscape would be in terms of telling stories from the diverse communities that make up te ao Māori.

The desire to improve regional outreach is shared by many Māori Television staff, including former staff member Julian Wilcox, and current staff member Mahuta Amoamo. In a 2012 interview, Wilcox described one possible way of enhancing regional news media coverage that would draw on the existing expertise and resources of iwi radio:

> We wanted to commit more regional reporters, but one of the [ways] we were looking at was perhaps looking at Māori radio. [W]e give them a human resource and they provide the base. We would give them a Canon DSLR and train them up (you can get a good camera and sticks and a lighting rig for, like, $8000 now) and so they just operate at a Māori radio station. But the issue was in video transmitting everything back to base. The Punga Net is not ideal at the moment. (J. Wilcox, interview, 2012)

While the technological constraints of Te Punga Net (the iwi radio distribution network) may have been a key factor in this vision not being realised, the idea of harnessing the talents, resources and experiences of other Māori media broadcasters seemed to many interviewees to be a good idea in light of the under-resourcing of Māori media in general. In addition, the missed opportunity for cohesion across the Māori media sector was perhaps compounded by the lack of a cohesive language strategy to support the first ten years of Māori Television's existence.

Mahuta Amoamo (Whakatōhea, Ngāi Tūhoe) recalls the early days of Māori Television staff's efforts to forge relationships with communities:

> When Māori Television was fresh and new, with the news and government going ra ra ra, iwi were very hesitant in letting us come to their events because they thought we were TVNZ, and that's the way we were going to roll. So it was an achievement to get iwi like, say, Maniapoto – because this was my first event that I remember very well – [they] have a hunting competition every year. We went with a kaumātua and she told them why we were there, we're here to make sure your people know what you're up to – they can hear your dialect, they can see you on television, they can find out why you do this competition, we'll be able to capture all of your rangatahi. (M. Amoamo, interview, 2013)

At some point in the development of Māori Television programming initiatives, Amoamo noted a shift away from covering such community events. For Amoamo, as well as for many other interviewees, Māori Television has the potential to bring more programming to the screen that tells stories about the successes of, and challenges facing, whānau, hapū and iwi.

According to Cathy Dewes, Māori Television needed to be wherever Māori people were doing well, and Mahuta Amoamo gave a specific example:

> I'm talking about iwi events like the Tūhoe Ahurei, which is a biennial event that celebrates being Tūhoe, where we have kapahaka, sports, netball, tautohetohe, debates, we have our babies involved. You've got every Tūhoe person in one rohe. Could you imagine how many interviews you could do? (M. Amoamo, interview, 2013)

Amoamo's kōrero is an invitation to imagine how Māori Television could act as a vehicle for giving voice to the rich fabric that makes up te ao Māori. Yet, as many stakeholders noted, this kind of community-based television would most likely require more resourcing than Māori Television currently has access to. The issue of limited funding was also raised by Dewes when she discussed the imperatives placed on Māori Television staff members to support the kaupapa of Māori Television as a revitalising agent of te reo and tikanga.

Te reo in the workplace

> [T]he vast majority of us here don't see this as being a job, we don't see this as being a part of our career, but firstly a privilege. A crusade is probably a good word to describe how we feel about what we do here. (J. Mather, interview, 2013)

Former CEO Jim Mather has consistently described his team as more than simply media professionals; they are advocates and champions for the kaupapa that grounds Māori Television: te reo me ngā tikanga Māori. If the initial phase of Māori Television's development was to consolidate its identity as a viable Indigenous national broadcaster, and to be a 'flagship for Māori development' (J. Mather, interview, 2013), another early ambition was to normalise te reo Māori in the workplace and to provide staff with opportunities to upskill in te reo Māori (Māori Television, 2005). According to Māori Television Board member Cathy Dewes, this ambition was thwarted by funding limitations:

> I think Māori Television is hugely limited by its funding resources. I think that the ideal is to have the whole of Māori Television, in time, speaking Māori, and by saying that I mean I assume if a person is speaking Māori they have an understanding of tikanga Māori and te ao Māori which non-speakers don't have. And so ideally, the whole of Māori Television are Māori, and everything they do, their thinking, their way of life, their ordinary daily being is Māori. Ideally, that's what should happen, and it's my understanding that the culture within Māori Television is changing, so that there is more emphasis and value being placed on becoming a Māori speaker – from the Chairperson of the Board to the person who cleans the toilets, everybody is speaking Māori. (C. Dewes, interview, 2012)

While there have been discussions about instituting language zones in parts of the building, as well as setting up kura within the organisation, the ambition of making te reo Māori the day-to-day language of Māori Television staff has yet to be achieved. According to media scholar Ruth Lysaght, in-house efforts have been made to upskill in te reo Māori:

> Charles Berryman (Ngāti Awa), former General Manager Reo and Tikanga (2007–2010) at Māori Television, designed language courses for people who had no background in te reo. Whilst there is a general willingness to learn and improve, the biggest problem with some staff is the bane of the adult language-learner: a lack of sustained motivation. (Lysaght, 2010, p. 163)

As media professionals driven by the work routines dictated by a content-hungry television programming schedule, the task of upskilling in te reo Māori is an additional pressure. According to former executive producer of current affairs Hone Edwards (Ngāti Hikairo):

> The thing that fascinates me about Māori Television is that given the clarity of the brand, I hardly hear the language being spoken, and I find that fascinating. I commend Jim [Mather]. He came in and he didn't speak the language, and he's learnt it and he speaks it whether it's right, wrong, upside down, back to front. But he leads by example. But that example isn't filtering down into the rank and file here. (H. Edwards, interview, 2012)

Edwards went on to describe what it was like to be a fluent speaker in a workplace where others were employed for their skills in broadcasting, not necessarily their expertise in te reo Māori. These comments again reveal the fine balance Māori Television staff must achieve between their identity as media professionals and the cultural imperatives conditioning their labour:

> Those of us who are fluent do speak te reo to each other, but you hesitate to speak to others because they don't have the language – they don't want to speak Māori. They just want to be here, to do the job, and go home. They don't want the cultural tangents that go with the job, and often I think people here are being employed because of that other aspect – they're being brought in because they have the skills to do that particular job. But they don't have the cultural background, which could make this place unique. (H. Edwards, interview, 2012)

The aspiration to be a te reo Māori-speaking organisation is a commendable one, but as Edwards notes, the practical day-to-day demands of making and broadcasting television content often override more cultural ambitions. The many different motivations for being a media professional are also at play, as well as the difficulty of finding trained media professionals who have expertise in te reo.

While experiences at Māori Television demonstrate the challenges of balancing the professional standards of a media industry with cultural imperatives, some Māori Television stakeholders think that the organisation should have considered alternative structures and alternative ways of making television from the very start.

Tikanga and the norms of television

For some, Māori Television took a wrong turn in the early days when it decided to broadcast English-language content, and employed non-Māori broadcasting experts to help generate content and establish production processes. Independent producer Quinton Hita has been public in his concerns about the route Māori Television has taken:

> [I]f you watch Māori Television in its current form, it is a Western model that has had brown faces and te reo Māori laid over the top. I think it represents our biggest

missed opportunity – to create something from the inside out, rather than the other way round. (Q. Hita, interview, 2014)

While Hita acknowledges the strategic value of Māori Television's approach to gaining industry credibility by drawing on established industry expertise, he regrets that the people who set up Māori Television did not provide a 'more Māori' structure for it. Hita's comments about working from the 'inside out' imply a structural realignment of television-industry practices that would result in a form of media-making with te reo and tikanga at the forefront, creating the grounding norms for the television that is made.

Another vision for how television might be structured differently is captured in the 2009 Te Kāhui o Māhutonga report, which highlights the risks of te reo Māori becoming a broadcast language that reflects the logic of the majority culture of English speakers:

> One of the dilemmas that face all who are engaged in the revitalisation of the language [is] that the Māori words we speak should reflect a Māori way of thinking, [but] the well-meaning attempts to preserve Māori grammar and vocabulary will come to nought if the language that we vocalise reflects English thought processes instead. The panel believes that the unique value of the Māori language is in danger of being diminished, perhaps fatally, by foreign thinking. One of the disturbing features of the modern Māori spoken by many learners of the language is that in syntax and idiom it sounds like Māori, but [it] feels like English. This could be perceived as a . . . colonisation of the Māori mind. Grammar is the soul of a language and the words its bones and flesh. (Te Kāhui Māhutonga, 2009, p. 14)

A further tension arises not from the audio component of television technologies, but from the visual aspect, and the industry norm of privileging a camera-ready personality over that of a fluent speaker of te reo. Language expert and former Māori Television general manager of te reo and tikanga Joe Te Rito (Rongomaiwahine, Ngāti Kahungunu) made this observation:

> [T]here is a thing in Māori Television, a tension if you like, between a pretty face and beautiful te reo Māori, and to me Māori Television has often tended towards the prettier face with the poorer-quality language. (J. Te Rito, interview, 2012)

Former TPP and current board member Piripi Walker made a similar observation when he noted:

> I would have hoped within Māori Television that we would have never lost the daily diet of the sound of the knowledgeable, truly culturally Māori person, and keep faith with the native speakers of the language who are the cradle essentially, of the culture and of tikanga Māori. And they're not allowed in many ways, to get to air because [of the] requirement [to] have pretty faces. (P. Walker, interview, 2013)

The requirement to have 'pretty faces' is one of the many unwritten norms of the television industry, and Māori Television is at the forefront of rewriting these norms by drawing on te reo and tikanga Māori, even as the norms of the industry at times appear to prevail. An example of such tensions can be found in Māori Television's efforts to produce news and current affairs programming that reflects Māori world views.

Acknowledging the crucial role the revitalisation of te reo Māori plays in Māori Television practices, Jim Mather described his staff's investment in their jobs as a 'crusade'. One long-time crusader is Julian Wilcox. When asked about his start at Māori Television, Wilcox noted: 'When I came into this job, it was all about reo, tikanga and getting into our communities and telling our stories' (J. Wilcox, interview, 2012). Alluding to the broader social environment out of which Māori Television emerged, he noted:

> For me it was like 'us against the world', and showing that not only should we have a place as an independent television service, we're the ones that have the responsibility of telling our stories to our people in *our* way. Because I think it is a different mode of journalism or television than the way mainstream tells our stories. (J. Wilcox, interview, 2012)

Dedicated to Māori news and current affairs until his departure in 2014, Wilcox had a commitment to telling Māori stories to Māori people in a Māori way, which, while seemingly straightforward, encompasses a range of persisting complexities. For how do you tell stories from the perspective of the diverse communities that make up te ao Māori, in te reo Māori, and using tikanga, when the very media systems and structures you inhabit have been shaped or sourced by non-Māori?

For example, news media norms include a tightly structured news bulletin format, which restricts the kind of in-depth discussions that need to take place in order to understand the full weight of a Māori story. Think of the resources needed for a broadcaster to turn up to, and record, multiple community events occurring across the country. Stakeholders expect Māori Television to tell stories on television in ways that align with Māori world views and practices. Flagship current affairs programme *Native Affairs* has been at the forefront of these kinds of stories, even as it attracted criticism in 2013 for its coverage of events involving Te Kōhanga Reo National Trust and Te Pātaka Ōhanga, which for some Māori commentators was too 'Pākehāfied'. In many ways the controversy surrounding *Native Affairs*' treatment of a peer language organisation reflects the complex desire of many stakeholders for a more 'Māori' form of Māori Television. This desire goes beyond simply expecting Māori Television to provide quality te reo Māori media content, but also to operate as an organisation in which Indigenous values prevail. The struggle to balance tikanga with the embedded norms of media storytelling is one faced by all state-funded Māori media makers.

Tikanga-based production practices

The challenge to produce media that is expressive of the values, world views and spirit of a specific people is a daunting one, and requires time, commitment, connection with community and the correct approach, drawn from cultural knowledge. According to Barry Barclay, the institutional norms of media industries (both nationally and internationally) include forms of institutional racism that privilege one mode of storytelling over others, and these norms were the sites of combat for Barclay (1990). Barclay's media practices assert the importance of telling stories that respect and maintain a deep link with the people and their histories (S. Murray, 2008). Joanna Paul echoed this approach when she described aspects of her media-making process:

> I learnt Māori all through school, through university and I've kept it up. So tikanga has become second nature to me, and so when I embark on a project say, like, for instance, with *Māori Boy Genius*, I called the family first. Flew down to see them, spent a couple of days with them. Made sure they were happy about it, met their tūpuna, went to their places that are sacred and tapu to them, and then brought the film-maker in and then checked in with them. There were things that happened along the way, and you would just show up and be there, and I think that it's a cultural mosaic that once you know how to read that road map then you kind of go along that road map. It's just a different way of making programmes. I mean it's not

to say that you don't use all the skills that you do making other programmes, it's just that there's an understanding of what to do and what not to do and how to awhi things along, how not to push when you don't need to push, how to allow people to have the time, and often times it invariably takes longer, it costs more, but I think the results are worth it. (J. Paul, interview, 2012)

This approach requires access to a community of relationships, additional time spent in pre-production, and an acknowledgement of, and empathy with, values and issues that may seem tangential to the storytelling process.

There are industry guidelines on how to maintain cultural integrity when making media productions related to te ao Māori. The *Urutahi Koataata Māori / Working with Māori in Film and Television* handbook (Haami, 2008); the 2012 report *Working with Māori in Screen Production* (Ngā Aho Whakaari) and *The Brown Book: Māori in Screen Production* (Henry and Wikaire, 2013) offer good primers on the cultural dimensions of working with Māori on media productions.

Haami's handbook includes guidelines written by Tainui Stephens, which include the following criteria.

- Me hui a kanohi – ahakoa te aha [*meet face-to-face – no matter what*].
- Me ū tonu ki ngā tikanga Māori [*demonstrate respect for Māori custom, that is ask advice of kaumātua*].
- Me mātau ki tō te kaupapa [*understand what the project is about*].
- Me mārama ki ngā wero mai o te ao pāoho [*understand the challenges of broadcasting, that is explain clearly to non-professionals and members of the public what will be involved, to enable truly informed consent*].
- Me whai mana tonu ngā mea e mana ana [*ensure authority is appropriately acknowledged, including intellectual property*].
- Me whai hua te katoa – mai runga mai raro [*something should come of the project for all involved*]. (Haami, 2008, p. 39)

Yet the practicalities of trying to integrate Māori values and world views into production and distribution practices require a great deal of creative thinking, as well as a strong commitment to the kaupapa. Attention must also be paid to the different production practices required to make feature films, television drama series and news media, as well as the links and continuities between these genres when producing Māori-media forms. Former *Native*

Affairs producer and independent film-maker Sharon Hawke (Ngāti Whātua) says of her time at Māori Television:

> I have a lot of fond memories of the place, but there was still lots of work to do, and there were a lot of challenges to be made to get us out of just duplicating what TVNZ and TV3 were doing. Because for me the likes of Merata [Mita] and all our pioneers of the moving image – the Don Selwyns, the Tama Poatas, the Tungia Bakers – they instilled in us, the next generation, a need to perfect our Indigeneity through the moving image. (S. Hawke, interview, 2012)

Reflecting on Māori Television's attempts to foster tikanga through their in-house productions, Hawke sets out an ideal case scenario while first admitting that incorporating tikanga into production processes is one of the hardest things to do:

> [E]ven though we've all seen and heard television for some 35-odd years, it's just hard to put those intangible values on a screen. I think that the whole process of gathering a story, of mixing with the community, you can translate the tikanga of things Māori by following through. So you go in with a crew into the community and then you leave. Like say *Marae DIY* – once they're gone, they're gone. So the follow-up back to that one community around, Okay, your programme's coming up, here's something out of the box. That producer goes back to that marae, and watches them watch it. Sits with them in the marae and watches it when it first goes to air. . . . So you know, that would cost money to send that producer back there, and that producer would have to be fairly thick-skinned to take the criticism, whether it's good or bad, and to put it into perspective, and to answer some of the questions around it. What damage would that be? Not much to that person if they had the skills to let it not affect them too personally, [and] to actually make use of that feedback. (S. Hawke, interview, 2012)

This kind of television production has the potential to produce stronger links between audiences and producers than those that exist in the current television climate, and yet the constraints of funding limit this kind of community engagement.

According to CEO John Bishara (Ngāti Tūwharetoa), Te Māngai Pāho receives around 40 per cent less than NZ On Air to fund programming (J. Bishara, interview, 2012). While comparisons between the two funding agencies must be nuanced in light of the struggles facing the New Zealand media-production sector more generally, former commissioning agent for Māori Television Annie Murray also referred to the impact of tight budgets on the development of the Māori media sector:

> Because our programmes are funded at around 60 per cent of [funding for] mainstream, all of the profit margins are squeezed so you get what's called a PCO, Production Company Overhead. It used to be called a management fee, which is the profit line in a budget, up to 10 per cent of below the line. In mainstream, it is a lot more money than it is for Māori productions, so that's how you fund your development, that's how you buy your equipment, that's how you upgrade your edit suite, it's out of your PCO. (A. Murray, interview, 2013)

The production company overhead is used to develop projects, and on pitches for future funding. Murray suggests that due to the level of funding, Māori media producers are more dependent from funding round to funding round:

> They're not very robust businesses compared to mainstream ones, because they're underfunded. So for them to invest a significant amount of time in a proposal, and usually it's the producer themselves who writes it, they really want to have a fair idea they're going to get it funded, because when they get it turned down, that money basically gets written off and all that time that's gone into it. So while it's disappointing as a network person not to get that commission, it's far more disappointing for the producer. (A. Murray, interview, 2013)

In addition to these fiscal constraints, the Māori media sector must do more than simply make television programming. They have to make television that contains an accessible, attractive and educative language curriculum. Since 2012 Te Māngai Pāho has asked independent producers to include a language plan in all proposals, measuring the extent to which a programme promotes te reo Māori. The producer must also make sure the quality of Māori spoken on the show is of a suitable standard. This sometimes requires contracting a consultant who can advise on these matters. This kind of media practice is difficult to achieve when dealing with broadcast production schedules that demand a certain length of programming, at a particular time, or when dealing with studio crews who are juggling multiple demands. Producers must also comply with funding agents by measuring the amount of reo Māori content on screen as well as its quality. Commenting on challenges that bilingual media-making poses for the independent producer, Kay Ellmers, director of Tūmunako Productions, described the impact of language requirements on the creative process:

> [I]t's not a satisfying experience for most programme makers walking that line of meeting the language numbers, because you're not just narratively telling the story how it naturally unfolds, you're also then having to massage it around meeting your language requirements. I think my analysis would be that there's far more voice-over consequently on Māori Television programming than [there] would be in mainstream, or than there would be if those programmes were allowed to just naturally evolve. (K. Ellmers, interview, 2012)

As well as the struggle to incorporate te reo Māori into production practices, there is another aspect of the Te Puni Kōkiri criteria for funding (the ultimate source of Te Māngai Pāho monies is Te Puni Kōkiri). This requires Māori media producers to contribute to capacity building within the sector, for example, by upskilling employees. Framing all these activities is the producer's commitment to the kaupapa of nurturing and sustaining te reo Māori. Cinco Cine director Nicole Hoey (Ngāti Kahu, Te Aupōuri) has been a long-standing member of the independent production sector and has helped to mentor other Māori production companies in the industry by providing financial services, access to studios and industry advice based on more than 25 years' experience. Commenting on her in-house staff mentoring processes designed to pass on financial literacies, Hoey noted:

> By the time [staff] leave the company, most of them own houses and a car; it's not unusual for them to be leaving after [a period of time] and they don't leave that quickly. They stay. We don't have a very big turnover – about eight to nine years – which is not the best thing sometimes because you do want a slightly bigger turnaround. But we get ten to twelve years [of] people staying. And we very much encourage people to buy houses – that's the big thing, especially with the Kiwibank, bank-savers and that sort of thing. And we teach them how to actually utilise their contractor status, about saving their receipts and doing everything and running it as a business, that they're mini-businesses. So that's very big for me, to make sure that they really understand that. (N. Hoey, interview, 2013)

These kinds of capacity-building strategies link the Māori media-production sector to wider community concerns, such as whānau wellbeing, through financial security and the ability to foster sustainable industry work. This whakawhanaungatanga ethos flows through to Cinco Cine's organisational structure, which Hoey described in the following terms:

> [W]e work on a circular business model. And at the very core of that is aroha. It's a bit like tough love with kids. With kids, whatever you're doing work-wise or if you're in a work situation, if you come from a base of love – and you may have to deal up very bad news to somebody – if you come from that base of love when you're doing it and make sure that you put every cloak around that person. Or whatever you're having to do, to ensure that it's done with integrity first and foremost. If it's done with love, and it's not done from a vindictive perspective, then everything will be fine. So that's the middle or the centre of the company. The next circle out is whānau. So anyone who works for Cinco Cine is whānau and stays whānau. . . . And the next circle out is hapū, so all our productions are hapū, so they have their own autonomy and rangatiratanga status. Then in the last circle out is the iwi, which is Cinco Cine, and that's the only circle that works inwardly and outwardly, and it's the cloak that protects and nurtures the company. . . . And that's the company structure – circular. (N. Hoey, interview, 2013)

The incorporation of tikanga into the organisational structure of the company, as well as a broader commitment to Māori development, is echoed throughout the production sector. Lara Northcroft (Tūhourangi–Ngāti Wahiao, Tūwharetoa, Tainui), a Rotorua-based independent producer of shows such as *Kapa Haka: Behind the Faces*, described her commitment to Māori development in the following way:

> At the beginning I'm not sure what it was – it was more, I want to be my own boss, I want to work in the industry and I want to work in Rotorua. Now that we have been going for nearly seven years, I like to base my kaupapa around four pou, which are whanaungatanga, to connect; mātauranga, to educate and grow; rangatiratanga, leadership; and kaitiakitanga, support and sustainability. Those things mean to me a number of things. It's not just in the screen industry. I am passionate about Māori in business. I'm involved in Takiwai [a Māori business network based in Rotorua] and we are always trying to provide opportunities of networking for Māori business, for wāhine Māori and anything they want to do – women leadership, and Rotorua in general, Rotorua business community and, within that, Rotorua Māori business

community. Even though it's Velvet Stone Media, I still like to be a wheke [*octopus*] and do some other things as well. (L. Northcroft, interview, 2014)

The kōrero of independent producers attests to the difficulties of a media-production sector grounded in the kaupapa of supporting the revitalisation of te reo and tikanga Māori, and charged with producing high-quality television content that meets the sometimes shifting demands of both broadcasters and funders, whilst also supporting and mentoring other Māori media professionals, and bearing the costs of such support themselves. According to Quinton Hita:

> There's no stability in the industry structure, and you've got a hundred people out there all vying for the three pieces of bread. That's how the Western model works, as a business model, and I think the argument for that is that it creates competition and you get a better end product. I'm not convinced that's a good business model to build an industry on, from my personal experience. It's very volatile – you can't do any future planning based on that model. There are expectations on us as producers to offer professional development – language development – to staff, and really that's ridiculous, because if you don't have a stable business structure you can't really do that. I've always thought that a much better model – if we go with the current status quo – is something more like tourism, where you have preferred providers that get three-year contracts, while still having room in the funding structure to support innovation. (Q. Hita, interview, 2014)

Shifts in the wider language and broadcasting sector also unsettle those media professionals whose revenue depends on having confirmed funding from Te Māngai Pāho on a yearly basis. Just as Māori Television has expressed a desire to have more long-term planning opportunities (J. Mather, interview, 2012) rather than being tied to Te Māngai Pāho and its annual review of funding, so too do independent producers desire a more stable economic structure to help support their practices.

∼

If events prior to Māori Television's emergence in 2004 involved a struggle for greater forms of Māori programming, since Māori Television's arrival the network has faced the challenge of 'perfecting' its Indigeneity in the face of stakeholder and audience expectations. The guiding kaupapa of protecting and promoting te reo and tikanga Māori is a kaupapa that unites not only Māori Television staff, board members and Te Pūtahi Pāoho, but also the funding agency, Te Māngai Pāho, and the independent Māori media sector.

This kaupapa impacts on the working conditions of Māori media producers, as well as the economic viability of the sector. As media scholar Mary Debrett has argued, due to the modest level of funding received by Māori Television, 'the service depends on considerable industry good will which raises questions about the long term sustainability of its funding model' (Debrett, 2010, p. 180). Māori media makers are required not only to make quality television content, they must also meet Te Māngai Pāho's language requirements, at the same time as addressing the needs of Māori Television's programming schedule. This involves designing language plans, and having the necessary language skills and quality assurance processes, which all have an impact on production costs.

Māori Television, as a flagship Māori media entity, is obliged to uphold the mana and prestige of te reo and tikanga Māori. While the network did much in its first ten years to carry the kaupapa, it has drawn criticism from members of Māori communities who want more tikanga-aligned practices behind the screen.

Chapter Three

To Zig Where Others Zag – Māori Television Programming Strategies

Jim Mather has often referred to Māori Television's capacity to 'zig' where other channels 'zag' as a prime programming strategy to build an audience and to demarcate the differences Māori Television offers (J. Mather, interview, 2007). The organisation works within a larger free-to-air media landscape, where commercial imperatives reign and where international English-speaking content dominates. Under such conditions, Māori Television has established itself as an innovative provider of local content (86 per cent in 2014), a source of quality international programming and a valued contributor to, and facilitator of, an emerging global Indigenous media landscape.* At a time when public-service-styled television is in decline, Māori Television has established a reputation as an important New Zealand public broadcaster.

This chapter uses a programming framework to consider the practices of Māori Television across a ten-year period, and to consider the wider shifts in the Māori-language and media sectors that may have helped shape those practices. To zig where others zag describes not only the kind of content commissioned and produced by Māori Television, but also helps to explain aspects of the network's scheduling strategies over time. Yet how might this zig-zag model change as audiences increasingly engage with television online and via on-demand platforms? Examining the resulting shifts in programming strategies across the 2004 to 2014 period suggests that Māori Television's initial focus was to secure a broad audience base for its ongoing operations, and build a respectable brand. In recent years the network has

---

* The local content statistic of 86 per cent in 2014 is according to a NZ On Air report (NZ On Air, 2014b, p. 6).

described itself more often as a Māori-language organisation, and the focus has shifted to ensure an improvement in the quality of language programming as well as online offerings (Freeman-Tayler, 2014). These shifts can be understood in relation to wider changes in the Māori-language sector and New Zealand's media culture. This chapter develops a programming framework for understanding:

- Māori Television's target audience(s)
- programming for language and for broad appeal
- programming strategies across ten years
- future programming challenges in an era of 'digital plenty'.

Māori Television's target audience(s)

The legislation governing Māori Television in its first ten years included a range of imperatives: to promote te reo Māori me ngā tikanga Māori, and to provide high-quality and cost-effective programming, in both Māori and English, that 'informs, educates, and entertains a broad viewing audience' and 'enriches New Zealand's society, culture and heritage' (Māori Television Service Act 2003). In addition to these general aims, the act requires Māori Television to broadcast mainly in te reo Māori during prime time, and at other times to have a substantial portion of other programming in te reo Māori. Provision is also made for children who have come through immersion education programmes and who seek to continue to learn te reo Māori.

The act also ensured that a review of the service would take place within six years of Māori Television's commencement. The panel of Te Kāhui o Māhutonga conducted the 2009 review and described the mixed mandate of the act in the following way:

> Language revival and television broadcasting are two significant and quite separate endeavors that have been brought together under the mantle of one piece of legislation. In practice, the MTS has had to deal with two competing and occasionally contrasting imperatives: to use an unpopular language of the minority to make popular television for the majority. (Te Kāhui o Māhutonga, 2009, p. 8)

A key task for Māori Television programming is to find a balance between the language requirements that dictate the network's practices, and the need to attract and maintain an audience that can support broader language strategies as well as help to justify further government funding.

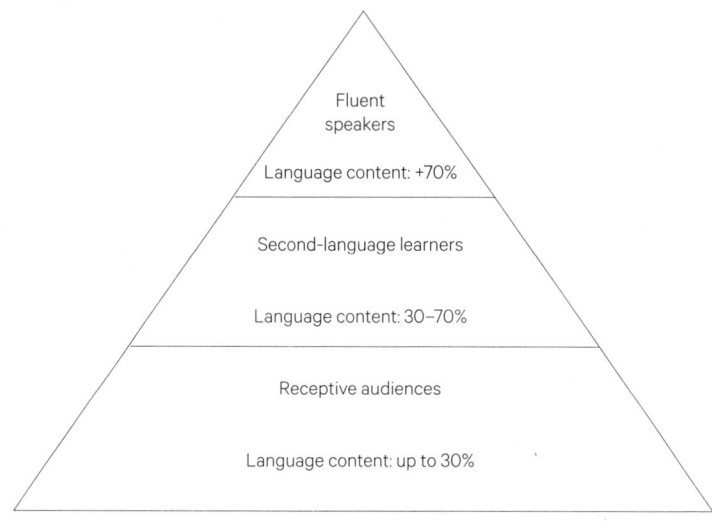

FIGURE 4.1 **TE MĀNGAI PĀHO PURCHASE AND FUNDING FRAMEWORK: LANGUAGE CONTENT (2010–2015)**

The network's varied appeal is encapsulated in its original tagline: 'Mā rātou; mā mātou; mā koutou; mā tātou', later shortened to 'Mā tātou'. For independent producer Kay Ellmers, making broadly appealing television content is a logical extension of being a media provider, even as this approach brings with it certain tensions that need to be constantly negotiated:

> I don't know how it would not be 'mā tātou' when it's a broadcast platform and that's the nature of a broadcast platform, it's open for anybody to come and see. I guess again it's just always that tension between staying true in what we want to do and what we want to discuss with ourselves, and then making it palatable to someone else which is the line I was constantly walking in mainstream broadcasting. (K. Ellmers, interview, 2012)

Ellmers's comments neatly summarise the competing tensions of an Indigenous media entity that must attract a broad audience in order to remain a viable organisation which is making good use of government funding, while also catering to the expectations of a niche Māori audience who constitute 14.9 per cent of New Zealand's total population, with a smaller niche audience of te reo Māori speakers and learners.

Over the years Māori Television has made programming which appeals to three different audiences, as determined by the funding agency Te Māngai Pāho:

- a receptive audience (appealing to beginner language learners with 0 to 30 per cent te reo content)
- second-language learners (appealing to intermediate learners, with 30 to 70 per cent te reo content)
- fluent speakers (over 70 per cent te reo content).

The youth market (audiences aged 14 to 29) is a long-standing priority for Māori Television, as intergenerational language transmission across whanāu is a key language revitalisation strategy.

Programming for language, culture and a broad audience

Funded by the state, Māori Television is not tied to the needs and demands of advertisers in the same way that commercial operators are, and yet audience share and ratings do have a role to play. According to *Hunting Aotearoa*'s producer Piripi Curtis:

> Ratings are important, because it means that people are watching your show and even more importantly it means that all our strategising and planning for reo outcomes has a better chance to have an impact. If we have only a few people watching, what's the point? Ratings also signal that people are enjoying what they are watching. When people enjoy what they are watching then they are more likely to accept te reo and tikanga as a natural form of Kiwi language and culture. (P. Curtis, interview, 2014)

Curtis's comments remind us of the balancing act Māori Television must constantly perform to reconcile its responsibilities to te reo and tikanga Māori with the need to maintain a consistent and growing audience. According to the Te Kāhui o Māhutonga report:

Conventional wisdom also suggests that a medium like Māori television will only survive if what is on offer to the viewer has popular appeal. Any television entity (even a public-service one) operates in a commercial environment. Broadcasting is an expensive business and attaches value to anything that generates revenue. (Te Kāhui o Māhutonga, 2009, p. 10)

Programming general manager Haunui Royal puts this dynamic another way when he states:

> But I think one of the questions to note here, probably one of the biggest questions, is language versus audience. It's the biggest – it is a dynamic tension and that's a strategy of programming. We describe our schedule as a Rubik's Cube. Scheduling just for audience? That's easy. Schedule for 51 per cent te reo programming in prime time catering for fluent speakers versus receptive Māori and non-Māori audiences? That's really hard. But what's interesting is that people go, 'Oh it's too much te reo Māori, it won't rate well.' But that's not necessarily the case. *Kai Time on the Road* for example is one of our most successful shows and it has a very high reo content. The skill of the presenter in presenting reo within the show is crucial. (H. Royal, interview, 2012)

As Royal's comments make clear, the language imperatives underpinning Māori Television pose challenges to programming and to scheduling staff, and also give rise to some innovative and creative programming practices.

The original legislation stipulated that Māori Television must broadcast the bulk of its language programming at peak viewing times, between 6 pm and 10.30 pm, a requirement since amended in light of online television content and on-demand viewing practices. Scheduler Greg Traill describes the competing demands that affect scheduling:

> We have got a lot more criteria compared to TV3. Their scheduling is compared to ratings and commercial sales. So for us, we have the act of Parliament, we have the Statement of Intent, programming strategy, genre, demographic, cultural sensitivity of Māoridom, language constraints; we've got language levels we have to think about, censorship, [and the] delivery of the programmes. (G. Traill, interview, 2012)

Royal further unpacks the dynamics of Māori Television programming practices in light of commercial industry norms:

In a commercial channel the programmer is god to a certain extent – you're given a contract, they say, 'Here's your job. You're going to give me 2 per cent more share of the market place. Here's your gun and you shoot anybody that's in your way.' That's pretty much how it works, and the programmers have a huge amount of power. Here, though, it's a very collaborative role and I have to bring everybody with me, and that can be quite tiring when you're trying to bring the executive, the board along with you. I've probably presented this [current] programming strategy about fifteen times. [Te Māngai Pāho] have been over it, the staff over it, the executive over it – eventually you just want to say, 'Can we just get on with it and do it?' But it's collaborative – we have a very collaborative way of working. (H. Royal, interview, 2012)

Solutions to these diverse demands have involved developing a scheduling strategy that offers a point of difference on the free-to-air television market, one that might attract a broad viewing audience as well as cater for language and cultural requirements.

In general, the art of programme scheduling follows two broad assumptions: that one is more likely to watch a programme that occurs before or after a programme most recently watched (adjacency), and the subsequent logic of flow that accompanies such viewing practices (Havens, 2006). Originally, programme scheduling was designed to mimic the rhythms of an average household, and offer programming to suit these rhythms. Hence, magazine shows on non-Māori networks tend to occur in the early evening when attention spans are distracted by household activities (coming home from work, preparing dinner), while the storytelling appeal of longer-form television is scheduled for the mid evening once household members have settled in for the night (Ellis, 2000).

At a time when media consumption occurs across such a range of different spaces, places and screens, the art of scheduling faces challenges. These challenges are intensified when you are a minority-language media producer working within a popular entertainment medium such as television. Yet Māori Television has initiated a range of programming innovations that have drawn audience attention. Think of the diverse sports programming on offer in the early days of Māori Television, or the innovations in the cooking show genre offered by *Kai Time on the Road* and *Marae Kai Masters,* or the coverage of various regional, national and iwi events over Māori Television's first ten years. To zig where others zag, in a programming context, means to divert the flow of audience attention away from mainstream media providers, using new and novel content as the bait. Think of the schedule decisions surrounding *Native Affairs*. Initially screened on Sunday nights at 8 pm, with a repeat screening at 10 pm on a Monday, in 2008 the show shifted to Monday nights at 8 pm and then to 8.30 pm in 2010. This is a distinctive programming decision given that other free-to-air providers often screen drama series such as *Desperate Housewives* or *Criminal Minds* in the Monday-night time slot. Another scheduling strategy established in the early days was to offer an international art-house film at 9 pm. Greg Traill notes how: 'The thinking in the early years [was] when audiences go mainstream, they check what's on, watch for half an hour, if they don't like it they come to us at 9 pm. And it's worked' (G. Traill, interview, 2012). Once audiences switch over to Māori Television to watch content that may have a general appeal, it is hoped that they might stay on for more reo- and tikanga-styled programming. While these strategies are constantly evolving, the craft behind scheduling on Māori Television's first channel in 2012 was described by Traill as follows:

> All our days are themed. On Sunday night we have reality/whānau-styled programming in the early evening. Monday night we have *Native Affairs* and current affairs programming. After *Native Affairs* we tend to go for the older audiences. Tuesday night is our international night so we would ask for programmes that have some issues with an international skew. Wednesday night is our 100 per cent reo night, so we have all our Māori programmes on that night. Thursday night's our sports entertainment night. Friday's entertainment night, family entertainment like *Hōmai te Pakipaki*. Saturday night we have our Saturday feature which plays at 9 pm. Sunday night, again, is the Rialto-style movies, and whānau again in the early evenings, such as *Kai Time on the Road*, *It's in the Bag*, those kind of programmes. (G. Traill, interview, 2012)

This programming strategy helps to create a vertical flow across the programme schedule, and to build and retain audiences. Screening family-styled programming is an important strategy to engage the notoriously difficult youth market. For an audience segment attracted to populist programming on channels such as TV2 and TV4, Royal used family-friendly programming, particularly on a Saturday night, to capture a multi-generational viewing audience.

Although language requirements add complexity to the already challenging task of providing programming content in an aggressively competitive environment, Māori Television's status as a state-funded organisation means that the network has a stable funding source, which means that their schedule can be planned between three to six months in advance. For long-time media producer and former Māori Television Board director Ian Taylor (Ngāti Kahungunu, Ngāpuhi), this is an advantage for Māori Television and could help foster innovations in programming, compared with commercial operators, who have to drive big numbers to generate advertising revenue: 'You know TVNZ, TV3, Sky, all of those people have to be really careful about when and where they move, because they risk losing an audience. We have the huge advantage that we don't face that risk; there is only an upside' (I. Taylor, interview, 2013).

This schedule stability has enabled the network to develop strengths in the area of extended coverage of one-off national events. According to the general manager of production from 2009 to 2014, Carol Hirschfeld (Ngāti Porou), working at Māori Television has led to new opportunities for television production:

> There's a lot of youthful vitality here, and a lot of originality that isn't immediately stifled as it can so easily be with bigger, more commercially driven broadcasters. And there's a wider brief in what you can do here. For example, one reason our bid to broadcast the 2011 Rugby World Cup was supported was that we could guarantee we'd run it free to air in prime time. Other broadcasters can't do that. Same with the Christchurch telethon, and our extended coverage of things like Anzac Day and Waitangi Day. We can turn over entire days of programming to covering those things in depth, and commission associated programmes to support that coverage. ('The Little Station that Could', *Sunday Star-Times*, 23 March 2014)

In the current climate, where public-service television is in decline, Māori Television has established itself as an innovative and public-oriented media organisation.

Programming across the years

In its first ten years Māori Television's programming and scheduling helped the network to establish its audience and it built a reputable brand for the network. An impact survey conducted in 2010 by Te Puni Kōkiri, together with Māori Television, Te Māngai Pāho and Te Taura Whiri i te Reo Māori, described Māori Television as having a 'marked positive contributing impact on Māori language revitalisation' (Te Puni Kōkiri, 2010, p. 4). Māori Television's programming strategies no doubt contributed to this positive impact. The strategies across a ten-year period can be roughly organised into three distinct periods: a start-up phase (between 2004 and 2007), a period of consolidation (2008 to 2011), and a third phase characterised by a closer focus on the language remit, and efforts to extend a digital presence (2012 to 2014).

To understand Māori Television programming practices in its start-up phase we have to remember that the network was functioning in a political climate where the Labour-led government had an investment in the idea of public broadcasting and a fondness for nation-building rhetoric. Sue Abel suggests that this might account for the emphasis on nationhood noted in the policies and documents concerning Māori Television at the time, as well as the focus on nationhood in the language of the 2003 act (Abel, 2011). The network is also part of a wider Māori-language sector, and the 2003 Māori Television Service Act emerged in the same year as Te Rautaki Reo Māori, the Māori Language Strategy, which was the main policy guiding the language sector at this time. The strategy highlighted techniques for language revitalisation that included strengthening language skills, usage, educational opportunities, community leadership and recognition of the language, but it provided little detail on how these techniques might be implemented (Freeman-Tayler, 2014). Subsequent reviews of the strategy occurred in 2009 and 2010, but with no action taken by Te Puni Kōkiri until December 2013, when the government announced a new strategy that is still the subject of much debate in te ao Māori, with outcomes yet to be decided.

With no firm implementation plan for how te reo might be revitalised, organisations such as Māori Television had to develop their own strategies, in unison with the demands placed on it by funding agent and fellow language organisation Te Māngai Pāho. According to Hone Edwards, the challenge of finding quality programming content in the early days of Māori Television was exacerbated by this lack of cohesion within the larger Māori-language broadcast sector, and an independent Māori media sector that was not yet firmly established:

> I think there were only about four of us to start getting stuff onto the shelf and at the time there weren't any guidelines around requests for proposals. They didn't really

know what they wanted and how much money... Te Māngai Pāho was willing to put aside for programming. (H. Edwards, interview, 2012)

Under these conditions Māori Television still managed to broadcast 7.9 hours of programming on average per day, with more than 50 per cent of the content in te reo Māori, and with two of these broadcast hours dedicated to children's programming (Māori Television Service, 2005b).

Programmes such as news show *Te Kāea* (an in-house production), language-learning show *Kōrero Mai* (Cinco Cine Film Productions), cooking show *Kai Time on the Road* (Maui Productions), reality television show *Marae DIY* (Hula Haka Productions) and GBLT magazine show *Takatāpui* (Front of the Box Productions) emerged between 2004 and 2007. According to Te Māngai Pāho's 2005 annual report, Māori Television's cumulative audience showed an increase in its viewership of 28 per cent in its first year, and the report described the network as providing 'the kind of programming that brands Māori Television as a station for all New Zealanders' (p. 7). This focus on a broad appeal to New Zealand audiences was echoed in the network's 2005 annual report, in which normalising te reo Māori among non-Māori audiences was discussed as a key language revitalisation strategy:

> Normalisation of te reo Māori will occur if people are given the opportunity to increase their knowledge and understanding. Given the small percentage of fluent te reo Māori speakers in New Zealand, we must find ways in which to ensure more New Zealanders are able to access and understand our programmes. We will continue existing and implement new initiatives such as increasing levels of English sub-titling, captioning and sign posting, to meet the needs of our non-fluent viewers. (Māori Television Service, 2005b, p. 14)

Māori media veteran Larry Parr held the position of general manager of programming between 2005 and 2008 and was responsible for significant programme innovations such as the all-day coverage of Anzac Day, a television event that 'secured the place of Māori Television in the NZ broadcasting landscape' (www.nzonscreen.com). The start-up phase of Māori Television also included the popular sports show *CODE* (2005–2016), with its relaxed and whānau-oriented presentation style and catch phrase 'Mean Māori Mean'. This phase also included agony aunt series *Ask Your Auntie* (2005–2007), *Hunting Aotearoa* (2005–) and children's programme *Mīharo* (2006–). Other live and extended coverage included events such as Waitangi Day celebrations, the biennial Te Matatini festival and the 2005 national election, the latter covered by news and current affairs shows *Te Kāea* and *Te Hēteri*.

In 2006 the network provided extended coverage of the tangi of Te Arikinui Dame Te Atairangikaahu, hosted in both English and Māori by Julian Wilcox and Wena Harawira. This period also saw attempts to establish Māori Television as the 'home of Māori sports', including league and rugby coverage, waka ama championships and the Māori Sports Awards. In keeping with Māori Television's tendency to zig where others zag, 2007 saw the launch of current affairs show *Native Affairs*, at a time when TVNZ was restructuring its news and current affairs department, involving a loss of more than 50 jobs.

Under a newly elected National government, the public broadcasting sector experienced a budget freeze in the wake of the global financial crisis of 2007/08 as the government took a 'value for money' approach to the public sector. A 2010 NZ On Air report on Māori programming, *Ngā Matakiirea*, noted that '[w]ith the entire television industry affected by the global economic crisis, a reliance on government funding is an obvious threat to mainstream Māori programming' (NZ On Air, 2010, p. 34). The report went on to refer to stakeholder feedback on the broadcasting climate at the time:

> This government seems to be about measurable results. I don't think you can measure everything, especially cultural enrichment. Be careful about using hard and fast measurements. Bureaucrats can end up not measuring the true value. (p. 34)

While fiscal constraints began to mark the public broadcasting sector at this time, the review of the Māori Television Service Act also took place. The 2009 review found that:

> Despite difficulties in the beginning, MTS has broadcast a comprehensive bi-lingual television service for five years. The MTS has a dedicated and growing audience. It provides a programme schedule that is an alternative to the offerings of mainstream television. It has given the Māori language a heightened presence in broadcasting, and a consequent public profile. (Te Kāhui o Māhutonga, 2009, p. 2)

Among other recommendations, the review found that many stakeholders were concerned with the overall quality of te reo Māori being broadcast. Feedback from one stakeholder contended that:

> There needs to be higher standards regarding the language. There should be an increase in the number of Māori language presenters as well as a standard proficiency testing of presenters. There is a high percentage of cheap Māori language programming which affects the way you ingest it – it makes the language unattractive. The measurement of language quantum levels should be infused with the measurement of the quality of the language. (Te Kāhui o Māhutonga, 2009, p. 11)

In light of this review, Māori Television annual reports at the time referred to the development of a Māori Television language strategy. Further commitment to quality language-learning programming came in 2010 in the form of *Kōwhao Rau* (Kura Productions) and *Ako* (Māori Television Service).*

Veteran broadcaster and te reo expert Quinton Hita devised and presents *Kōwhao Rau*, which features intimate kōrero with Ngāpuhi kaumātua who have led 'extraordinary lives'.† In 2013 this series inspired a spin-off programme, *Taniwha Rau* (Kura Productions, 2013–), which focuses on the mita of the Tainui peoples.

The 2010 language-learning programme *Ako* was part of the network's attempt to increase the amount of quality te reo content and strengthen its language revitalisation focus. *Ako* featured one of the most revered te reo Māori speakers of contemporary times, Pānia Papa, who also played a central role as a language-plan adviser to the independent Māori media sector. *Ako* is set in a classroom-like context, with six students at varying levels of te reo skill. This set-up is to encourage the idea that the audience is part of the class. 'Passionate about language revitalisation', Papa hoped that *Ako* would 'raise the [te reo] proficiency level across the board'. Furthermore, she noted in a media interview that there 'is a lot of focus on beginner level te reo speakers, but we want to provide something to those who have shown a commitment to getting themselves fluent'. This is achieved through a programme that 'has a grammar focus', which is important to 'improving accuracy'.‡

---

* Shown in 2010. http://www.maoritelevision.com/tv/shows/ako
† As described in promotional material for the programme which can be found at http://www.maoritelevision.com/tv/shows/kowhao-rau
‡ http://www.nzine.co.nz/features/maoritv_sucesses.html?PTPFrom= percent2Findex percent2FTravel_N_Leisure.html

Between 2008 and 2011 Māori Television continued its tradition of offering bilingual programming content that reworked existing television formats and genres. Since its launch, Māori Television has drawn on established global television formats (lifestyle programming, reality television and game shows) to make programmes that appeal to a broad audience. The recycle and re-use of television formats has been a global phenomenon since what some scholars describe as the 'communication revolution' of the 1990s, which resulted in the global spread of a commercialised mode of broadcasting, together with fears of cultural imperialism and an attendant increase in national regulatory measures to protect local content (Oren and Shahaf, 2012). Māori Television programming that reworks global formats includes sports programming (*Hunting Aotearoa* and *CODE*), food television (*Kai Time on the Road*, *Kai Ora* and *Fusion Feast*) and the talent-show format (*Hōmai te Pakipaki*, *Kanikani Mai* and *Māorioke*) among others. In 2009 Blue Bach Productions (run by Otaki-based Libby Hakaraia, and Tainui Stephens) secured the rights to a fondly remembered New Zealand game show, *It's in the Bag* hosted by Selwyn Toogood. The newly revamped *It's in the Bag* featured Pio Terei and Stacey Daniels Morrison. Libby Hakaraia described the show as an 'antidote' to reality television despite having a game-show format. This is illustrated in the way that the show has a 'completely different reference point and construct' to that of typical reality programmes. When rejuvenating *It's in the Bag*, Hakaraia made a conscious decision to move away from city-centric production and values in a number of ways, taking the programme on the road to small and more rural communities. The values of community are supported during the filming and broadcast of the programme, with a notable example being that all the money collected at the door from the audience is given as a koha for local projects or charities. Hakaraia has stated that you can 'go anywhere in New Zealand and there are real people wanting to say something' and that for many of those people, a 'bag of kina is more real ... than winning *X-Factor*'.*

In 2013 Tūmanako Productions (run by Kay Ellmers) continued the tradition of reworking reality television formats with *Marae Kai Masters*, a cooking show featuring head-to-head cook offs between eight marae-based teams of four and presented by Te Kohe Tuhaka and Nevak Rogers.

---

* See Hakaraia's 2011 Radio NZ Interview accessed at http://podcast.radionz.co.nz/sat/sat-20110917-1105-libby_hakaraia_-_in_the_bag-048.mp3

According to Ellmers, the objective of *Marae Kai Masters* was to 'create a show that promoted community building and encouraged rangatahi to gravitate towards the kitchen'. Ellmers explained that, 'at its heart, *Marae Kai Masters* is all about celebrating our ringawera . . . the men and women who give tirelessly to keep the home fires burning and manaaki manuhiri up and down the motu'. As such, the programme reflects the values and objectives of Tūmanako Productions with its long-term production of factual programming that represents Māori in diverse and meaningful ways.*

During its period of consolidation, Māori Television also launched its second channel, Te Reo, in 2008 on the Freeview platform (and via Sky) with funding assistance from the outgoing Labour government. This two-channel strategy now enabled the network to deliver 70 per cent te reo language programming during prime time (Māori Television, 2009). New programming for Te Reo included *Te Pātaka Kōrero*, an oral history series, *Ko Tawa*, a series depicting the stories behind taonga collected by Captain Gilbert Mair, and *Ngā Pari Kārangaranga o te Motu*, a series produced by iwi, for iwi and about iwi, and aimed at promoting the diversity of dialect.

For the executive producer of Te Reo, Eruera Morgan (Te Arawa, Tainui), *Ngā Pari Kārangaranga* is an opportunity for iwi to record their people, their histories and their mita before it gets lost. When discussing the meaning of the programme's title, Morgan explains:

> 'Ngā pari kārangaranga' is a traditional metaphor that refers to the echoing cliffs facing us. Many years ago, that was a way of transmitting voices – from the cliff faces. 'Pari' is the cliff face. 'Kārangaranga' is when the voice projects outwards to the rest of the valley or the community. It's a means of communicating in their own language. (E. Morgan, interview, 2014)

When asked to describe the difference between Te Reo and the bilingual Māori Television channel, Morgan said:

> Kiwi and iwi – that's how I view the two channels. So Kiwi is Māori Television, and iwi is Te Reo channel. When I say 'iwi' whether you are kōhanga reo, kura kaupapa, wharekura, wānanga, iwi, as in all of our various iwi throughout the country, various

---

* See Ellmers's interview in *Mana: the Māori news magazine for all New Zealanders*, Jun/Jul 2013, pp. 58–60.

regions, so it appeals to a Māori-speaking community – that is what Te Reo is all about. (E. Morgan, interview, 2014)

While Te Reo consolidated its programming schedule in this period, extending its broadcast hours from 7 pm to 11 pm daily in 2010, between 2009 and 2010 Māori Television devoted 12 per cent of its total hours to international drama, documentaries and film. This included global Indigenous content, such as the Aboriginal Australian-themed series *The Circuit* (SBS, 2007–2009), a legal drama about an Aboriginal lawyer who moves to the remote Kimberley region in Western Australia; and *East West 101* (Knapman and Wyld, 2007–2011), a culturally diverse detective drama. By including global Indigenous content as part of its programming strategy, Māori Television helped to strengthen its global profile as a media maker and curator of global Indigenous content, a profile that bypasses the constraints of national borders to affirm the shared predicaments across nations experienced by some Indigenous peoples. A further strategy to enhance global connections with Indigenous communities occurred in this period with Māori Television's launch of the inaugural World Indigenous Television Broadcaster's Network in 2008, with a conference hosted by Māori Television on the theme of 'Reclaiming Our Future'.

Between 2008 and 2011 the network continued to make appeals to New Zealand nationhood by adapting a much-loved New Zealand author's children's novel, by hosting the 2011 telethon *Rise Up* for Christchurch on the third anniversary of the city's earthquake, and by making a bid to broadcast a global sporting event (the Rugby World Cup) close to the nation's heart.

In 2009 Māori Television embarked on a co-production deal with Te Māngai Pāho and NZ On Air to adapt Margaret Mahy's novel *Kaitangata Twitch* into a thirteen-part children's drama. The production team were largely non-Māori but included the scriptwriting talents of Briar Grace-Smith and the digital effects expertise of Ian Taylor's Animation Research Ltd. This was Māori Television's 'first "high-end" drama production', predominantly in English, that appealed to a general audience (McLeod, 2013, p. 75), and it was subsequently nominated for the Prix Jeunesse, an international children's television award.

Perhaps the most high-profile programming strategy in this period was Māori Television's bid to secure exclusive free-to-air broadcasting rights to the 2011 Rugby World Cup (a tournament eventually won by the host nation,

New Zealand). The possibility of having 10 per cent of the World Cup commentary spoken in te reo Māori was enough to generate a public outcry that went far beyond the confines of the nation's television industry, with many complaining vociferously that Māori Television could only transmit to 90 per cent of the population, a complaint that conveniently overlooked the fact that two other broadcasters (the privately owned TV3 and Prime) had similar transmission restrictions.* Other questions were raised about the financial backing that Māori Television had received from the Minister of Māori Affairs, Dr Pita Sharples, and Te Puni Kōkiri. The National government quickly responded by offering financial backing to rival state broadcaster TVNZ, a move that threatened to create a bidding war between the two institutions. Māori Television CEO Jim Mather subsequently expressed disappointment over the level of political management that occurred around the bid.

National Party leader and Prime Minister John Key ultimately prevented a bidding war by offering Māori Television symbolic leadership of a three-way deal with TVNZ and TV3 – a resolution which, while still claimed as a political victory, fell far short of Māori Television's original bid for exclusive rights. Pita Sharples drew attention to the fact that the 2011 World Cup event would occur in election year – as indeed it did – and saw the government's panicky reaction as being about control, and fear of the impact of rugby commentary including an element of te reo Māori. According to press reports, the subsequent coverage provided by Māori Television yielded positive ratings results for the network, with an average audience of 402,206 viewers per game.† The hosting of this global event also confirmed Māori Television's expertise in multicam and live-action television production, further enhancing their esteem within the media industry.

Between 2012 and 2014 Te Māngai Pāho began to introduce the requirement for independent media producers to include a language plan in their applications for funding of productions, and the 'ZePA' language of 'right-shifting' began to circulate within the Māori media sector. In a briefing to incoming ministers in 2014, Te Māngai Pāho stated:

---

* *Dominion Post*, 15 October 2009.
† http://www.nzherald.co.nz/entertainment/news/article.cfm?c_id=1501119&objectid=10751300

In 2012/13 Te Māngai Pāho adopted the ZePA model and the Right shift approach. The ZePA model highlights how Right-shifting the position of an individual from Zero to Passive to Active can strengthen the position of the language within society. The key difference is that the emphasis is not simply on moving directly from Zero to Active. Right-shifting an individual from Zero to Passive can generate increased awareness and support for language revitalisation more broadly, and the subsequent right-shift from Passive to Active is then easier to achieve. (Te Māngai Pāho, 2014, p. 16)

Changes to the Māori Television Service Act also took place on the basis of the 2009 review. Removing 'broad appeal' from the legislation, the revised wording of the Act read:

> The principal function of the Service is to contribute to the protection and promotion of te reo Māori me ōna tikanga through the provision, in te reo Māori and English, of a high-quality, cost-effective television service that informs, educates, and entertains viewers, and enriches New Zealand's society, culture, and heritage.*

While the shift in wording now freed Māori Television from the need to appeal to a 'broad' audience, incoming CEO Paora Maxwell (2014–) raised concerns on behalf of the Māori Television Board, about the shift from 'te reo Māori me ngā tikanga' to 'te reo Māori me ōna tikanga' (the altered wording meaning 'the Māori language and its accepted linguistic norms'). This change was never part of the recommendations made by Te Kāhui o Māhutonga, but was added once the Māori Affairs Select Committee consulted with governing body Te Pūtahi Pāoho. In a 2014 *Briefing to Incoming Ministers*, the Māori Television Board argued that the act should revert back to the original wording 'te reo Māori me ngā tikanga' (meaning 'the Māori language and Māori traditional cultural practices'). Claiming that the original wording better reflects the aims of those who initially fought for Māori broadcasting, the briefing noted:

> In the Māori world view, Māori culture itself, and traditional practices at the core of being Māori, were taonga equal in value to the language. This belief was at the foundation of the Māori effort to reclaim and reassert Māori values and culture through

---

* Māori Television Service Amendment Act 2013.

the language. Retention of the two taonga, the language and the culture, was the true purpose of those long campaigns. The Waitangi Tribunal Wai 262 decision in 2010 offered the following summary: 'In July 1991, Cabinet took its undertakings on Māori broadcasting to the High Court. These included, amongst other things, the development of special-purpose Māori television. The Crown accepted that "the Maori language and culture were taonga, and hence entitled to the protection of the Crown in accordance with article 2 of the Treaty"'. (Māori Television, 2014a, p. 20)

Acknowledging that 'normalising te reo was always its major purpose' in the fight for Māori media, this document also argued that a major secondary role was 'the promotion of Māori traditional culture . . . and informing both Māori and non-Māori about it' (p. 19). For Maxwell and the board, the new wording was 'profoundly important', because it 'serves as the primary principle from which a host of resourcing and programming decisions are made' (p. 21). That is to say, the new wording of the act might have implications for the kind of funding the network can access as well as the kind of programming it can offer. In an aggressively competitive market, where audience share still matters to a non-commercial television provider, the network's ability to access funding from a range of sources (including NZ On Air, sponsorship and advertising) is of great importance.

This period also witnessed a further extension of broadcast hours for Te Reo to enhance its children's and youth programme offerings. The live infotainment talkshow *Mataora* was launched on Te Reo in 2012 and was initially hosted by Eruera Morgan. On the bilingual channel a daily five-hour language tuition block, under the sponsorship of Te Wānanga o Raukawa, replaced infomercials. According to Julian Wilcox, audiences received these changes positively:

> I think the change that the executive incorporated this year by extending the hours of broadcast – namely 9 to 12 having the three hours of acquisition, and then 12 to 3 having mainly application language programmes – I think that was a positive thing and the audience numbers are certainly higher than when we had Guthy-Renker infomercials. (J. Wilcox, interview, 2012)

This programming strategy was designed to enable those viewers who wanted an immersive flow of te reo to tune into the language block on the bilingual channel and then switch to Te Reo for further immersive language content.

For Wilcox, Te Reo was one of the major achievements of the network's first ten years, as it offers the kind of 100 per cent television programming that advocates of the language have long desired.

With the government's decision to complete the digital switch over by December 2013, another of Māori Television's focuses for the 2012 to 2014 period included developing its profile as a digital media provider. In July 2011 former assistant CEO and head of content at TVNZ, as well as former group head of digital for Fairfax Media, Stephen Smith, joined Māori Television as general manager of the digital strategy (a position since reorganised as head of multi-platform in 2014). One of the prime elements that attracted Smith to Māori Television was the organisation's strong sense of identity and clear sense of purpose, a coherent 'brand' necessary in a media era where 'content is king'. According to Smith, Māori Television has a very clearly laid out content proposition, based on the legislation governing its practices, which emphasises 'the recognition and rejuvenation of language and tikanga (culture) Māori'. Reflecting on the difference between TVNZ's identity and Māori Television's, Smith stated:

> If I said to someone, 'Well, what's TVNZ's identity?' I think that the majority of people, even within the industry, might struggle a little. They'd be able to talk to you more about what it was, than what it is. They definitely wouldn't be able to tell you what they think it's going to be. Whereas I think defined by its content proposition, and where it has been able to position itself with its audience, I think the identity for Māori Television is evident in the ease by which people give you a sense of their own relationship with it, in a way that is increasingly more difficult with other [New Zealand] media entities. (S. Smith, interview, 2013)

Māori Television's coherent identity enables the network to provide niche media content that sets a high level of expectation about tone, quality and theme that can then be harnessed across a range of media platforms. Another strength Smith sees in Māori Television is the fact that it is the 'originator, the producer, the curator of content that it has and manages' (S. Smith, interview, 2013). In an era when media providers are often the aggregators of media content produced elsewhere, being the originator of media content contributes to its authority and credibility. As such, the aphorism 'content is king' needs to be nuanced by the need to understand the context in which the content emerges.

Māori Television has worked on improving its online presence. Until its re-launch in 2009, the organisation's website appeared to be little more than a digital container for the programming schedule, policy documents and statements of intent. However, by 2010 its annual report noted that 'a total of 2779 hours of video content have been made available via the website. This content is comprised of 453 hours of 100 per cent Māori-language programmes and 2326 hours of bilingual programmes' (Māori Television Service, 2010b, p. 20). The report also noted the lack of geo-blocking on the website, which means that access to media content is not restricted by geography and can help accomplish Māori Television's vision to deliver 'Māori language and culture programming to the global community' or, at the very least, to the New Zealand diaspora (Māori Television Service, 2009b, p. 2). According to its 2010 Statement of Intent, following the website's re-launch, visitors increased 2.5-fold, with one-fifth of them coming from Australia (Māori Television Service, 2010b).

In 2013 Māori Television conducted an overhaul of the website, which now arranged media content according to language competencies, and provided more opportunities for audience participation. Online viewers were able to provide feedback in real time, comment on selected news stories, use the 'Share Your News' function, and tweet, share and recommend Māori Television content. These strategies align with Jim Mather's 2013 vision for the network:

> So we need to adapt and adapt in a true sense of the word, not just pay lip service and think that by taking a programme off our broadcast schedule and putting it on our website that's meeting the requirements of our viewers. We need to go much, much further than that. So I think in five years' time Māori Television will be probably more focused on producing or acquiring or commissioning content and actually having a different mentality associated with that, as opposed to being a traditional television broadcaster that has an audience waiting for us to release our weekly schedule and who will sit there and watch a programme, a line-up, because that's what's been decided by our programmers. (J. Mather, interview, 2013)

Digital media provide opportunities for greater audience engagement and interaction and complement Māori Television's governing commitment to revitalise and rejuvenate Māori language and culture, as well as the service's status as an Indigenous media entity. According to Haunui Royal:

I suppose the dream is having an interactive hosting presence that can utilise digital technologies to enhance the learning experience and create second-screen experiences. The TV medium is largely passive and this is where the digital space has so many advantages. I think the website ultimately is the tool to take teaching te reo to the next level because of its ability to engage in online and active conversations, and the use of gameplay as well. This crosses over to the areas of children's programming and we are very pleased [now] to be able to bring four top children's programmes in te reo for our tamariki and mokopuna: *Dora the Explorer*, *Sponge Bob Square Pants*, *Team Umizumi* and *Penguins of Madagascar*. (H. Royal, interview, 2012)

In addition, the network now has the capacity to use online analytics and software to track audiences, particularly rangatahi, to learn more about audience behaviour and how they consume media. The promise of greater interactivity between audiences and programming content in a digital era is best encapsulated in the 2014 series *Swagger* (Raukatauri Productions, 2014–), a programme directed at the youth audience and made by youth themselves.

The 2014 emergence of *Swagger* signalled Māori Television's commitment to programming that might appeal to a youthful, media-savvy demographic. Part of the appeal included highlighting the role of media technologies as storytelling vehicles for youth. Drawing on digital media was a language-learning strategy directed at youth, as the mystique surrounding digital technologies could help to generate positive feelings about a minority language (Cormack, 2007). Or, as Gearóid Ó Tuathaigh has argued – in the context of Irish-language media – media technologies provide 'acoustic credibility' to younger viewers so that they may see their language as part of the contemporary setting (Ó Tuathaigh, quoted in Lysaght, 2010). Accordingly, *Swagger* involved a core group of youth ranging in age from nine to 26, drawn from various parts of the North Island. Equipped with an iPhone 5, external microphones, tripods, steady-cams, and after two workshops with professional media makers, the participants delivered media content for the thirteen 30-minute episodes. According to the introductory voice-over from one of the participants (and production assistant), Ngawaero Maniapoto (24), *Swagger* offered:

a whole new way of thinking about television. We have technology at our fingertips and we are already using it. We make movies to go on YouTube, Facebook, Vine,

Snapchat, Tumblr and Instagram. We are already putting things that are important to us online. So why not put it on television?

Each contributor produced original material in te reo Māori or English, from their own perspectives and interests, and their stories spanned the thirteen-week episode structure and included a range of topics. Huia Mace (17) provided stories based around her parents and their Auckland store Native Agent. Teina Terei (15) offered exercise and diet tips for those wanting to get in shape, while Te Kaha Jonathan (12) went to various sporting events, including ki ō rahi (a ball game) and theme park Rainbow's End. Ngawaero Maniapoto (24) shared her daily routines with her child, Finau, and Kevin Harrison (22) provided coverage of the ceremonial waka taua *Te Hono ki Aotearoa* (the link to New Zealand) and its journey to the River Thames in London for Her Majesty Queen Elizabeth's Diamond Jubilee Pageant. The range of material gathered by the *Swagger* team included travel reports from Berlin and Switzerland, anti-drug messages, makeover fashion segments, and food and study tips. A second season was launched in 2015 suggesting that the first series was well received.

By promoting a close relationship between online media and television, *Swagger* raises questions about the role that user-generated media content might play in shaping future television practices. Such practices might lead to different forms of television with lower overheads, and which are more responsive to the needs and views of audiences. However, media scholars argue that user-generated content can also lead to exploitation, as audiences draw on their own free time and energy to make media content for professional media providers (Petersen, 2008; Van Dijck, 2009; Hearn, 2010).

Future programming challenges

In an era when the range of media content continues to expand, Māori Television must compete with other free-to-air providers, as well as the dominance of Sky in New Zealand's media market. Emerging online businesses such as Netflix and Lightbox, which provide global media content at competitive prices, will further intensify competition.

The governing logic of Māori Television programming has been to 'zig where others zag', meaning that Māori Television has provided programming not offered by other media organisations, a strategy that has diversified New Zealand's television culture. Yet this kind of programming strategy may need to be revised in light of what some scholars call an era of digital plenty. Trisha Dunleavy and Hester Joyce define this era as including 'a vastly increased channel and programme menu, alternative delivery platforms' and 'an increased sense of "me-TV control"' (Dunleavy and Joyce, 2011, p. 173). In such an era the promise of greater consumer interactions and alternative ways of producing and distributing media are framed as attractive options in the wake of waning state interest in public-service media. Indeed, Peter Thompson has argued that when the incumbent National government was asked about the civic rationale for its media policies, National politicians resorted to invoking 'myths about market competition and digital plenty' (P. Thompson, 2012, p. 6). These are the conditions under which Māori Television currently labours.

Māori Television has proven itself able to excel at extended coverage of national and cultural events such as Anzac Day and Te Matatini, and in 2011 demonstrated its ability to compete with other free-to-air media providers in its bid for exclusive rights to the Rugby World Cup. These media events certainly chime with research on the role played by television in minority language wellbeing. As discussed, research suggests that the public visibility of a minority language helps to reassure speakers that their language is relevant and significant (Lysaght, 2010; Cormack, 2007). According to former Māori Television Service research manager Coral Palmer (Waikato–Tainui, Ngāti Maniapoto), Māori Television's Rugby World Cup coverage raised the network's national profile significantly, and by extension that of te reo and tikanga Māori. But Palmer also pondered how sustainable such brand awareness can be when she noted: 'The Rugby World Cup was good for bringing in a large number of viewers, but it wasn't in line with our normal programming, so it is not just about attracting new viewers but more importantly about retaining them' (C. Palmer, interview, 2012).

Hone Edwards offered a similar point of view when he suggested that the ratings spikes generated by the Rugby World Cup coverage needed some additional programming momentum behind them in order to hold the audience:

> Our audiences definitely increased during the Rugby World Cup but I think being able to measure the success of the Rugby World Cup lies in the aftermath not right then,

when the game was going to air. It was after, when the Rugby World Cup was over. What did we have to offer up to keep those audiences there? We had nothing. So I think it's a grand idea to go out and do all of that sort of stuff, I think it's great – but how do you hold those audiences there? (H. Edwards, interview, 2012)

High-status media events such as the Rugby World Cup do important work in promoting awareness of Māori Television among national and even international audiences, but the problem of retaining viewers remains. Perhaps to zig where others zag is no longer the best way to describe programming strategies at a time when on-demand delivery allows consumers and audiences the freedom to organise their own flow of media content.

Recent audience surveys suggest that more traditional viewing practices still dominate in New Zealand (NZ On Air, 2014a), or, as the director of Australian ABC said in 2008, '[t]here is no doubt that the bow of the ship is still the television in the corner of the living room' (quoted in Turner and Tay, 2009, p. 86). However, media providers, including Māori Television, increasingly straddle the space between 'old' and 'new' media processes. Imagining Māori Television in the year 2018, Jim Mather noted:

> I would want to see Māori Television being a different type of organisation, to have completed its transition from being a traditional broadcaster to being a new media organisation, a completely relevant media organisation. By that I mean we're in an industry that's changing significantly and television hasn't really changed so much in the preceding 60 years from when it was first introduced in New Zealand through to five to ten years ago. The internet has been the key driver of that change, but also I think the relationship has changed between ourselves and our viewers. It's no longer a one-way, static broadcast situation. Now the expectations upon us are just so much greater and we need to realise that television is no longer the most powerful medium in the world, and it's been a long time since it has been, actually. And so our organisation needs to adapt to reflect the fact that traditional linear television is only going to meet the requirements of a part of our audience, and that part is diminishing. With the generation of digital natives that are evolving, television is not even their primary means of information and entertainment – it's just one of a range of options. (J. Mather, interview, 2013)

To remain 'completely relevant', Māori Television has to keep expanding its audience reach, particularly among those younger media consumers who make up a significant proportion of the Māori population. The youth demographic is crucial to any minority-language strategy, as intergenerational transmission is an important tactic to ensure the survival of a language (Fishman, 1991). Coral Palmer described audience feedback from younger viewers in the following way: 'They want to see themselves on TV. They want to see their friends and their whānau. They're the "me" generation, so we are trying to integrate more of that into programming' (C. Palmer, interview, 2012).

While *Swagger* is one way in which Māori Television has appealed to the youth market, the programme's creator and producer Hinewehi Mohi highlighted the difficulty of creating programming that can deliver on the language mandate required by the funder and network, at the same time as appealing to those rangatahi who are the targets of such language objectives. Commenting on her experience of working with, and raising, rangatahi, Mohi notes how English-language or bilingual media content is the preferred form of programming, even for those rangatahi who have proficiency in te reo Māori. When asked why, Mohi reflects:

> Possibly popular culture and Americana has become more influential than their own culture. It's all the slang that they can use and they just want to be cool and the same as everyone else. They possibly take te reo Māori for granted because they haven't had to fight for it, struggle for it. (H. Mohi, interview, 2014)

Mohi's comments allude to the intergenerational tensions experienced by second-language-learning parents who have struggled to achieve fluency in te reo Māori, and who have supported their children through kōhanga reo and kura kaupapa Māori schooling systems to become fluent Māori speakers. Mohi's comments also hint at the symbolic power of global media content and the value attributed to such media content. When asked what potential solutions she might see to this dilemma, Mohi said:

> We need to get them excited about integrating the language with popular culture, because they largely see it as ceremonial and instructional. And there are few young Māori who instinctively speak Māori as their first language with others . . . I think because schools are earnest in their approach to the protocols, because they're desperate to make Māori a priority, this might sometimes make it boring and some kids are sort of switching off. They know they've got the language anyway, so it doesn't faze

A poster from the 1980s celebrating protests of the 1970s. Reproduced with the permission of the Alexander Turnbull Library, Wellington, New Zealand.

Te Reo Māori protest petition, 1972. Reproduced with the permission of Auckland War Memorial Museum–Tāmaki Paenga Hira, *Auckland Star* collection.

Te Reo Māori petition 40th anniversary, 14 September 2012. Former Te Reo Māori Society members John McCaffery, Lee Smith, Roger Steele, Rangi Pouwhare, Joe Te Rito and Andrew Robb, accompanied by Paul Diamond, curator Māori at the Alexander Turnbull Library, and Glenis Philip-Barbara, then CEO of Te Taura Whiri i te Reo Māori. Photograph by Dylan Owen. Reproduced with the permission of Dylan Owen and the Alexander Turnbull Library, Wellington, New Zealand. Ref: PADL-000808.

Merata Mita being filmed by Barry Harbutt and others at the entrance to Kawiti Marae, Waiomio, in February 1984. Reproduced with the permission of John Miller.

Eva Rickard being interviewed by Derek Fox for TVNZ at Kawiti Marae, Waiomio, in February 1984. Reproduced with the permission of John Miller.

Barry Barclay with Denis O'Reilly at a training hui held at the Hawke's Bay Community College, October 1985. Reproduced with the permission of John Miller.

A group shot of members of the Kimihia scheme in the gardens of the Avalon Studios in Wellington, February 1988. Crouching, left to right: Gabrielle Huria, Poto Stephens, John Miller; standing, left to right: unidentified, Makere Henare, Arihia Bristowe, unidentified, Paora Maxwell, Rangimoana Taylor, Nan Wehipeihana, Tainui Stephens, Tammy Painting, Sean Ruatara, Whetu Fala. Reproduced with the permission of John Miller. *All effort was made to identify the participants in this photograph; please contact the author if you have any information related to this image for inclusion in future research.*

Merata Mita at the editing suite in 1989. Reproduced with the permission of the *New Zealand Herald*.

Barry Barclay protesting outside NZ On Air offices, 16 December 1996. Photograph by Philip Reid for the *Evening Post*. Reproduced with the permission of Alexander Turnbull Library, Wellington, New Zealand. Ref: EP/1996/3620/7-F.

Don Selwyn on a drama shoot mentoring novice director Moana Sinclair and DOP Davorin Fahn, late 1990s. Reproduced with the permission of John Miller.

TIME	MONDAY	TUESDAY	WEDNESDAY	THURSDAY	FRIDAY	SATURDAY	SUNDAY
5.00 - 6.00 pm	E Tipu e Rea (Kids Show)	E Tipu e Rea (Kids Show)	E Tipu e Rea (Kids Show)	E Tipu e Rea (Kids Show)	E Tipu e Rea (Kids Show)	5.30 pm Manu Tioriori	5.30 pm Game of Week
6.00 - 6.45 pm	Tai Ohi (Youth Lifestyle)	Tai Ohi (Youth Lifestyle)	Tai Ohi (Youth Lifestyle)	Tai Ohi (Youth Lifestyle)	Tai Ohi (Youth Lifestyle)	E Tipu e Rea (Kids Show)	Sports Game of the week
6.45 - 7.00 pm							Te Heteri (News)
7.00 - 7.15 pm	Te Heteri (News)	Te Heteri (News)	Te Heteri (News)	Te Heteri (News)	Te Heteri (News)	Te Heteri (News)	Billy T (Entertainment)
7.15 - 7.30 pm						Sport	
7.30 - 8.00 pm	Te Kaahu (Current Affairs)	Te Kaahu (Current Affairs)	Te Kaahu (Current Affairs)	Te Kaahu (Current Affairs)	Te Kaahu (Current Affairs)	Puku Kata (Comedy)	Hauora (Health)
8.00 - 8.30 pm	Sports Action	Billy T (Comedy)	Sports (NBA)	Te Tumu Korero (Maori Drama)	Wahine Toa		
8.30 - 9.00 pm		Mana Tangata Indigenous	Billy T Special Te Toki	Wananga		Te Ao Marama (Movies)	Te Ao Hou (New Doco's)
9.00 - 9.30 pm	Te Ao Marama (Movies)	Docos	(Panel debate of Issues)	(Exist.Docos)	Te Ao Marama (Movies)		Kahurangi (Arts Programme)
9.30 - 10.00 pm			Billy T Special				Waka Kai-Pakihi (Business)
10.00 - 10.25 pm		Toi Whakaari (Haka)	Toi Whakaari (Haka)	Toi Whakaari (Haka)			Nga Tapuwae (Archival)
10.25 - 10.30 pm	Karakia	Karakia	Karakia	Karakia	Karakia	Karakia	Karakia

Aotearoa Television Network (ATN) programming schedule published in *Te Maori News*, April 1996, vol. 5, no. 7. Collection of National Library. Reproduced with the permission of editor Andrew Tumahai.

ATN staff featured on the cover of *Te Maori News*, April 1996, vol. 5, no. 7. The photo was taken in the initial studios set up in one of the upper floors of the Heards Building in Parnell Road. Those shown include: front row (left to right): Potaka Maipi, Virginia Edwards, Eruera Morgan, Pita Pewhairangi (on floor), Puhi Rangiaho, Peata Melbourne, Sonya Haggie, Godfrey Rudolph; back row (left to right): Tawini Rangihau, Tania Morgan, Maringi Houkāmou, Maui Tate, Mihingarangi Forbes, Vince Heperi, Maaka McGregor, Shavaughn Ruakere, Ngawini Shortland, Te Hira Henderson, unidentified, the late Jason Rāmeka, James Caldwell. Collection of National Library. Reproduced with the permission of editor Andrew Tumahai. *All effort was made to identify the participants in this photograph; please contact the author if you have any information related to this image for inclusion in future research.*

Allan Hawkey's cartoon 'Maori Television is born . . . .' *Waikato Times*, 29 March 2004. Reproduced with the permission of Allan Hawkey and the Alexander Turnbull Library, Wellington, New Zealand. Ref: DCDL-0002207.

The dawn launch of Māori Television on 28 March 2004. Reproduced with the permission of Gil Hanly.

Te Huirangi Waikerepuru and then Minister of Māori Affairs Parekura Horomia at the launch of Māori Television on 28 March 2004. Reproduced with the permission of Gil Hanly.

Julian Wilcox, Joanna Paul and Sharon Hawke behind the scenes at the Māori Television launch day, 2004. Reproduced with the permission of Gil Hanly.

Behind the scenes at the 2004 Māori Television Service launch.
Reproduced with the permission of Gil Hanly.

Māori Television reporter Jodi Ihaka interviewing Frank Graham at the tangihanga of Te Arikinui Dame Te Atairangikaahu, August 2006. Reproduced with the permission of John Miller.

Above: Jim Mather, CEO of Māori Television from 2005 to 2013, featured in a *Dominion Post* article entitled 'From Political Football to Part of the Furniture', 4 May 2013. Reproduced with the permission of Lawrence Smith / Fairfax Media NZ. Ref: 627915220.

'RWC TV', a Chris Slane cartoon depicting media coverage of the bid to gain broadcasting rights to the 2011 Rugby World Cup, *New Zealand Listener*, 16 October 2009. Reproduced with the permission of Chris Slane and the Alexander Turnbull Library, Wellington, New Zealand. Ref: DCDL-0012704.

Haunui Royal, Carol Hirschfeld and Julian Wilcox at Māori Television. 'The Little Station That Could', *Sunday Star-Times*, 23 March 2014. Reproduced with the permission of Lawrence Smith and Fairfax Media NZ and the *Sunday Star-Times*. Ref. 629116922.

Producer Kay Ellmers and camera operator Steve Fisher interview contestant Zayde Taurima from Mohaka Marae for season two of *Marae Kai Masters*. Reproduced with the permission of Tūmanako Productions.

The 2014 *Marae Kai Masters* presenters Te Kohe Tuhaka (left) and Nevak Rogers at Waikare Marae. Photograph by Peter De Graaf. Reproduced with the permission of the *New Zealand Herald*.

It's in the Bag hosts Pio Terei (left) and Stacey Morrison (centre) with a contestant. Reproduced with the permission of the *New Zealand Herald*.

Production stills from episode eleven, season five of *Kōwhao Rau* featuring Quinton Hita and Herewini Tarawa. Reproduced with the permission of Kura Productions.

Production still from episode ten, season five of *Kōwhao Rau* featuring Quinton Hita and Frank Taipari. Reproduced with the permission of Kura Productions.

Director Dan Mace, presenter Huria Chapman and producer Kay Ellmers check out a shot on a studio shoot for *Mīharo*. Reproduced with the permission of Tūmanako Productions.

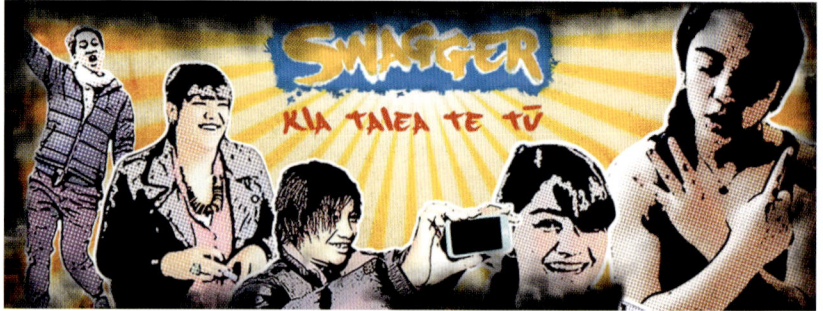

Season one *Swagger* promotional material. Reproduced with the permission of Hinewehi Mohi.

Mihingarangi Forbes' Twitter post stated, 'Locked out of Kōhanga Reo press conference in Ngāruawāhia today' and featured this photo of Forbes and Semi Holland. Reproduced with the permission of Mihingarangi Forbes.

them. But it's not growing and it's not becoming a part of our daily lives. And that is the secret that the network and funders need to unlock as well. (H. Mohi, interview, 2014)

∼

Using a programming framework shows how the legislation governing Māori Television poses a puzzle to the network, which must be worked through by developing innovative programming practices that use 'an unpopular language of the minority to make popular television for the majority' (Te Kāhui o Māhutonga, 2009, p. 8). To zig where others zag in the early days of Māori Television's production practices meant to offer points of difference in a media market that were not offered elsewhere. The 2007 emergence of *Native Affairs* and its placement in the Monday-night line-up secured Māori Television's reputation as a leader in the field of New Zealand current affairs television programming. The network's skills in delivering extended coverage of national and live events developed over the years, culminating in its success in making a viable bid for the rights to the Rugby World Cup.

By using national events to appeal to the nation, the network captured a non-Māori audience receptive to Māori language and culture. It could be said that the network consolidated its contribution to language and cultural revitalisation by enhancing the visibility of the language, enabling te reo and tikanga to circulate more broadly through the nation's public sphere (Lysaght, 2010; Cormack, 2007), and, in its online and on-demand developments, enhanced the prestige and relevance of te reo and tikanga Māori through association with digital technologies (Bell, 2010). In light of technological shifts in the way television content is produced and distributed, and the 'me-TV' control enjoyed by current media audiences, the temporal dimensions of Māori Television's zig-zag model might now need revision.

While the appeal to nationhood has been a successful strategy for building an audience, Māori Television has also developed significant language programming content for fluent and second-language speakers. Te Reo offers an immersive space that provides the opportunity for a continuous flow of te reo Māori programming, while *Mataora*, *Ako* and *Kōwhao Rau* build on earlier language programming innovations such as *Kōrero Mai*, *Tōku Reo*, *Mīharo* and *Te Tēpu*.

Programming strategies that ensure a vertical flow across the weekly schedule may function to enhance the provision of language outcomes, even for content such as international art-house films and documentaries. When considering the role that international documentaries might play in providing language outcomes, one can draw on existing research on minority-language media and argue the value of such content to language outcomes. If Allan Bell argues that the prestige of a minority's language is enhanced by its association with technologies, it could be argued that prestige is also accrued when associated with television content from overseas. When receptive audiences come to Māori Television to watch festival documentaries on a Tuesday night, or the international art-house film on Sunday's 'Cinema' slot, it could be said that the act of hosting such content enhances the standing of not only Māori Television, the network, but all that is associated with the network, primarily te reo Māori. Yet providing meaningful evidence to substantiate such claims remains a challenge for Māori media scholars.

If the start-up phase of Māori Television involved the task of producing enough te reo programming for a content-hungry schedule, and building a reputation as a viable public broadcaster, in recent years the network has focused on improving the quality of te reo programming and responding to shifts in the larger Māori-language sector, including Te Māngai Pāho's move to the ZePA model, and various reviews of the Maori Language Strategy. Shifts in legislation relating to the broadcaster (for example, from 'te reo Māori me ngā tikanga' to 'te reo Māori me ōna tikanga') reflect these wider dynamics. Recent efforts by the Māori Television Board to revert back to the original wording suggests that such changes to legislative wording might restrict the current board's vision for Māori Television.

Chapter Four

Audience Engagements with Māori Television Programming

Kōrero from Māori Television staff, board directors, Māori media producers, academics and commentators provides various frameworks (historical, tikanga-based and programme-oriented) that illuminate the challenges facing an Indigenous media organisation such as Māori Television, as well as its successes. Such kōrero illuminates what goes on *behind* the screen, as well as *on screen*. This chapter focuses on dynamics in front of the screen, and explores how some audiences engage with Māori Television. Previous chapters allude to Māori Television's audiences indirectly, through reference to the importance of ratings statistics concerning programming, or research to do with the ethnic make-up of audiences. These references to the audience use quantitative data collection processes, and many media scholars have issues with this approach to the idea of television audiencehood.

Take, for example, the AGB Nielsen company, which provides ratings statistics for the majority of New Zealand media outlets. In a commercial environment, these statistics help determine the kinds of programmes that get funded. Nielsen uses an electronic monitoring device known as a people-meter to track the viewing behaviour of individuals in households, as well as their guests, through the use of a remote control. All household members and guests have their own allocated button on the remote that registers their viewing practices. When a viewer begins to watch a programme, or when they have finished watching, they must press a numbered button on the remote control. Nielsen retrieves this information remotely at 2 am each day. The New Zealand people-meter panel is made up of 600 households and is said to constitute around 1500 individuals. Media industries use the viewing habits tracked in these households to make more general statements about New Zealand television audiences overall.

Critics of the people-meter system claim that this means that statements made about New Zealand television ratings are drawn from information gleaned from approximately 0.014 per cent of the New Zealand population (Hunkin, 2015). The number of Māori and te reo Māori speakers included in New Zealand people-meter panels is also a concern, deserving more research. Beyond the specific example of ratings, media scholars such as Ien Ang have argued that mechanisms for measuring television audiences in no way capture the complex, contradictory and ephemeral experiences of living with television, they merely count the audience. As Ang notes:

> In the everyday realm, living with television involves a heterogeneous range of informal activities, uses, interpretations, pleasures, disappointments, conflicts, struggles, and compromises. But in the considerations of the institutions that possess the official power to define, exploit and regulate the space in which television is inserted into the fabric of culture and society, these subjective, complex and dynamic forms of audiencehood are generally absent; they disappear in favour of a mute and abstract construct of 'television audience' onto which large-scale economic and cultural aspirations and expectations, policies and planning schemes are projected, allowing these institutions to govern and control the formal frameworks of television's place in contemporary life. (1991, p. 2)

Ang acknowledges a significant difference between the everyday habits of watching television and official discourses about audiences that draw on ratings statistics. For Ang, the media industry's reliance on ratings constitutes an 'institutional point of view', which 'colonises' knowledge about television audiencehood. She calls for more research focused on actual audience experiences (1991, p. 160). Her audience-centred approach does not attempt to make broad generalisations about viewing habits, but rather brings to light the everyday details of particular people, at particular moments, reflecting on their viewing practices, and examining common themes.

Currently, a small body of existing research explores the habits and perspectives of Māori Television viewers in the manner advocated by Ang. One such study examined the reasons why non-Māori watch Māori Television (Turner, 2010). The study included 66 participants who took part as interviewees or focus group members or via questionnaires. The study found that

Māori Television programming is popular with non-Māori: because it offers content for those who are nostalgic for local and 'New Zealand' programming in a pervasively commercial environment; because of a desire to be more informed about things Māori, global Indigenous cultures and 'minority affairs'; and because it offers public-service-style broadcasting that has an ethical and ideological balance (Turner, 2010). Another study examined 312 email and online responses to the 2007 Anzac Day coverage. The study suggested that non-Māori viewers identify a kind of 'New Zealandness' within the programming, and this 'elides the very obvious Māori nature of the programming' (Abel, 2013a, p. 111). The study contends that such viewing practices do not enable non-Māori to 'connect with the Māori world' in meaningful ways (2013a, p. 119). An audience study involving individual interviews with five Māori women living in Ōtepoti (Dunedin) found that Māori Television helps to strengthen Māori identity, particularly for those living amongst a non-Māori majority (Poihipi, 2007).

This chapter contributes to emerging Māori Television audience research, with a focus on Māori viewers due to the scarce existing research involving Māori participants. This provides insights into how primarily Māori audiences view Māori Television content, and its institutional presence, by offering stories, insights and anecdotes from diverse Māori communities.

Based on themes emerging from the kōrero of eight focus groups, this chapter develops an audience framework that considers:

- the educative dimensions of Māori Television programming and its contribution to language and cultural knowledge
- Māori Television's contribution to Māori wellbeing and whanaungatanga
- the network's role as a cultural bridge and benchmark for non-Māori media providers
- future challenges for Māori Television.

Between 2012 and 2013 the research team held eight focus groups to explore questions related to the impact and significance of Māori Television. Ranging in age between 20 and 80 years, focus group participants were drawn from both urban and rural environments, and from both Te Ika-a-Māui and Te Waipounamu (North and South Islands), including Ōtepoti, Tāmaki Makaurau, Hangatiki, Kawakawa, Te Whanganui-a-Tara and Whakatāne. Forty participants (16 men and 24 women) took part, 36 of whom self-identified as Māori. The questions we asked of participants were generated from a range of sources, including interviews with Māori Television stakeholders, scholarly literature on global Indigenous media, what other media said about Māori Television, trends in television viewing, and what Māori Television has said about itself and its television programming. We asked about viewing habits and how people use Māori Television, what people had learnt from Māori Television, what Māori Television does well, what it could do differently, and the significance of the broadcaster's appeal to a range of audiences and identities. The kind of programming mentioned in focus groups included (among others) long-standing shows such as *Waka Huia*, *Kai Time on the Road*, *Pūkana*, *CODE*, *Marae DIY*, *Native Affairs* and Anzac Day coverage. Participants also referred to more contemporary programming, such as *It's in the Kete*, *Songs from the Inside*, *Kōwhao Rau*, *Tautohetohe* and *Iwi Anthems*.

The range of responses gathered in these groups reveals that Māori Television is a media organisation that provides language-learning resources, cultural knowledge and strength-based representations of te ao Māori, which have the potential to help shift the thoughts and actions of audiences in ways that could benefit local, national and global cross-cultural relationships. Kōrero from the focus groups also expressed aspirations for more diverse representations of te ao Māori, better use of existing and emerging media resources, and innovative television productions that express the distinctiveness (creatively, ethically and otherwise) of te ao Māori.

The following quote from one focus group participant helps set the scene. Reflecting on her viewing habits as a Māori living in a non-Māori-dominated household, this participant commented:

> I also remember that when we lived at that house we had a TV that when you turned it off and turned it back on, it would come back on the channel you'd left it on. Because I lived with Pākehā people and this was Māori Television – so different from their perspective – I would change the channel. I'd be watching Māori TV and I'd change the channel to TV One or 3 or 2 before I turned it off so that when they turned the TV on it would be on a normal [sic] channel. It was when I realised I was doing that I was like, 'I've gotta move places'.

In this household, the participant experienced some tacit social pressure to make sure the television was set to a 'normal' (read non-Māori) channel. This brief comment provides insights into television's role in establishing and normalising the everyday habits of people and households, and the kinds of unconscious actions that ultimately contribute to the cultural norms and power dynamics of a society. Themes arising from kōrero from focus groups offer partial insights into how Māori Television's programming, as well as its symbolic presence as a Māori media organisation, has affected a range of viewers.

Māori Television's contribution to language learning

The first major theme to emerge from audience kōrero was Māori Television's role in supporting more formal language-learning strategies offered by schools, wānanga and night classes. For those committed to active engagement with te reo, programming content such as *Tōku Reo*, *Ako*, *Kōrero Mai* and *Pūkana* aids language usage and contributes to the written, visual and oral resources of the language. These programmes help audiences to test their understanding of words and sentence structures. One participant (a teacher) noted the improvement, across a term, in her student's ability to kōrero Māori after watching Māori Television content:

> I think [Māori Television's] important because, educationally it's important for the kids, cos I know of one of my boys in my class, he came with no reo. A term later his kōrero was like pretty much all day. They said a big part of it is he has to go home and he has to watch *Tōku Reo* every day before he watches cartoons.

This story demonstrates the value of having te reo programming on in the home after school. By establishing a routine in the household, as well as providing incentives such as cartoons once the reo homework was done, this student was able to use television to complement his school-based language journey with whānau-based activities in the home. This sense of everyday-ness, as well as the use of te reo in a range of contexts, is a vital part of language learning.

Another participant's kōrero provides insights into Māori Television's role in supporting university-based language acquisition:

> I can distinctly remember when Māori Television started in 2004 because that's when I was going to Waikato University. I chose to take a whole year off to do te reo Māori and that was the year that Māori Television came in and so for me it was just fantastic because all we could get down there was Tainui FM. So being able to come home and to watch Māori Television even though I didn't really know how to understand it all ... Back then they didn't have the subtitles underneath so you sort of just sat there. But just that fact that you could listen to the reo in its varying forms – like the different mita that come from the different iwi – it was good.

This same participant also noted that another member of his whānau felt frustrated by the speed of the reo on television and the unfamiliar words used to describe things:

> But for my mum at the time she would get hōhā with the way that they would talk because, either it'd be too fast or some of the kupu were just totally different from what she knew.

This observation was supported by comments made by a participant in a different focus group:

> Sometimes when you hear someone speaking who's really fluent they go really fast and you only pick up the odd word but yeah – sometimes I've just got my ear out for it rather than sitting and watching it. I might be doing something then I'm thinking, oh I know that I've got the gist of that sentence.

The speed of speech on screen, as well as an ever-evolving vocabulary (appropriate to te reo as a living language), frustrated some focus group participants. Television's one-way transmission of content reveals the medium's limits as a language-learning tool, even as participants widely recognised the benefits of having te reo programme content on screen to support language aspirations. The importance of 'having an ear out' in relation to te reo as background sound suggests that te reo programming content in the home has a role to play in creating an immersive whānau space supportive of language use.[*]

---

[*] These audience experiences are also reflected in the research on Māori radio conducted by scholars such as Rangi Matamua and Jo Mane. See R. Matamua, 'Te Reo Pāho: Māori Radio and Language Revitalisation', 2006 (PhD thesis) and J. Mane, 'Pāho Māori: the Impact of Māori Language Broadcasting on Māori Language Survival', 2009 (PhD thesis).

While some focus group participants made efforts to sit and watch shows specifically to learn, or as a mandatory after-school task for children, other participants used te reo Māori programming content as ambient background sound while conducting domestic activities. These stories suggest that having televised te reo Māori as an accessible and everyday resource that can be taken up as needs demand is important to some Māori Television audiences.

Māori Television's contribution to cultural knowledge

According to focus group kōrero, Māori Television's educative potential is not restricted to language learning. Kōrero suggests that Māori Television acts as a conveyor of cultural knowledge, as an archive of material important for future generations, and as a site of authority on matters concerning Māori. When asked, 'What does Māori Television teach you?' one participant replied:

> Well almost everything on [Māori Television] is teaching you something. Whether it's supposed to be or it's indirectly. So on the Te Reo channel they play re-runs of *Waka Huia* from back in the day, and there's always something of interest on that. So the last one I watched on there ... it was the history of Te Matatini and it was ... I never knew half of that stuff. Whenever I watch *Wairua* I learn about a whole different way of looking at the world because that's what that show's about. On *Pūkana* I always pick up new colloquialisms, new words, heaps of little things like that.

These comments underscore Māori Television's role as an important source of te reo and tikanga Māori content, providing contemporary audiences with kōrero, faces and activities from the past. Māori Television's re-runs of the long-standing *Waka Huia* also makes the organisation the kaitiaki of an existing taonga, the voices and perspectives documented by this long-running programme. *Waka Huia* also provides historical background to contemporary popular events such as Te Matatini. *Wairua* (featuring experts such as Patu Hohepa discussing the spiritual dimensions of te ao Māori) provides knowledge and expertise difficult to access otherwise.

Another participant appreciated *Iwi Anthems*, because it offered a deeper understanding of the history surrounding certain waiata:

> I like [*Iwi Anthems*] because it starts to make you understand that that waiata came from that area. It was Kahungunu's turn last night. So yeah, we have those melodies in our own head that we've heard when we were young and things like that, but to actually put a place to where they come from – it's nice. And to see old kaumātua and kuia with grey hair standing on the stage singing.

This comment suggests that shows such as *Iwi Anthems* play an important role in not only honouring the skills, wisdom and mana of kaumātua and kuia, but also in deepening the existing knowledge of a participant who may know the words of a waiata but not the historical context.

This programming example also demonstrates Māori Television's additional role as producer or commissioner of contemporary Māori programming, providing documentation of te ao Māori today. In doing so, the network continues and extends the archive tradition set by *Waka Huia*. Such programming includes content unseen elsewhere, as one participant noted:

> There was one [programme] on making fire and I think a Tūhoe guy on horseback going around showing which woods made fire – how to do it and how to keep it for weeks, and it was amazing. I'd never seen anything quite like it. I think [television's] a real good way of conveying some of that knowledge. I haven't seen any other show quite like that on in terms of someone having so much knowledge about one aspect of life.

Participants acknowledged the importance of the archival and documenting role of Māori Television when they reflected on how valuable it was to see and hear kōrero from kaumātua that might otherwise be lost. Having such content played on screen provided these participants with intimate access to the wisdom of esteemed experts. One participant, when reflecting on things only ever seen on Māori Television, noted:

> Rongoā programmes with Kāterina Mataira, all of those old kōrero. Some of those were probably what was most interesting to me because you wouldn't just normally have those conversations with those people, so being able to see and have that type of resource available is really important.

The access to significant experts, as well as the ability to record their kōrero for the future, was important to members of another focus group:

> I learnt a lot of things that our kaumātua hasn't got around to telling us all yet, and it's cool to have it recorded because sometimes when they tell us things you forget it, but if you start to forget you just watch the recording of it again and it's just so valuable.

The value of documenting the knowledge held by kaumātua suggests that Māori Television and funder Te Māngai Pāho play a significant role in gathering and storing knowledge for the use of future generations.

Comments in another focus group suggested that Māori Television programming content can provide difficult-to-find knowledge that even a keen researcher could not access. Referring to *Kōwhao Rau*, one participant noted:

> He [Quinton Hita] was talking to this lady up in Kaikohe, I think, and he goes on his horse and has a cup of tea with the old people. He was talking about tikanga of the tangi up there and how it has changed over time. I did some of those studies in one of my papers – some of the stuff she was talking about I had never heard of before, even though I researched a whole essay and project on it, so it is quite useful. If she didn't have that opportunity to go and have that interview on TV, then that knowledge would have died with her. She was quite old. She said that her family and the younger generations weren't quite interested in it.

Māori Television's capacity to screen the recorded knowledge and wisdom of those kaumātua still with us today is a bitter-sweet observation in light of the length of time it took to establish a Māori-operated television channel, as this comment from another participant suggests:

> They talk about it like there's a recorded history now in their visual eyes that they see that they're talking to these elders. So that's recorded and they honour those. They think that if they were to pass tomorrow at least we've got something down, whereas you know that would have been nice in the '60s and '70s when a lot of them were alive.

While *Waka Huia* and documentary series *Tangata Whenua* contributed much to this televisual archive, Māori Television continues this tradition on a new scale.

Another participant noted how the network provides opportunities for being updated on contemporary as well as historical issues. This participant suggested that the kinds of conversations hosted on Māori Television would only be otherwise accessed through specialist Māori spaces:

> It is an amazing way to get an insight into te ao Māori, and contemporary issues, as well as historical issues. . . . Unless you went to the Poukai [hui on marae – usually for the Kīngitanga], you probably wouldn't actually be engaged with that kind of content.

Māori Television enables viewers to listen to the voices of notable experts and acts as a repository of cultural knowledge that can aid whānau memories and histories. While linking present-day audiences with voices and faces from the past, Māori Television also transmits information across the generations. One such example involved an older whānau member who has a different relationship to te reo and tikanga than those growing up with kura and kōhanga reo. While first acknowledging the role Māori Television plays in valuing Māori identity, this participant suggested that Māori Television provides cultural knowledge for a grandparent who feels the pressure to keep up with the mokopuna:

> I think the thing for my family and my mokopuna is to reaffirm the fact that it's great to be Māori. We don't have to apologise for who we are or we don't have to blame who we are. The kids just own it in a way that we were never allowed to. I never knew that my children's afterbirth was anything of value. It was not something that was discussed. My parents decided that what you don't know won't hurt you. I didn't know anything about Tāwhirimātea, all of the gods that we have out there, because it was never discussed. So when it became the current conversation, I would think, 'How did we miss the bus?' My mokopuna are coming home and saying things to me that are completely beyond anything I was ever taught, and I'm having to say, 'I better find out what this kid's talking about so that I'm on the same page.' They've heard it on Māori TV and it's been OK-ed.

This story highlights the intergenerational differences between whānau members in terms of mātauranga and te reo Māori. It also reveals a perception of Māori Television as a site of cultural authority. The cultural confidence of this participant's mokopuna may be the result of better access to education that affirms Māori ways of being, or it might be due to exposure to more informed representations of things Māori post-2004. According to this participant, Māori Television has the ability to make up for the shortfall in cultural knowledge experienced by earlier generations with only mainstream media to watch. The final sentence in this kōrero ('They've heard it on Māori TV and it's been OK-ed') is an important reminder of the role that Māori Television plays as a site of cultural authority on things Māori due to its very public role as a source of Māori representation. It reminds us of the power and authority that some audiences invest in the network, as well as the attendant responsibility Māori Television has to these audience investments.

Another strong theme to emerge from focus group kōrero related to Māori Television's role in providing content and knowledge about tikanga and reo:

> I wasn't brought up immersed in the culture, other than going back home for a few tangi and stuff, but we didn't have the reo at home or any sort of tikanga, so a lot of what I have learnt is at uni, at wānanga and off Māori TV.

Under these conditions, Māori Television acts as a cultural proxy for many of those Māori who have not experienced a marae upbringing or had te reo as a first language. As we shall see, Māori Television's capacity to support cultural knowledge across the diverse experiences of being Māori plays an important role in acknowledging the distinctive concerns and varying standpoints of Māori community members. Other members of this focus group backed up this participant's observation:

> Yeah, we weren't brought up speaking te reo or anything like that. The only interaction we really had with te ao Māori, was for tangi, unveilings and that kind of stuff, even though we lived relatively close, like within an hour or so of our marae. Because my father didn't speak te reo, and his father was told not to speak te reo, there was no real connection to our marae or anything like that. I wouldn't say Māori TV fills that gap, but it goes some way towards reconnecting you with tikanga and te ao Māori.
>
> Participant: I'd probably agree with that, in terms that it doesn't fill that gap – it kind of supplements.

The theme from this aspect of focus group kōrero is how Māori Television exposes audiences to new ideas and old knowledge of te ao Māori, and how this content supplements the many different forums for exploring cultural identity. Programming that features kaumātua and kuia brings their expertise, experiences and mana to wider audiences, as do programmes that showcase the specialist knowledge of experts in the field of wairua, rongoā, woodcraft, atua and tikanga.

Focus group members also valued Māori Television's ability to facilitate links between the diverse experiences of being Māori, and to transmit knowledge across generations. This linking function also relates to the viewing experience of participants whose comments suggest that watching Māori Television can facilitate and deepen connections between whānau, friends and community members.

Māori Television's contribution to whanaungatanga

Māori Television operates in a media environment where it is now the norm to access other forms of media when viewing television content. Responses from focus group participants suggest that Māori Television content stimulates links with whānau members, who feel compelled to text, post or call whānau and friends when they see content that might be of mutual interest:

> My Mum and aunts ring me up all the time, and they're always uplifted by what they see on Māori TV. They're excited, uplifted because they're human and it's their ways.

The causes of these impulses to connect with whānau are multiple, but could include the idea that the programme concerned contains a whānau member or friend, or addresses an event on the whānau marae or an issue that affects their community or iwi. When asked whether or not participants talked to other people about Māori Television, one participant noted how she would discuss the content of language-learning programme *Ako* with her sister:

> Yeah, we do that all the time, me and [sister who works in the same rumaki unit] cos she doesn't get to watch it much, yeah I update her.
>
> Interviewer: So that's your fullas' *Shortland Street*? [laughter]
>
> Yeah, aw that's, yeah, our *Shortland Street* talk, be like, aw [sister] I learnt that blah-blah-blah, and she'll go, 'Awww, yeah', so yeah, we talk about it a lot.
>
> Interviewer: And it obviously helps you like with key things?
>
> Yeah cos usually things that I'm not sure of, she probably isn't sure of either, so we both learn from it.

These shared viewing experiences demonstrate Māori Television's capacity not only to facilitate whānau connections, but also to enhance shared understanding of te reo Māori and attendant cultural knowledge. Many of the participants discussed watching *Hōmai te Pakipaki* and sharing their responses with friends and family as the show progressed:

> I'd be texting up my sister like, 'Oi are you watching this on Māori TV?' and she's like, 'Yeah.'

This desire to reach out to discuss *Hōmai te Pakipaki* with other viewers is not restricted to Māori, but can also be found in the cross-cultural viewing practices of the non-Māori audience:

> Our neighbour across the road, she very rarely has anything to do with the Māori world. Nothing. She'll push it away as far as she can, typical Pākehā lady. But she'll watch *Hōmai te Pakipaki* and her . . .
>
> Interviewer: How do you know this?
>
> Oh we're very good friends with our neighbour. But she'll watch *Hōmai te Pakipaki*, and she'll be texting my mum all night. 'Oh did you see this one. This one's horrible, this one's good.'
>
> Interviewer: While it's happening?
>
> While it's happening. And you go on Facebook and you'll see comments coming up all about it, and it's just a show that's just gone so mainstream. Whenever you hear someone singing that's cool, the first thing you say to them is, 'Oh you should go onto *Hōmai te Pakipaki*.' It's just a part of New Zealand culture now.

It is not surprising that *Hōmai te Pakipaki* (2007–2015) inspired viewers to engage with each other via text or phone during the course of the show, because it was a community-based form of television programming designed to showcase amateur talent, and because audiences got to vote via text. The show's long-standing popularity demonstrates Māori Television's ability to appeal to communities, with crowds gathering outside the network's Newmarket studios to get a chance to compete for the evening or to support a whānau member.

With the development of a core loyal audience for shows such as *Hōmai* te Pakipaki, Native Affairs and other popular programming, Māori Television has the capacity to become a topic of conversation in varying social spaces, including the workplace. One participant touched on the power dynamics that help shape everyday conversations when she admitted to only talking about Māori Television to select people in her workplace. In the process of hearing what others were saying in her focus group, this participant noted how she might now talk to more people about Māori Television content while at work, and that this might help change non-Māori attitudes to Māori Television, and, by implication, attitudes to te ao Māori:

> I'm gonna watch it more now! Actually, just talking about everything today, I didn't realise how much I did watch Māori TV, and it's kinda made me want to watch more now? . . . I said before that I only select certain people to talk to and when you brought up, or someone brought up the word 'engage', awww man I'm gonna shove it in their faces and just go, 'Are you fullas gonna watch this?' [laughter], so it's kinda made me think, nah . . . I am gonna just like, 'Aw man, cool', cos they all come to work and say, 'Aw did you watch *Shortland Street* or *Home and Away*?' Which I always watch anyway, but yeah, so now I'm like, shit I might start doing that to them and they might . . . You know? It might interest them one day to change the channel.

By talking about the media content seen on Māori Television, focus group participants help to spread the enjoyment they have experienced and the knowledge they have gained, or help set the agenda for workplace conversations that centre on things Māori. These shifts in media consumption – the ability to access social media sites such as Facebook to share links to programming, the texting of whānau members when something of shared interest is on-screen – complement an emerging body of research to do with e-whanaungatanga, which examines how digital media can extend Māori cultural concepts and practices (O'Carroll, 2013a, b, c, d, e; Waitoa, 2013). If e-whanaungatanga relates to social media's capacity to enhance whānau connections across space and time, then Māori Television content, as it is shared, commented on and dispersed across diverse audiences, including Māori whānau, non-Māori neighbours or workplace colleagues, suggests that Māori Television programming has the potential to inhabit everyday spaces in ways not seen before.

Three themes from focus group kōrero emerged in relation to Māori Television's role: as a language-learning aid, as a source of cultural knowledge, and as a mechanism for extending whanaungatanga. A fourth theme arising from participant kōrero relates to the role played by Māori Television in disseminating positive representations of diverse Māori worlds that can enhance a sense of personal and collective wellbeing.

Māori Television as a source of wellbeing

Twelve years on from its emergence, Māori Television is now a taken-for-granted player in New Zealand's media environment, but comments from focus group members remind us of the novel and effective impact of having te reo Māori and Māori perspectives on prime-time television in the network's early years:

> When Māori Television came out it was: te hari, te koa [o] te ngākau – kei te haere mai tētahi, tō tātou reo, tō tātou reo, kei te kōrero a tātou [i tō tātou] anō reo, ki te kōrero ngā hītori, ngā whakapapa, ngā waiata tawhito – ngā mea katoa. [*Happiness and joy filled the heart – here was something in our very own language, that let us speak our own language, that let us speak of our history, our genealogy, of our ancient songs – all those sorts of things.*]

A participant in another focus group reflected on the impact of having te reo and tikanga on screen and expressed a sense of personal connection to aspects of Māori Television programming, as well as a hope that such content might act as an aid to self-improvement:

> I can comment on the fact that the programmes that I see on Māori TV are the programmes that are generally personal, that evoke types of emotions, and I suppose that contributes to the connection I feel to my culture and I suppose in that way keeping me connected . . . I think of Pānia's [*Papa*] programme and all those different programmes that teach you different aspects of the reo or of different things [that] could be useful for taking out of that context to self-improve.

More than simply entertainment, this reflection confirms Māori Television's impact at a personal level and its provocation to viewers to begin, or to continue, the journey of learning te reo.

A theme common to another focus group (and also present in Vanessa

Poihipi's study) addressed the idea that Māori Television offers counter-images and different ideas about te ao Māori from those stereotypes fostered by non-Māori media providers:

> What I liked about Māori TV is that it gave a more positive outlook on Māori in comparison to mainstream, where all you see is mainly Māori on the news and ...
>
> Other participants: 'On *Police Ten 7*!'
>
> or something like that. Whereas on Māori TV they show more Māori, and they show positive Māori and those that are doing well and um you know, that have careers ...
>
> Other participants: 'Māori sports stars!' 'Yeah!'

One participant noted how Māori Television takes certain stereotypes about Māori and reclaims their meanings:

> It breaks down all these stereotypes you see in the mainstream media about Māori being criminals, being dumb, being poor and all these types of things – you'll see a very different Māori on Māori TV. Even some of those negative stereotypes that you see in mainstream society, they're actually broken down and [are] being reclaimed on Māori TV. I grew up and people said, 'Boil up is a food for poor people', but now on Māori TV you have *Boil Up* as a show. They're reclaiming those things [like cuisine] that people tell us are negative about ourselves. Like *Native Affairs* – the word 'native' has [had] this negative loading to it.

This ability to re-vision mainstream Māori stereotypes also accompanies the network's capacity to throw light on contemporary debates within te ao Māori:

> One thing I just wanted to comment on was a [2013] investigation that *Native Affairs* did on the Kōhanga Reo Trust. I think it is an interesting news item because before we were talking about how Māori TV challenges stereotypes or presents Māori in a positive light, perhaps it's signalling a shift into a second stage of Māori TV's development where they're actually able to critique Māori society a little bit more than they have in the past. I feel like Māori TV presents one part of Māori society really well but doesn't cover other aspects and doesn't challenge where power lies within Māori society – I think this sort of investigation where we actually were challenging

some of that. So people have very different perspectives [on *Native Affairs*' coverage] but I just think it's a very interesting thing to note. We're critiquing our own power structures a little bit.

According to this participant, Māori Television's representational powers should not be restricted to simply providing positive stories that combat a history of negative representation; the network must also throw light on, and raise debate about, matters internal to te ao Māori (a topic discussed in more detail later).

As well as Māori Television offering content that can act as an antidote to prevailing negative portrayals of Māori and te ao Māori, and have the potential to provide a Māori analysis of Māori issues, participants also noted the importance of seeing Māori role models on screen and how they have achieved their successes:

They showcase the ones that stand out, what do you call them? The talented ones? Yeah, all of the talented people and the high achievers. They show their side of the story – they share it with the whole country. Whereas you wouldn't even know about them [*all other participants agree*] if there was no Māori TV. . . . Yeah, it gives them the opportunity to show what they've achieved and how they've got there and who their inspiration was.

One cannot underestimate the value of strength-based representations of Māori people and things Māori when we take into account the longer history of Māori media representations, as well as the hostile environment that some Māori initiatives endure. The importance of pride in things Māori is registered in the following comment:

It's the same old story that if you produce something that gives you pride and dignity around owning it, it's got to be constructive and it's got to be positive. I think our kids would thrive on that, rather than being portrayed as statistically the most people that go to jail, the most people that are sick, the most people that are ill-educated and that sort of crap.

The theme of pride in Māori Television programming was also present in kōrero from another focus group:

> I'm proud a lot about Māori Television. Like Anzac Day. Man, when I first saw that, the first programme they put out on Anzac Day, that was just awesome because of how they presented everything on that programme. And then, it's funny because the next year, I noticed that the Pākehā were doing the same thing on TV. So Māori TV led the way.

As kōrero from participants suggest, Māori Television plays an important role in providing a space for Māori to celebrate, debate and promote things Māori – on Māori terms. According to these comments, making space in the mediated public sphere of Aotearoa for Māori voices and experiences can only lead to an enhanced sense of wellbeing for Māori.

A fifth theme to emerge from this kōrero concerns the role that the network might play in informing non-Māori of the values, practices, concerns and ideals of te ao Māori, and the ways in which Māori Television's broadcasting practices act as a benchmark, and a challenge, to other television providers.

Māori Television as a cultural bridge and a challenge to other media

For many participants, Māori Television plays a vital role in teaching non-Māori about the culture of tangata whenua and helps set the scene for greater tolerance of cultural differences within New Zealand society. For example, some participants noted how prevailing stereotypes about Māori (as seen on shows such as *Police Ten 7*, a reality television programme that profiles wanted criminals) encourage misinformation about things Māori. When Māori Television offers counter-narratives and positive stories about the diverse worlds that make up Māori communities, it offers non-Māori an easily available window into te ao Māori. One self-identified Pākehā participant argued that non-Māori need a greater understanding of Māori, and that this should be supported through Māori media programming that is available on all free-to-air channels, not just Māori Television:

> That's what I think Pākehā need, is some understanding. That's why I think that there should be more Māori TV on free-to-air, not just on a specific channel, because it's a bit like saying to a Pākehā on the street, 'Come into the marae.' And I think it's a bit

the same for Māori TV, 'Come have a look at this channel.' They don't want to do that, but if it's easily available in a different way.

While watching Māori media content may not necessarily lead to greater understanding of things Māori, this comment also raises the issue of the risk of Māori media content becoming ghettoised on Māori Television or on early-morning slots of mainstream providers.

Participants generally agreed that Māori Television provides information about the Māori world for non-Māori audiences. However, it was also noted that the international art-house films and documentaries screened on Māori Television, as well as global Indigenous media content, offer a broader education about cross-cultural differences that might have benefits for those living in Aotearoa. According to the same Pākehā participant:

> So [Māori Television's] really helpful in understanding a culture which is not the one you grew up in. I think that's one of the things that New Zealanders need to be tolerant of. It doesn't matter whether we're talking with someone who's come from mainland China, or from Sāmoa or from Tūhoe or from wherever, we need to be able to talk across those cultural divides. Māori TV helps enormously there.

This theme of enhanced cross-cultural understanding links to comments made in another focus group about the benefits of culturally diverse programming:

> Yes, yes. Yeah I think it's interesting because it's culturally diverse. It's not just Māori, there's a whole lot of other things that [they] bring in from foreign films. You've got *Tagata Pasifika* on and those kind of things. It's for all people, it's not just directed at Māori. It's Māori TV for everyone. That's the thing that I like.

In addition to Māori Television's inclusive, informative and culturally diverse programming, participants commented on the challenge posed by Māori Television to other media institutions to provide more informed (and better-pronounced) Māori-related media content. Across all eight focus groups a general sense came through that Māori Television 'ups the game' for Māori media content across the free-to-air sector:

> I think Māori TV sets a precedent for other journalists and media people that actually this is a quality service and it's a valid service and we are robust professionals in that industry – we can do it, what are you doing? I think – I'd like to read [Māori Television's presence] as a rationale behind why mainstream has sort of picked it up a little bit.

Another participant in this same focus group agreed, suggesting that a market logic may inform the drive for non-Māori television makers to improve reo pronunciation:

> And as you're saying, other TV channels are upping their game because they're saying that actually we do have to do the pronunciation correctly otherwise we'll lose a sector of our audience.

A participant in a different focus group made a similar comment about the necessity of other free-to-air television providers changing their work practices in light of Māori Television successes:

> I think that kind of challenges mainstream TV stations to up their game a bit when they do have Māori content. They can't just continue to present it from a Pākehā perspective now, because there's this alternative and viewers are being drawn to Māori TV, so they should have Māori programmes and I imagine present more thorough research from a Māori perspective.

At one point another participant in a different focus group noted how impressive she found the bid for the 2011 Rugby World Cup coverage made by Māori Television. Reflecting on the ways in which non-Māori television might now respond to things Māori in the wake of Māori Television, she stated:

> Yeah, and so they have to show how they are demonstrating that, so yeah, maybe it is competition too, and certainly when they had to compete for the rights to the World Cup I thought that was awesome – I thought they really upped the ante. They were joining forces and they were ahead of everything, and they were as competitive as any other channel and I thought that was really very cool – very cool.

According to these views, Māori Television leads the way in representing Māori perspectives in the media; it has proven equal to the competitive edge of other media institutions, and it has set the benchmark for other media organisations to try to match.

What Māori Television could do differently

In the course of discussions about the significance and impact of Māori Television, participants also raised issues about – or noted aspects of – Māori Television's programming and practices that could be improved to better reflect the desires of various audiences. These suggestions included the desire for:

- a greater range of programming
- more representations of, and better engagement with, diverse Māori communities
- the enhancement of links with other media
- more programming innovations that reflect Māori ways of doing things, and Māori values.

Many participants wanted to see a greater range of programming in the schedule, including one participant who wanted content that contained more useful information, such as weather reports:

> One other thing I think that Māori TV doesn't do so well, you can't get everything that a person might 'need' from television from Māori TV. For example, I want to know what the weather's going to do in the morning – I can't turn on Māori TV and find that out. I can turn on Māori TV but it's just songs and the upcoming programme, but why don't they have at least weather? ... [T]hat could be a good time for them to just show the weather, so I can turn on Māori TV and say, 'What's the weather doing? Sweet.'

Possibly underlying these comments is a vision of Māori Television as a type of media organisation not limited by a language or culture mandate, but one that embraces all aspects of television provision including issues facing the nation as a whole. While acknowledging that one channel cannot serve all purposes, this participant made an additional comment on content:

I can't really satisfy my entertainment needs on Māori TV. I can get information, I can get news, I can get heritage and all these things but I still need entertainment.

A desire for more drama was a common theme among participants, who suggested that Māori Television could include more films based on Māori literature, or re-run domestic film-festival product:

Wouldn't it be great if they could make more movies or more programmes about our great books that we've had written, or something like that . . . you know how you see them in the film festivals – maybe after about three years, why don't they buy them or run them?

Another participant suggested that Māori Television could improve its competitive edge with a soap to rival that of TVNZ's *Shortland Street*. Reflecting on the tendency to change channels to watch a popular programme, this participant noted:

At a certain timeframe, we all do it, we transfer over to the mainstream television, like *Shortland Street* or something. So I don't know, maybe just a stable series? A *Shortland Street* for Māori . . . a soap that would just compete with *Shortland Street*.

While participants suggested the need for more varied programming (including a flagship soap opera to rival that of *Shortland Street*), they also hoped that Māori Television could more comprehensively acknowledge the diverse realities of Māori communities.

Some participants felt excluded from the kinds of on-screen worlds seen on Māori Television. As one participant put it:

It's so North Island focused . . . they should [have been] there filming when we had our waka ama wānanga, when we had the opening of the marae, when we had this unveiling or this exhibition. They should be here because you only have to watch it and they're in Tūhoe, they're in Ngāpuhi, they're in Te Tai Tokerau – they're doing it all up there but there's no one down here [in Te Waipounamu].

In a different focus group, a participant expressed the desire for images of Māori that span the full spectrum of Māori identity. Fellow focus group members supported this desire:

I wish it would sometimes have a few more fair-skinned Māori, being quite fair-skinned myself, and knowing that a lot of Māori are quite fair-skinned.

Participants: Yeah.

But because of that stereotypical 'Māoriness' and colour comes with that.

Another focus group questioned Māori Television's outreach to communities and wondered how the network could develop new relationships that might grow and support the generations to come. One participant asked, 'I see Māori TV as a potential developer and nurturer as well [as a] creative outlet – what are they doing to build our next generations or to support the next generation?' She went on to say:

> We keep talking about building relationships, and I think maybe that's what Māori TV need to start now doing after more than ten years on air – where are their relationships in the community? Are they relying on their old networks, or are they building new ones for a new vision of what sort of programmes they [are] going to be producing in ten to fifteen years with a new emerging population?

This same group discussed the constraints of Māori Televison, as a state-funded entity, being representative of te ao Māori. One participant suggested that Māori Television leaders should visit communities outside of Auckland to learn about existing resources and create better networks from the flax roots up:

> I'm thinking that's slightly outside the box thinking about where Māori Radio came from – where it is currently – your conversation around why don't we have a voice in Māori TV. Part of me just thinks actually that it will always just be a commercial body – it will always be a government-owned industry. Part of me wants those and the creative thinkers to actually get out of Auckland and come and visit people, and I know that type of work is ... important, but actually when you start exploring the land and seeing who's out there, I think you get a better idea of what resources are available.

Another focus group raised issues about the quality of engagement with Māori communities by Māori media production teams. Participants referred to the reality makeover show *Marae DIY*, which visits different marae throughout the country and conducts a makeover of parts of the marae complex. When the name of the show came up, one of the participants immediately responded, 'Ae, *Marae DIY* – Marae rip-off [*laughs*].' The following exchange ensued:

> It was alright at the time, but we were going through a process of trying to upgrade our whole marae complex and when [*Marae DIY*] finished doing their upgrade we were in the process of building a new marae altogether anyway, and so a lot of the things they did were actually taken out.
>
> Participant: It was too fast, eh? They built it too fast, because you only can do it – they only do it half pie. So you end up having to rip it all out . . .
>
> Yes. And very hurried – a lot of their work. But in the end it turned out okay, we did our brand new marae and it cost us a couple of million but . . . unfortunately a lot of their work was kind of . . .
>
> Participant: Bulldozed it over – be honest. Bulldozed it over – all those lovely trees and all that mahi they put in.

This exchange suggests that the on-screen content of some Māori Television programming has off-screen realities that may not enhance community wellbeing or community agendas. As such, the Māori media sector face the persisting challenge of how to meaningfully consult with people within short production timeframes.

In many ways the concerns about enhancing Māori Television's engagement with more diverse communities chimes with participant interests in how Māori Television might make better connections with existing Māori media resources such as iwi radio. One self-identified Pākehā participant observed:

> I'm surprised that iwi radio hasn't come up at all in the conversation, but that's probably because people don't listen to radio that much these days. But there ought to be – as part of Māori cultural development, there should be a link somewhere between iwi radio and Māori TV.

The capacity for Māori Television to provide programming that could connect across a range of platforms was a topic also raised by this participant and pursued by a fellow focus group member:

There's *The Nutters Club*, eh? That's really cool. I think that's broadcast on Radio Live and Māori TV. They could do something like that on iwi radio and Māori TV.

Participant: So, if Māori Television's getting a feed, why can't they link in with a Māori network and help strengthen both the causes of Māori Television and Māori radio ... Instead of reinventing the wheel, use the network that's been established for just that – the iwi network.*

The desire for greater cohesion across the Māori media sector also chimes with other comments made about Māori Television's engagement with emerging online content sources. The changing nature of media production and consumption practices, and the rise of online media as an aid and vehicle for television today, led to this comment:

Maybe Māori TV could do like a talent scout through that site [Vimeo] and be pulling off what they want there and then paying that person $100 for five repeats or whatever it is.

This approach to acquiring television content from Vimeo (a video-sharing website run by a niche community of film-makers) signals the kinds of expectations audiences have of how television might change in a digital era and how Māori Television might incorporate these changes. It also suggests that new media forms such as Vimeo have a role to play in enhancing Māori Television's engagement with its many publics.

Another participant from a different group suggested that Māori Television has some work to do in its engagement with social media. Commenting on the sharing of media content online, he stated:

If it was a bit more consciously in social media then I think we would probably watch more. Because every time I see something posted from Māori Television it's easier for my group of friends who all think and feel basically the same things – so what they're interested in, I'm usually interested in – they've picked it up and said, 'Oh, yeah I can

---

* Te Whakaruruhau o Ngā Reo Irirangi Māori (the Iwi Radio Network) allows radio stations to share and simulcast content across the network. In 2011 the network was able to simulcast live te reo Māori commentary on the Rugby World Cup by linking up with Māori Television's immersion channel Te Reo.

actually access Māori Television without having to shuffle through what's on today – oh that's a repeat that I saw last year.'

In addition to these desires for greater connectivity across regions and communities, and via different media platforms, some participants looked forward to seeing more television programming in the future that reflects Māori creative energies, talents and values.

Participants across all focus groups agreed that some Māori Television content enhances language and cultural knowledge and contributes to a sense of pride and Māori wellbeing. However, some participants expressed mixed feelings about other aspects of Māori Television programming. Across the focus groups, participants noted how Māori Television's production values sometimes make the content difficult to watch. One participant noted how the quality of set design often impaired her ability to engage with the programme:

> Some of the staging for the shows makes me a bit sad because we're so spoilt, I think, with the quality of talk-back style shows that we've had in from overseas rather than the talk-back shows that we get on Māori TV. I don't know, the quality of staging could just be a little bit more . . . It does make me sad, because those who are being interviewed have so much mana to them or they wouldn't have been brought in, and so actually I would have watched this but actually I'm being really distracted by the setting – and I know they've pulled it back and cut it back because they want, well I'm assuming that they want the kōrero to sit with this person, but an empty chair? Or you know a chair and a chair? I think, come on – you know production-wise let's . . .
>
> Participant: It makes you feel like it's the poor relation.
>
> I do . . . I expect a certain amount of production value, so I flick off.

Such kōrero demonstrates how aspects of Māori Television programming can be perceived as diminishing feelings of Māori wellbeing in a range of ways. In this instance, set design devalued the kōrero from studio guests and raised concern about how viewers might perceive the mana of the kaumātua involved. A fellow focus group member reflected on how set design can impact on self-perception, and create the feeling of Māori Television being a 'poor relation' to mainstream television providers.

Māori Television programming can also impact on the wellbeing of audiences by repeating stereotypes that confirm normative notions of Māori identity, including gender typecasts. One participant expressed a certain cringe factor when viewing aspects of 'old-school style' programming in shows such as *Hōmai te Pakipaki* and *It's in the Kete*. When asked to explain what 'old-school style' meant, this participant replied:

> Yeah, old school. So *Hōmai te Pakipaki* and *It's in the Kete* have this – and I'm sorry, and you guys can smack me out for this – but the Billy T-type persona of being Māori. The hahahaha – the jovial . . . I often times cringe because I think we're stereotyping ourselves. Is that a behaviour that we truly have? . . . Is this really our people, or is this our people taking on colonial perceptions of who we are and so we are that now? We're the Billy T culture – or are we?

These comments highlight Māori Television's ability to perpetuate images and ideas about Māori that have been generated by earlier New Zealand television culture, and pioneering Māori celebrities such as Billy T James, with the ambivalent outcomes of such repetitions. The participant acknowledged the difficulty of asking such a question with her apology to her fellow focus group members, which suggests a concern that she was out of step with the opinions of the group. However, this same participant continued to ponder whether or not Māori Television is making content that reproduces tired stereotypes, or if it has the capacity to make television that is better aligned with Māori creativity, beliefs and values:

> Are we making Māori TV from a Pākehā perspective, or an interpretation of that, or are we actually using our beliefs and values in the way that we develop and provide the stories? Are we using our pūrākau to develop our programmes? Are we using our myths and legends to develop contemporary youth programmes about those beliefs and values?

Declaring her hope that Māori Television might be a conduit for expressing Māori world views, this participant stated:

> I want us to have the ability to re-present ourselves, and if Māori TV's our mechanism, to have a voice for how *we* perceive ourselves and how *we* want to represent ourselves without being told how we should be looking – I think that's where I come from because I want us to have a voice, I want us to have our own voice.

These comments reflect a desire for more programming that reflects the distinctiveness of Māori culture and knowledge, and is driven by the talents and traditions of the diverse communities that constitute te ao Māori.

A different focus group participant echoed these sentiments when he discussed the risk of relying on non-Māori-defined ways of making television:

> They are Māori, too. For them to be Māori and to reach other Māori they have to become Māori, not another TV station just doing what Pākehā say . . . They have the potential to do that – get out of the Pākehā way and move into their own.

These focus group aspirations recall the activist roots of the organisation and the Tiriti-based politics underpinning Māori Television's 2004 launch. While many participants acknowledged the hauora benefits of Māori Television, others suggested areas where Māori Television needs to improve its engagement with audiences, and provide content that meets the needs of diverse Māori communities. Focus group kōrero suggested that developing greater links with audiences would enable this Māori media organisation to better deliver on its responsibilities.

Māori Television acts as a site of cultural authority for many of its viewers, including non-Māori. This means that the network not only has the potential to cultivate and enhance a sense of wellbeing for its Māori viewers, and greater understanding among non-Māori, the network can also potentially cause harm by repeating entrenched stereotypes about te ao Māori. As a commissioner of content, Māori Television is responsible for ensuring that production companies do not privilege on-screen content at the expense of off-screen relationships. As a Māori media organisation dedicated to the uplift of te reo, tikanga and the voice of te ao Māori, Māori Television is obliged to produce television programming that reflects the norms, values and priorities of Māori audiences. Given the diverse nature of its audiences, as well as the diversity within te ao Māori as to what 'Māori' means, this is a perpetual challenge.

This audience framework provides partial insights into how some audiences have engaged with Māori Television. Where institutional discourses about audiences draw on ratings statistics to make broad claims about audience habits, this survey provides snapshots of the everyday habits of Māori Television audiences that highlight the ephemeral nature of media consumption. While acknowledging the important work done by Māori Television, the focus group participants also suggested ways that Māori Television might develop, suggesting that Māori Television should:

- support aspiring language learners and the work of kōhanga reo, kura, whare wānanga and universities
- extend and enhance Māori knowledge
- function as a kaitiaki of earlier forms of Māori media
- act as a documentarian and archivist for future generations
- transmit intergenerational knowledge
- be a site of cultural authority
- enhance whanaungatanga across diverse communities
- contribute to Māori wellbeing
- bridge diverse cultural communities
- set a benchmark for other media outlets when addressing Māori matters and when pronouncing te reo Māori.

In discussion on ways in which Māori Television might develop in the future, participants wanted Maori Television to:

- provide more informational media content, drama (including a soap opera) and New Zealand festival films
- provide programming reflective of diverse Māori worlds and devise more community-outreach practices
- expand existing professional networks to include the creative potential of flax-roots communities
- connect with other media such as iwi radio and digital media
- develop more tikanga-based media practices to enhance the wellbeing of Māori audiences and to align with Māori values.

Chapter Five

Māori Television and a Politics of Culture Framework

A range of voices including the Māori media sector, politicians, commentators, language experts and audiences have demonstrated the many different visions of what Māori Television should do and be, and the contribution it makes to Māori language and culture, as well as to New Zealand nationhood. While it was established by Tiriti-based activism, and by the desire for more potent forms of cultural and political representation for te ao Māori, in its first ten years Māori Television pursued an inclusive approach to audiences, and became a respected part of New Zealand's media culture. This inclusive approach enabled Māori Television to establish itself as a viable minority-language media organisation within an English-speaking non-Māori majority culture.

However, as interviews and focus group kōrero have suggested, while an inclusive approach has many political benefits, some Māori stakeholders aspire to forms of Māori media that express distinctly Māori ways of making television, drawing on te reo and tikanga in a more concerted way. What a distinctly Māori form of television might look and sound like is an issue up for perpetual debate. The struggle for greater opportunities and spaces where diverse Māori world views can be expressed, reflected on, and debated, on terms determined by Māori, is a persistent challenge. This chapter examines Māori Television's contribution to a politics of culture, which provides a framework for examining the assumed relationships between artistic and cultural practices, as well as more overtly political outcomes. In particular it focuses on a decolonising theme that runs through much of the kōrero from stakeholders. Understanding the implicit links that people make between cultural production and politics helps shed light on the utopian dimensions of politics (defined in its broadest sense as the desire for transformation) and the material constraints facing Māori Television.

As we have seen, the idea of Māori Television has mobilised many political desires over the years. For broadcaster and founding member of Ngā Aho Whakaari Ella Henry, the fight for Māori Television was more than a fight for broadcasting; it was part of a wider struggle for greater autonomy on Māori terms. According to Henry, 'by revitalising our language and culture [through television] we would strengthen our identity and our resolve for sovereignty, for self-determination, for tino rangatiratanga' (E. Henry, interview, 2012).

Yet, former CEO of Māori Television Jim Mather prioritised the network's ability to independently decide what best serves the interests of Māori viewers, not the promotion of Māori self-determination as such. While respectful of the long struggle to establish Māori Television, Mather used his time as CEO (from 2005 to 2013) to focus on the future and what sorts of broadcasting could be done (Abel, 2013b). As we have seen, the interests of Māori viewers are extremely diverse and difficult to anticipate. Some viewers want entertaining programming, not politics. Others want more civic-minded programming that can contribute to Māori wellbeing. These competing visions of what Māori Television should be reflect the varying political and cultural powers accrued to television as an agent of social change and as a conduit of tino rangatiratanga.

When Piripi Walker said that Māori Television was 'worth 25 MPs to Māori' (P. Walker, interview, 2013), he was assuming that Māori Television has a significant political role to play to support Māori interests and perspectives. When Maria Bargh suggested that Māori Television might help non-Māori think differently about Māori matters, she was alluding to television's ability to help shape public opinion and to make visible Māori-oriented agendas. When Quinton Hita described Māori Television in its current form as a missed opportunity, he was suggesting that there is a form of television that can more closely express Māori values and viewpoints. This kind of kōrero treats Māori media as a vehicle that enables Māori to take up a symbolic space within the media landscape of Aotearoa, in ways that affirm and assert Indigenous perspectives and purposes.

These political aims chime with Linda Tuhiwai Smith's notions of a politics of decolonisation, which place Indigenous concerns and world views at the centre, and produce knowledge that expresses Indigenous perspectives for Indigenous purposes (Smith, 1999). When stakeholder kōrero is considered in relation to academic literature on decolonisation, four dimensions of a decolonising political agenda arise. These include: focusing on achieving greater forms of cultural and political representation (Thiong'o, 1986), creating spaces to retell Indigenous stories (Mita, 2000; Hutchings, 2002; Lee, 2009), making visible Indigenous agendas for social and political change (Smith, 2000), and enabling a form of anti-colonial struggle that grows from grass-roots spaces (Zavala, 2013). Such a decolonising political agenda is aspirational in that it offers a utopian horizon to which people might aspire in order to effect changes at the level of the everyday. So these four dimensions are part of an iterative and dynamic model of political change, which understands that decolonisation is not a process that one eventually arrives at the end of, but is ongoing, dynamic, and with outcomes that are difficult to anticipate. Such a politics involves a perpetual struggle to attain the cultural ideals and aspirations of a people in the face of persisting constraints. This chapter discusses these four dimensions of a decolonising agenda in relation to Māori Television programming and practices, highlighting the network's achievements as an agent of social change, and pointing to the work that remains to be done to meet the decolonising expectations that some Māori stakeholders have for Māori Television.

Greater cultural and political representation

The struggle to establish Māori Television included the struggle for the right for te reo Māori to be heard on the airwaves, in schools as part of Māori-led curriculum innovations, and in parliamentary and court settings. The struggle was also to give voice to Māori concerns, and to help strengthen the political and cultural standing of Māori. How Māori Television has contributed to greater forms of cultural and political representation can be evidenced in a number of ways. One way would be to compare Māori-language programming offerings prior to the advent of Māori Television, with those offerings available afterwards. NZ On Air's 2010 report on mainstream Māori programming on other free-to-air providers noted that (excluding Māori Television programming) the number of hours of Māori broadcasting has 'remained relatively consistent at between 300 and 400 hours per annum since 2000' (NZ On Air, 2010, p. 10). In contrast, Māori Television offers approximately 7000 hours of broadcast content, with 70 per cent of spoken content in te reo Māori across both channels (Māori Television, 2014a). But does an increase in Māori media content necessarily mean enhanced political power?

Another way of thinking about Māori Television's contribution to greater cultural and political representation for Māori is to examine the news media coverage offered by Māori Television, and the opportunities that *Native Affairs*, *Te Tēpu* and *Te Kāea* provide for Māori politicians, for commentators, and for communities, to share the stories that concern their communities and constituents. The extended coverage of election issues provided by *Native Affairs' Kōwhiri* programming was an example of an overt way of informing communities on Māori issues, and offered a forum where politicians and their communities could engage on matters of public import. Māori Television therefore offers an important public space for debating Māori issues of the day, on Māori terms. The network also provides opportunities to flesh out the jaded stereotypes provided by non-Māori media providers, for example, the framing of Ngāi Tūhoe public figure Tame Iti as a folk devil (Devadas, 2008). Commenting on the programming content available on Māori Television, scholar Jennifer Lawn makes a case for the humanising and bridge-building function of such content:

> This mixture of homeliness, cosmopolitanism, and a mature and absorbing presentation of heritage have a cultural bridge-building function; it's hard to demonize Māori activist and performance artist Tame Iti as a terrorist, for example, when you've watched him demonstrate how to cook eels in the show *Kai Time on the Road*. (Lawn, 2016, p. 142)

Having access to more diverse and informed sounds and images of te ao Māori certainly provides a greater opportunity for productive cross-cultural exchanges, but how do you assess the political impact of such content in light of the network's niche audience?

Another example of Māori Television's cultural or political contribution can be seen in the ways that politicians talk about Māori Television. Māori Party co-leader Pita Sharples, when introducing the 2013 Māori Television Service Amendment Bill to New Zealand's Parliament, stated:

> The launch of the Māori Television Service in 2004 was a watershed moment for Māori people and, indeed, all New Zealanders. It transformed the media landscape in this

country. It made our language and culture accessible to a broad viewing audience. For Māori it has meant the celebration and normalisation of our language, our tikanga, and our people. I am delighted to celebrate its achievements. (Sharples, 2013)

Twelve years on, many politicians now regard Māori Television as 'the best public broadcaster' (Turei, 2013, p. 14921), and 'the best of the free-to-air channels' (Mallard, 2013, p. 8792) in a country where commercial imperatives dominate the media sector.

Yet the idea that Māori Television contributes to New Zealand public-service broadcasting needs to be understood in the light of the longer history of Māori exclusion from New Zealand's public sphere, and the continuing decline of public-television provision in this country. Using a public-service framework to describe Māori Television's significance obscures Te Tiriti o Waitangi-based struggles that inaugurated the network's emergence (J. Smith, 2015).

Focus group kōrero revealed the more intangible benefits of having more media coverage of things Māori. Many participants acknowledged feeling proud and empowered by seeing more Māori faces on screen, and hearing te reo Māori on the airwaves and in the home. The novelty of seeing Māori faces and hearing te reo Māori on screen should not be overlooked given the decades of invisibility experienced by Māori. Media commentator Morgan Godfery reminded us of this point in a documentary made for Māori Television's tenth anniversary titled *Through the Lens* (2014):

> I was twelve years old when the channel started, but my abiding memory was of Waitangi Day. For the first time here was a channel that was presenting a Waitangi Day that I understood, pushing back against those negative narratives. It was a Māori view, and that was something that was strangely subversive at the time and also really empowering.

Godfery's comments allude to the generation of young Māori now growing up with Māori Television. What possible long-term effects and influences will this media organisation have on the generations to come? While feelings of pride, recognition and empowerment may not directly link to overt political changes elsewhere, or immediately, many would agree that being affirmed in heart, mind and body by the things seen on screen can enhance the capacity to engage in other dimensions of life. One could argue that Māori

Television contributes to greater Māori wellbeing through its diverse depictions of things Māori. On-screen content draws on experiences that occur at the level of the individual, the hapū and the iwi, as well as portraying more global relationships with other Indigenous media providers.

Reflecting on typical non-Māori representations of Māori, Wally Penetito notes:

> You wouldn't think there are lots of ways to be Māori if you only relied on what journalists, researchers and politicians tell us about ourselves. You would think we are all the same – 'those Māori' in inverted commas, underlined, written in italics, made bold; you know what I mean? (Penetito, 2011, p. 38)

As Penetito's comments suggest, depictions of te ao Māori have often been framed in ways that reflect non-Māori perspectives. In the wake of a long history of such media practices, Māori Television provides insights into the diverse realities of those citizens of Aotearoa often conflated into a monolithic category, 'Māori'.

Scholars have drawn attention to the ways in which the category 'Māori' (a term originally denoting those who were 'normal' in early colonial times) has developed a racial and ethnic category over time (Matahaere, 1995). Now many scholars acknowledge the need for more expansive categories for understanding contemporary forms of Māori identity. Penetito argues that there is 'a dominant or pervasive view or paradigm of what it means to be Māori and that view is based around the idea that unless it is whakapapa defined then it is not really real, it is less than authentic' (2011, p. 39). While acknowledging that 'the whakapapa view of being Māori is our legacy, it is our inheritance, it is our taonga tuku iho' (p. 41), he notes that there are people who know they are Māori but who don't know what that means:

> They say they don't know what their Māoritanga is; that they don't talk about it because they don't know what it is; that they don't know how to join in or how to belong. They want to know the next step to take, and they argue that there is no use in somebody saying to them 'Go and learn your reo or go and learn your whakapapa'. They do not know what that is, where to get it if they want it, or even if it is something worth wanting. (Penetito, 2011, p. 40)

As focus group kōrero suggested, for those audiences who have not grown up knowing about their cultural identity, watching programming on Māori Television can complement the kinds of knowledge often found through kaumātua, on marae and in the activities of hapū.

Belinda Borell's study of South Auckland rangatahi reveals the diverse realities young Māori experience. Borell argues that conventional frameworks of Māori identity risk marginalising those who cannot perform the cultural activities of being Māori (including speaking te reo, knowing whakapapa and performing waiata):

> Those who are not seen as connected in this way are often defined by what they are seen as lacking, hence terms such as disconnected, distanced, detached and dissociated. Although young Māori may define themselves in terms of difference from others there is an increasing danger of some urban youth being defined as different from Māori who are 'culturally connected' and for this to be seen primarily as a negative demarcation. (Borell, 2005, p. 30)

Indigenous broadcasters such as Māori Television help address these negative demarcations. As comments from focus group participants suggested, for those not immersed in their culture, Māori Television offers knowledge that is difficult to access elsewhere, and on-screen content role-models diverse Māori experiences. These knowledge-sharing acts and role-modelling contribute to notions of Māori cultural citizenship, a form of citizenship that Māori Television programming demonstrates at the individual, iwi and global levels. As other Indigenous scholars have argued, Indigenous identities are '(re)constructed at multiple levels' (Alfred and Corntassel, 2005, p. 600), at global, state, community and individual levels, and they vary over time and place. Aspects of Māori Television programming reveal these varying levels of experience, contributing to more complex and variegated expressions of being Māori than those available prior to 2004.

Programmes that depict journeys of personal discovery are popular on Māori Television. The title of the series *Tātai Hono* (Bravestar Films) can be translated as 'joining the links' and relates to the programme's prime goal of answering the question 'Ko wai ahau?' (who am I?). The show's Facebook page states:

> This series will follow the journey of disconnected Māori as they rediscover their roots. With the help and support of a kaumātua led research team, the viewer will share the

pilgrimage back to the talents' marae and their iwi, hapū and whānau. We will hear the stories of Māori who have longed to fill the void in their life.*

Drawing on conventional notions of Indigenous cultural belonging (the assumption that there are 'disconnected Māori'), *Tātai Hono* takes as its subject those whom Wally Penetito identifies as people who know they are Māori but who do not know what that means. The half-hour programme focuses on the lives of Māori who have lost (or do not know the meaning of) the knowledge of their tribal links, language and tikanga. *Tātai Hono* involves ordinary people rediscovering their whakapapa, their marae and their tūrangawaewae, as well as their iwi, hapū and whānau links.

In one episode (series eight), former New Zealand hockey representative Bevan Hari, of Māori, Pākehā and Indian descent, embarked on a journey to know his whakapapa. While tracing his Māori ancestry through the Births, Deaths and Marriages registry was one approach, locating the marae that his family was affiliated with, holding an ancient taiaha in his hands, walking the lands of his iwi (Ngāti Awa), and viewing archival footage of his tūpuna, were framed as vital aspects of his journey to his identity. At one point Hari met with Ngāti Awa tohunga whakapapa Pouroto Ngaropo. He took him to his tribal lands, and recited the names of the mountains, islands and rivers that make up his tūrangawaewae. When they reached the hometown of Matatā, he told Bevan, 'It is great to have you home.' He then gestured to the landscape and said, 'This is us.'

Tātai Hono validates and welcomes those Māori who have not grown up within their hapū and iwi, and who are without connection to their tribal lands, and helps them to trace and build these connections. By modelling such experiences on television, *Tātai Hono* makes evident the ongoing impact of colonisation on contemporary experience. The show demonstrates the diverse realities of Māori, and offers pathways of connection and belonging for those who know nothing of their whakapapa. At the same time as offering conventional pathways to gaining knowledge about Māori identity (by visiting kaumātua, going to marae and learning from oral sources), *Tātai Hono* teaches the audience about those Māori who struggle with their identity. By showing experiences of cultural disconnection on screen, the programme normalises those experiences, and offers a better understanding of the many

---

* https://www.facebook.com/pages/T percentC4 percent81tai-Hono/373244903537?sk=info

ways that people discover their cultural identities. This normalising occurs through the medium of television, promoting increased cultural confidence.

Academic Margaret Mutu (Te Whānau Moana hapū of Ngāti Kahu, Te Rarawa, Ngāti Whātua) said when asked about the contribution Māori Television makes to developing notions of cultural identity:

> Māori Television normalises being Māori, and so it will give those who are perhaps a bit scared of going and finding out who they are, and where they belong and all that sort of thing – hopefully it gives them the confidence to do so. That is especially so for the programmes on people who are looking for their whakapapa and their background – they have given some stories of people who've gone through that path. (M. Mutu, interview, 2012)

The idea that *Tātai Hono* might imbue an audience with the confidence to seek out knowledge about their links to te ao Māori is one that alludes to Māori Television's role in supporting personal and individual agency. The stories told through *Tātai Hono* demonstrate how feeling disconnected from whakapapa and community is a common experience for Māori, but the programme's approach also raises a contradiction. By framing certain Māori as 'disconnected', the programme continues to reinforce normative notions of what it means to be Māori, and the solution to this 'disconnect' is framed in very conventional ways: better knowledge of whakapapa and engagement with whānau and hapū members, walking the land and experiencing the taonga of tūpuna. The solutions offered in this show cannot address the experiences of those Māori who will never know their whakapapa.

Other programmes on Māori Television are based on the specificities of particular iwi identities. For example, *Iwi Anthems* (Raukatauri Productions) features waiata and performances from particular iwi. As promotional material for the programme states: 'Our iwi anthems often tell a unique story about our tribe revealing who we are, where we're from, what we're like and what's important to us.'* Each episode is devoted to screening a performance in a hall or wharenui by the particular iwi. After each 'anthem', someone from the group explains the background to the song, thus providing the television audience with historical knowledge related to that iwi.

One episode featured a lament for one of Ngāti Ranginui's fortified

---

* http://www.maoritelevision.com/tv/shows/iwi-anthems

villages that had been devastated by colonial forces. While ostensibly a waiata dedicated to historical events, at the time of recording the episode Ngāti Ranginui had just signed their Treaty settlement with the Crown. So while the Crown had offered a compensation package, the screening of the lament functioned (as one iwi member framed it) as a 'reminder that these memories haven't left the heart and mind for those who lost their lives during that time of conflict identified in the claims'. In this example, Māori Television has functioned as an archivist for, and an educator about, the past, and its persistent relationship to the present.

Perhaps *Ngā Pari Kārangaranga* is the most compelling form of iwi programming offered by Māori Television. The programme is described as being 'made for the iwi by the iwi, an authentic collection of distinctive kōrero from around the motu.'* Made by different iwi groups, *Ngā Pari Kārangaranga* does not offer an overt account of tribal history or tribal traits, but draws on the kōrero of kaumātua or kuia talking about their own life experiences. These elders outline their whakapapa in considerable detail, they explain their ties to the whenua, and they tell stories about their lives, often with considerable humour. One kaumātua reminisces about the arrival of rock 'n' roll, when the boys all watched the girls spinning and their skirts going up. Another kaumātua describes milking the cows on cold mornings, and keeping his feet warm in fresh cowpats. While the stories may be those of individuals, the whakapapa and ties to whenua clearly link these old people with the wider iwi, as does the mita of their language.

By broadcasting diverse iwi realities, Māori Television promotes a more nuanced understanding of Māori identity, not only for non-Māori unsure of how a tribally based cultural identity might work, but also for those who have connections to things Māori. As interviews with Māori stakeholders and audiences of Māori Television demonstrate, seeing iwi members, iwi practices and iwi dialects on screen is a treasured phenomenon, one that leads to a greater sense of pride in iwi identity.

The global Indigenous media programmes that air on Māori Television are also a site of positive identification for Māori, as one focus group participant noted:

---

* http://www.throng.co.nz/2012/05/nga-pari-karangaranga-o-te-motu-7/

> Being Māori is about having the ability to explore the world and to find out [about] the bigger world. We were never so silo-ed, and so if [Māori Television] didn't have what it does – it does have other Indigenous perspectives [from] around the world. I think it makes it easier for us to engage ... whether it is kei roto i te reo Pākehā [*in English*], it's the [Māori] perspectives, and the way they're joined with other Indigenous perspectives [from] around the world that I think is far more valuable. When [non-Māori] see a range of other cultures and the affinity that Māori do have with a lot of other Indigenous cultures, I think that creates a new perspective on what is Māori identity.

The potential for building international links across Indigenous nations can be seen in the programming that shows the shared predicaments of colonisation and its ongoing impacts. Drama series such as *Redfern Now*, and the documentary series *First Australians*, help to strengthen viewer understanding of the political and cultural concerns of Indigenous peoples in Australia. In 2011 *We Shall Remain* offered Māori Television viewers insights into native American perspectives on the coming of European settlers to their lands. In 2013 the documentary series *Wabanaagig: Land of the Rising Sun* screened stories of the Wabanaki people of Canada (also known as 'The People of the First Light') and their storytelling practices.

The inaugural World Indigenous Television Broadcasters Network (WITBN) Conference, hosted by Māori Television in Auckland in 2008, revealed the network's global aspirations. As a founding member of WITBN, Māori Television is part of a network that shares native language and cultural resources with international Indigenous media communities. As part of this initiative, Māori Television has compiled and screened *Indigenous Insight*, a 30-minute news programme which broadcasts stories that make visible the everyday issues facing Indigenous communities.* Contributors to the programme include: Māori Television; the Aboriginal Peoples Television Network (APTN), Canada; TG4, Ireland; BBC ALBA, Scotland; and Taiwan Indigenous Television (TITV).

This kind of global programming provides opportunities for New Zealand-based audiences to make connections between local concerns and the recurring issues facing a range of Indigenous communities from around the globe. The sense of a shared predicament between peoples in Taiwan, Canada, Ireland, Scotland and Australia offers Māori audiences opportunities

---

* http://www.scoop.co.nz/stories/CU0906/S00165/a-window-to-the-world-on-maori-television.htm

to reflect on the links across nations that might unite Indigenous communities. One interview participant suggested when discussing international Indigenous programming:

> It is the voice of other Indigenous people and in some ways it's reflective of how we feel [here] and so you can kind of relate to things that other Indigenous people are going through, and just knowing what other Indigenous experience[s] [are] like.

As these examples demonstrate, having Māori programming on prime-time television that provides a diverse range of representations has positive effects for viewers who identify with the content. However as we shall see, although Māori Television offers content that many are proud of, some Māori stakeholders want more from the network. The contribution that Māori Television makes to cultural and political representations is tied to another dimension, that of a decolonising political agenda – creating spaces to retell Māori stories in Māori ways.

Creating spaces to retell Indigenous stories

While one aspect of a decolonising political agenda considers how Māori Television contributes to greater forms of cultural and political representation, a second aspect considers how Māori Television has created space (social, material and intellectual) to retell Māori stories in Māori ways.

One practical example of Māori Television's success in creating a space for Māori storytelling is the electronic programming guide (EPG) and the placement of the bilingual Māori Television channel. In a very material sense, Māori Television's presence on the EPG (as well as its presence in the TV guide published in daily newspapers) demonstrates the uptake of Māori space in New Zealand's mediated public sphere. Alan Witherington, former general manager of finance and administration at Māori Television, reflecting on the digital switch over (DSO), which was imminent, said:

> We were one of the original foundation members of Freeview and at that stage, it was TV One, TV2, 3, 4, and we came on as the first broadcaster, so we grabbed channel 5. We're not legally or contractually entitled to it, but that's our position, and I sit on the board of Freeview and 5 is our spot, and we'll work pretty hard to hold that. Channel

numbering is probably going to be a lot more significant when [the] digital switch over happens, because everyone's either going to have Sky or they're going to have Freeview. And in the analogue world, unless you pre-programmed your tele, Māori Television could be anywhere. Freeview – you go up and down in the channels, next button, Māori Television. (A. Witherington, interview, 2013)

According to Witherington, this electronic spatial setting may have benefits for the bilingual channel. Discussing the cumulative ratings system used by Māori Television, Witherington suggests:

Our 'cume' will probably rise significantly – our accumulative audience – purely because of people just channel surfing, going next, next, next, next, next, and a lot more people will at least pass through Māori Television. Hopefully some of them will camp a while and watch something. And whether that translates into average audience and audience share growing that's going to be the test, but it should be good for us in terms of awareness, exposure and those kinds of things, which we need to convert into actual audience. (A. Witherington, interview, 2013)

Another way of creating space to retell stories precious to Māori is the opportunity Māori Television provides to view earlier Māori programming such as *Koha*, *Waka Huia* and *Ngā Taonga Whitiāhua*, a programme made in conjunction with the then New Zealand Film Archive (renamed Ngā Taonga Sound and Vision in 2014). These re-screenings enable audiences of the present to experience the wisdom and insights of leaders and kaumātua from days gone by. The archives bring the past alive, and help to strengthen the cultural knowledge of younger generations. So Māori Television functions as a kaitiaki of Māori media from the past, to ensure those sounds and images still circulate among communities today.

Māori Television also commissions and screens new television content that develops aesthetic innovations in television storytelling, in ways that align with te reo and tikanga Māori. For example, Quinton Hita devised and presents *Kōwhao Rau*. On one level this is a programme where Hita visits kaumātua from Ngāpuhi in their homes, where they share their memories with him. On another level, the aesthetics of the programme (the way it looks and sounds) express a world view seldom seen on New Zealand screens. The one-hour programme has a leisurely pace, and the duration of camera shots is longer than conventional television pacing. Hita's aim for the programme is to capture the mita used by those kaumātua he sees as the last of the native Ngāpuhi reo speakers. Hita says:

> If you were to transcribe all of the interviews to date you would have hundreds of hours of kōrero, you would have a definitive source of te reo o Ngāpuhi as it exists today. I hope one day that I or someone else will be able to collate it all, and there's your definitive source, dictionary, phrase book. (Q. Hita, interview, 2014)

Kōwhao Rau appears to have struck a chord with audiences, and Hita has had iwi from all over the country approach him, partly, he says, because the format does the old people justice. He initially had difficulty getting this format accepted, as Māori Television tried to persuade him to confine the discussions to 30 minutes, because they did not think that an hour of talking heads was good television. Hita says:

> My argument was that in the Māori community I live in, our timeframes are different. People might accuse me of being old-fashioned and stuff, but there are still a lot of Māori families in our communities who feel that these things are important. You know an hour was nothing – we used to sit around a table and I'd have to listen to kaumātua talk for three or four hours. I think these days most people don't learn the language in that context, and that's what they miss . . . in terms of formal language acquisition – all the pauses, the silences, and the little words, and all the digressions in a conversation. These aren't relevant to the television style which says you have to stick to the kaupapa for half an hour and make it into something meaningful. But to me those distinctions are te reo o te kāinga – the language of home. (Q. Hita, interview, 2014)

Kōwhao Rau represents a success story in terms of showcasing the mita of Ngāpuhi, and hence the richness of iwi differences, as well as establishing a format that refuses to follow conventional Western models. As a result, it is one example of the decolonising potential of Māori media production. As comments from focus groups suggest, audiences desire more of this kind of storytelling and these kinds of aesthetic innovations.

Māori Television's flagship annual event, Anzac Day coverage, also demonstrates the network's capacity to reframe narratives of New Zealand nationhood in distinctly Māori ways. One of Māori Television's boldest strategic moves was to devote a whole day in 2006 to broadcasting remembrance services, interviews, and a range of other programmes related to the First

World War, as well as other wars in which New Zealand has been involved. At least half of the broadcast was narrated in te reo (not always subtitled), and at least half of the participants included in the programming for the day were Māori. The broadcast attracted a large non-Māori audience, and Māori Television's coverage of subsequent Anzac days became a widely followed and highly regarded annual event. This approach to programming demonstrates how Māori Television reconsiders national events from the perspective of te ao Māori. According to Linda Tuhiwai Smith:

> To me [Anzac Day's] their showpiece, and it brings a number of elements together, because it does have our stories, it does have good documentary, it's got pieces for people who speak Māori, and pieces for mainstream audiences, because we can see all our relations. (L. T. Smith, interview, 2013)

When asked to consider how Anzac Day might contain a nation-building agenda that taps into existing narratives of New Zealand nationhood, Smith replied:

> I don't see it as that. I mean, it might perform that role but that's not why we watch it. We watch it because we're watching the feats of our ancestors at some point, and their stories. (L. T. Smith, interview, 2013)

For independent media producer Kath Akuhata-Brown, Anzac Day is an opportunity to celebrate the deeds of those who have passed:

> Those soldiers. It is about aroha for those old people. And not a soft aroha, but a deep enduring whakapapa aroha. Even before Māori TV came along we were celebrating those old people and telling [these] stories. (K. Akuhata-Brown, interview, 2012)

Creating Māori spaces within a well-honed national narrative of New Zealand has been a successful strategy for Māori Television, and has earned the respect and praise of many. Yet this kind of programming also carries the risk of re-inscribing well-established tropes of Māori masculinity (the warrior figure) as well as shoring up national narratives of nationhood based on warfare activities offshore, while ignoring New Zealand's own history of warfare within the nation (Abel, 2013a).

Making visible Māori agendas for social and political change

The third dimension of a decolonising political agenda is the ways in which an Indigenous media organisation such as Māori Television makes visible Māori agendas for social and political change. To set an agenda is an expression of power and, indeed, a key aspect of self-determination. Yet how well can Māori Television assert a 'by Māori, for Māori, and about Māori' agenda when it exists within a Crown-based legislative framework and a Crown-initiated funding regime?

Constraints on Māori Television's ability to affirm Māori agendas for political change include: the legislation governing Māori Television's practices and objectives; the norms of the media industry, whose measures of value draw on ratings and audience share; and the production schedules and funder requirements that help shape what is seen and heard on screen. These constraints can be summed up by a recurring paradox: how to provide support for the wellbeing and health of a minority language using a medium that needs an audience to justify the funding it attracts. Understanding Māori Television within a politics of culture framework involves highlighting these persisting constraints, including the legislation governing Māori Television's practices in its first ten years.

Māori Television's capacity to affirm Māori agendas for social change has been shaped by its legislative imperative to make a 'broad appeal' to audiences, including non-Māori. While there are benefits to this inclusive approach, CEO of Te Māngai Pāho (TMP) John Bishara calls into question the emphasis on 'broad appeal':

> It's extremely difficult to sustain the funding without the buy-in from the wider community, taxpayers and government. And the government's commitment to te reo Māori, or obligation to reo revitalisation, had been fought out in court, and the government lost that battle. Currently, TMP receives approximately $50 million, which is the government's obligation to Maori-language broadcasting. Isn't it the government's job to make sure that the government wins over the taxpayers to ensure the obligation is maintained? Rather than give TMP and [Māori Television] the money, and suggest it's their/our job to win over the non-receptive audiences, the rednecks – even those Māori who reject their [own] culture? Bullshit, I say. The government has a huge role to play. (J. Bishara, interview, 2012)

Bishara's comments suggest that one must be suspicious of a government strategy that asks Māori not only to labour to revitalise a language and culture damaged by long-term state neglect, but also to win over a broad audience who might find such programming appealing. As Bishara's comments remind us, the Crown also has a substantial role to play in providing a supportive and safe environment for the flourishing of te reo and tikanga Māori. While the Crown may have delivered on its promise to resource Māori broadcasting after decades of Crown negligence, the establishment of Māori Television should not mean that the Crown can now rest on its laurels and avoid its ongoing obligations to te reo and tikanga Māori. Yet Bishara goes on to outline the ways in which a Māori media organisation must consistently remain accountable to the Crown, as opposed to the Crown's accountability to Māori:

> [W]e have to have systems and processes in place to make sure that [the spending of] this money is accountable and transparent, to maintain the government's trust and confidence that taxpayers' money is being spent appropriately. The whole Māori broadcasting sector has this responsibility when I think about it. Select Committee reporting provides the opportunity for government, coalition parties, the opposition and independents to question the agencies, and if all is good say, 'Look, this money is fully accounted for and it's transparent and it's doing many of the things that we asked it to do.' (J. Bishara, interview, 2012)

As Bishara points out, all state-funded initiatives must be accountable and transparent when dealing with taxpayer money. Bishara makes additional comments about the dilemma facing Māori Television in a media sector where audience share and ratings are the dominant measure of value:

> Unfortunately for Māori TV, they are part of the bigger television broadcasting and media sector where ratings remain king. But if we just measured Māori Television and the funded programmes by ratings, we'd shut down tomorrow, actually, we probably should have shut down yesterday. This is a dilemma our Māori broadcasting sector faces every day, including iwi radio. NZ On Air face the same issue trying to promote local productions. If it doesn't rate for the mainstream broadcasters, TVNZ and MediaWorks, the programme is cut. However, NZ On Air has ratings as a criteria and TMP, to a certain extent, includes ratings in their criteria. Television remains a very powerful tool to promote anything and we should just measure Māori Television like other mainstream broadcasters. [Māori Television] and TMP are all

about Māori-language revitilisation, and television, radio and new media remain very powerful tools to utilise for this purpose. Yes, we need better and clearer measures other than ratings, sure! But the programmes still need to appeal to wider audiences as well as Māori. (J. Bishara, interview, 2012)

These legislative, economic and institutional imperatives help shape Māori Television's activities, and make the network responsive to outside social forces. So Māori Television's ability to support and enable Māori agendas, or to be a vehicle for self-determination, must be considered in light of these larger constraints.

Take, for example, the normative audience measure of ratings. Primarily a tool for selling audiences to advertisers, many New Zealand-based media scholars have raised questions about the quantitative basis of the ratings system, which cannot account for the quality or level of attention experienced by survey participants (Lealand, 1998 and 2001; Zanker and Lealand, 2010; Dunleavy, 2012). Minority-language media providers in other countries must also deal with the rhetoric of ratings, and its historical basis as a commercial measure, not a social one. According to the chief executive of the Welsh-language media provider S4C, Ian Jones, it is 'no longer appropriate in today's multiplatform television environment to use one simple performance measure to assess success'* (Thomas, 2013). He goes on to say that 'success today is a combination of factors including audience reach, economic impact, audience appreciation, trust, a successful provision of content for learners . . . and contributing to a positive impact on . . . language and culture'.

While Bishara's point about the need for a wide audience makes pragmatic sense, viewing the institutional constraint of ratings through the lens of a decolonising political agenda would throw up the need for devising alternate metrics of success based on Māori values and priorities. When asked about the measures of success currently applied to Māori Television, Linda Tuhiwai Smith suggested:

> If we're going on ratings, that's an inappropriate measure for what [Māori Television are] actually funded to do, which is to provide a richness around the Māori language and culture. So they really need measures that capture what it is that they're trying to achieve. They're not about popularity, that's not their function. It seems to me that

---

* http://www.bbc.com/news/uk_wales_23343492

the better measure, or some other alternative measures, might be the quality of the reo as understood by reo speakers, the authenticity of the reo, the diversity of iwi reo and the reflection of that in programming, the range of ways that reo is represented as a living language, the use of appropriate archival material that shines the light on more classical examples of reo, the use of popular culture and the way in which young people are shown speaking Māori and functioning in [life using the] Māori language. Those are qualitative measures but you can put a measure on them. If you go by ratings you're basically [taking] a turtle and you're saying you've got to run up that tree and we're going to time you. Māori TV can't do those things. They've got one ankle chained down here and another ankle chained down there and they're being told to run. Well, that's impossible. (L. T. Smith, interview, 2013)

While the rhetoric of ratings significantly contributes to public debates regarding Aotearoa New Zealand's broadcasting sector, Smith's comments invite new consideration of the measures we use to frame the value of Māori Television.

In addition to these reo-focused suggestions on how to gauge Māori Televison's success, and in light of focus group and interview kōrero, consideration could also be paid to the ways in which Māori Television has helped to inspire and provoke greater discussions about Māori agendas for social and political change, how Māori Television has invigorated the growth of the independent Māori media, how it functions as a pathway to greater forms of Māori development, as well as the network's ability to offer programming that might set the agenda for workplace conversations, and its impact on non-Māori broadcasters who now use more te reo Māori in their workplace. These impacts need a more expansive framework than audience measurement in order for any significant assessment to take place. And, as Linda Tuhiwai Smith shows, it is Māori who need to determine these new measures of success.

When asked what underpins his commitment to the media industry, independent media producer Bailey Mackey (Ngāti Porou, Ngāi Tūhoe, Rongowhakaata) noted that while te reo was the original motivation, he now had a broader objective – that of Māori development. When asked what he meant by this, Mackey replied:

Well I think social, cultural [development] and less I suppose economic development, but for me economic development actually happens on a personal level. It's the by-product of those other things. If I'm actually participating in social and cultural development, the by-product for me is that I actually have a successful business. And on one level that's economic development for the Mackey family. And so my thing is that I'm actually involved in a wide range of things outside of TV. And I always find that they actually end up overlapping into my TV career – networks and things like that. (B. Mackey, interview, 2013)

Mackey's reflections suggest there is an intimate relationship between social, cultural and economic factors, and that support for te reo through programme-making can contribute to broader aims, including the economic advancements that occur when one is a successful business person. While chapter three highlights the challenges faced by many in the independent Māori media sector, the contribution that Māori Television makes as an outlet for the creative energies of the independent sector has significant implications for Māori development. Employment in this sector provides further opportunities to enhance the wellbeing of whānau and wider communities.

At the level of the everyday, Māori Television also helps set the agenda for discussions among whānau members and workmates about matters of concern to Māori, or about the entertainment value of Māori Television offerings. As we saw earlier, one focus group participant noted in her discussion of workplace conversations:

> I'm gonna watch it more now! Actually, just talking about everything today, I didn't realise how much I did watch Māori TV and it's kinda made me want to watch more now.
>
> Participants: Yup, mmm hmmm.
>
> And like, how I said before that I only select certain people to talk to, and when you brought up, or someone brought up the word 'engage', awww man, I'm gonna shove it in their faces and just go, 'Are you fullas gonna watch this?' [laughter], so it's kinda made me think, nah . . . I am gonna just like, 'Aw man, cool', cos they all come to work and say, 'Aw did you watch *Shortland Street* or *Home and Away*?' Which I always watch anyway, but yeah, so now I'm like, shit I might start doing that to them and they might, aw . . . You know, it might interest them one day to change the channel.

By speculating on how a workplace conversation might spark non-Māori to watch more Māori Television content, comments from this focus group participant throw light on the incalculable and everyday effects of having more Māori voices and faces on screen.

One final suggestion on how Māori Television might contribute to the conditions whereby Māori can set the agenda for social change is in the impact the network has had on other media organisations and their use of te reo Māori. Kōrero from stakeholders suggest that since 2004 there has been an increase in the use and quality of kupu Māori by non-Māori media providers. For example, presenters on Radio New Zealand now regularly include a mihi when introducing programmes such as *Morning Report* and hourly news bulletins. However, it is one thing to include a mihi in the preamble to a news story, and quite another to have the framing of that news story convey Māori experiences and points of view. How these everyday shifts in language use affect the stories this nation tells about itself in the years to come remains to be seen.

Māori Television and flax-roots spaces

The final dimension of a decolonising political agenda, the relationship the organisation has to its constituents, allows us to see the utopian dimensions of such a politics. As a state-funded media entity, Māori Television cannot be defined as a flax-roots organisation, and yet as feedback from focus groups and interviewees suggests, people expect Māori Television to represent, and be informed by, the diverse communities that make up te ao Māori. While Te Pūtahi Pāoho is the formal mechanism representing Māori communities in relation to the network, this structure has attracted criticism for its partial representation of diverse Māori stakeholders. Yet Māori Television attempts to be accountable to, and in touch with, its audiences and stakeholders in other ways. These include the relationships built up by news and current affairs journalists who rely on access to group members and spokespeople to provide content for news programming such as *Te Kāea* and *Native Affairs*. The network also connects with audiences online and at local events, and has systems in place to account for complaints about content. Discussing the connection with the public both onsite and online, former research manager Coral Palmer noted:

> When I used to work for another organisation we used to go out to events and have a stall there and try and encourage people to come and talk to us about doing our courses, but it was very difficult to try and get people to approach us. We would always have to go up to them and when you do approach them they are sort of like unsure. When I went out representing Māori Television, the difference was apparent straight away. People treat you like you're their best friend. You don't even know them but because you work for Māori Television – they have this real connection with Māori Television – they are really friendly, they open up to you and tell you everything, and that's the value of the brand, the Māori Television brand, and what it stands for. (C. Palmer, interview, 2012)

Palmer also developed an online mechanism for making contact and gathering feedback from audiences on programming content. Called the 'Whānau Forum', Palmer described it in the following way:

> We started that because the Nielsen panel was only giving us quantitative information so it was telling us things like how many people were watching. But it wasn't saying, for example, with a show, if the ratings decreased, it wasn't telling us why, so we developed the Whānau Forum so that we would have our own audience panel that complements the Nielsen ratings. And what we did was we recruited people from an advert on air saying, 'If you want to tell us your opinion, go to this website, join our Whānau Forum panel and we will send email online surveys out to you and you will also be in to win spot prizes.' We have got about 1100 people on it at the moment. They are all our viewers. We have only recruited them through our website and through our shows. Our live shows like *CODE*, we've got some viewers through there, and we send email surveys out to them once every two months specifically. (C. Palmer, interview, 2012)

The network also gathers feedback from audiences via emails and phone calls, particularly when viewers have a complaint to make about what they have seen on screen. Haunui Royal acknowledges the crucial task of engaging with audiences to ensure correct practices, or to address a mistake made:

> We had a situation earlier where there was some information that was wrong and one of our local communities up north got hōhā. I thought at the time there was just some issue around the subtitling – we got it wrong. But it turned out really what was at the heart of it was that they didn't like the informant, and they didn't want him talking about their story. It was being represented to me as, 'It's about this Haunui and that

one', and I asked, 'Are you sure it's not about the guy?' And sure enough when they finally came for the hui, they're happy I'm listening and I'm going, 'Oh okay yes it was about the guy, it wasn't about all this other stuff actually, it's just about he's the wrong guy to talk about that iwi' – he didn't have the right whakapapa and they didn't like him anyway. So that's how you can stop things. Things can snowball with communities like that. If you can get in really early – and generally sorry is a really good word – 'I'm sorry we did that, we're working for you, we don't want to whakaiti [*belittle*] you, we're here not to whakaiti you so what would you like and how do we manage this thing?' That's so much part of the job – how you manage people and more often than not people just want to have their mana respected. (H. Royal, interview, 2012)

Being accountable to viewers, seeking audience feedback and being seen within communities are all strategies that connect the organisation with te ao Māori. Imagine comparing this kind of public outreach with that conducted by fellow media organisations such as TVNZ and MediaWorks. Such a comparison would throw light on the time taken by the Māori media sector to develop financially viable yet civic-minded media that attempts to connect with its audience.

The desire for Māori communities to drive the decisions around media-making processes, complements current discussions globally about digital media's role in enhancing and extending grass-roots struggles (Dahlberg and Siapera, 2007; Morozov, 2011). A devolved and dialogic form of media seems a worthy vision, yet could easily be confounded by those economic, political and technological forces that condition New Zealand media industries. Yet, having a vision for how the future might look is a crucial aspect of a decolonising consciousness.

~

Let's be brave to identify what we need to transform and then dream about how we can transform it. (Moana Jackson, 2011, p. 77)

Moana Jackson's quote invites us to imagine the world in which we want to live, and suggests that dreams can lead to the building of these worlds. The ways in which people invest in creative, cultural products (in this instance, the art of television) as conduits to more overt political change should be valued. The politics of culture discussed here has focused on a decolonising political agenda, which is an aspirational and future-oriented form of change. While the feasibility of these decolonising aspirations can be challenged – by funding issues, production demands, institutional constraints and the long-term impact of the loss of te reo Māori – the focus should be on understanding how Māori Television currently contributes to a decolonising agenda for Māori, and the kinds of aspirations that stakeholders have for what Māori Television might be able to do in the future.

A politics of culture framework makes visible the dreams of diverse Māori stakeholders who might inspire new commitments and action from Māori Television as an Indigenous media network. Stakeholder kōrero provides a road map for how to achieve a form of Māori Television that is not simply television in Māori, but is continuing to develop Indigenous forms of media that are fuelled by the desires of stakeholders. Such Māori media would be organised along the principles embedded in te reo me ona tikanga, where day-to-day practices and long-term visions flow from Māori values, ideals and actions.

When considering Māori Television within a politics of culture framework, we could say that many of the decolonising aspirations surrounding Māori Television have yet to be achieved, but that this is the nature of such a political agenda. Rather than decolonisation understood as a process that one eventually arrives at the end of, Māori Television demonstrates how such a politics involves multiple sites of perpetual struggle, which are continually renewed and renegotiated. A crucial task ahead for all who care about the decolonising potential of Māori media is to dream about the kinds of structures, stories, sounds and images we would hope for in an Indigenous media network, and to have that network listen.

Chapter Six

Putting the Five Frameworks to Use

Māori Television faces multiple demands from its various stakeholders, at the same time as it must negotiate the embedded norms of New Zealand media industries, as well as governmental and flax-roots political aspirations, and persisting economic constraints. There is value in understanding these complexities through a range of frameworks, including matters to do with history, tikanga, programming, audiences and the political desires attached to cultural processes. A five-framework approach offers differing angles on Māori Television as a social and cultural phenomenon, and opens up fresh perspectives on matters often taken for granted. It makes space for the diverse voices of, and perspectives from, te ao Māori, as well as for the viewpoints of, and conditions facing, those who work in the Māori media sector.*

To demonstrate the value of such an approach, brief insights into how the five frameworks might be of use in relation to Māori Television news and current affairs can be obtained by looking at coverage of a pre-eminent peer-language institution, Te Kōhanga Reo National Trust. *Native Affairs*' 2013 coverage of the financial affairs of Te Kōhanga Reo National Trust (TKRNT) and its financial arm, Te Pātaka Ōhanga (TPŌ), generated much conflicting debate within te ao Māori and New Zealand's public sphere more generally. These debates raised questions about culturally appropriate news media practices, and the role of Māori journalism within a democratic society. A brief gloss of how the five frameworks could be deployed to throw light on the complex issues raised by *Native Affairs*' coverage, and on subsequent public discussions,

---

* It is my hope that the five frameworks proposed in this book complement the earlier work of authors such as Carol Archie, whose important text *Pou Kōrero: a journalists' guide to Māori and current affairs* helped to decentre a prevailing non-Māori perspective on New Zealand media.

follows. The *Native Affairs*–TKRNT media event demonstrated the contested expectations underpinning Māori news practices, and the impossibility of speaking of te ao Māori in monolithic terms. More than this, the debates and discussions inspired by the NA–TKRNT media event reveal the impoverished nature of New Zealand public-sphere discourses more generally, and prevailing perceptions of Māori news media and Māori institutions.

Setting the scene

In 2013 *Native Affairs* broadcast two stories ('A Question of Trust', which aired on 9 September, and 'Feathering the Nest', which aired on 14 October) dealing with the governance and management of language-revitalisation preschool organisation TKRNT, and its financial arm, TPŌ. Both stories investigated the concerns of 51 kōhanga reo members from Mataatua and Tauranga Moana rohe over issues relating to the financial structure of the organisation, lifetime membership practices, and personal loans to staff and board members to the value of $10,000. The story drew on information about credit-card expenditure given to the *Native Affairs* news team. When approached by *Native Affairs* to make comment on the story, TKRNT declined to engage. As the media event progressed, TKRNT applied for an interim injunction to prevent *Native Affairs* from covering the story; it banned *Native Affairs* staff from a subsequent press conference, and it laid a complaint with the Broadcasting Standards Authority over 'A Question of Trust', a complaint that was ultimately not upheld.

The coverage by *Native Affairs* sparked two inquiries. The Ministry of Education commissioned Ernst & Young to conduct an inquiry into the management of public funding by TKRNT, which found no wrongdoing. A subsequent inquiry into TPŌ by the Serious Fraud Office also found no evidence of criminality by TPŌ. While these inquiries took place, TKRNT held a national hui at Ngāruawāhia to address concerns raised by whānau. Meanwhile, 'Feathering the Nest' received international recognition as a model of good Indigenous journalism, and the *Native Affairs* team positioned itself as a champion of the flax roots. Many Māori and non-Māori shared opinions via television and radio news media, blogs, tweets and news-feed comments on the importance of holding those in power to account, even esteemed kaumātua. However, other voices from te ao Māori raised questions about the role of an Indigenous broadcaster when dealing with contentious Māori matters, and whether or not Māori news on Māori Television was being told in a Māori way.*

Five frameworks for understanding a Māori media event

Thinking historically
Many of the issues raised by the *NA*–TKRNT media event allude to the historical role of non-Māori media in depicting things Māori, and orthodox ideals about the role of news media in holding elites to account. To think historically about the *NA*–TKRNT media event one could consider:

- the broader media environment that has historically depicted te ao Māori
- the current climate that surrounds news media in New Zealand and globally.

As the work of scholars who research in the area of New Zealand news media suggests, non-Māori news stories often frame Māori in terms of conflict, as outsiders to the 'mainstream', or with news values antithetical to Māori social norms (P. Thompson, 1954, 1955; Te Awa, 1996; Abel, 1997; Walker, 2002; Gregory et al., 2011; Nairn et al., 2012). This history of misrepresentation is outlined by former Māori Party co-leader Tariana Turia when interviewed on Radio Waatea about *Native Affairs*' coverage of TKRNT. Radio Waatea stated:

> She said people in Māori institutions like Māori Television and kōhanga reo should be driven by kaupapa and tikanga. 'That is not the case in terms of Māori Television. For many of us who fought to get Māori TV, our firm belief was we wanted something that promoted mauri ora, the things that were important for us as a people, to paint the side of a picture so you wouldn't get the impression 90 per cent of our people were mad, bad or sad, which is how we are portrayed by the rest of the media. So yes, I must

---

* In June 2015 the *Native Affairs* team included another story about TKRNT featuring an exclusive interview with former trust board member Toni Waho, described by *Native Affairs* as Te Kōhanga's whistle-blower. One week prior to this screening Mihingarangi Forbes announced her decision to resign from Māori Television.

admit that as someone who totally loved those things, I think I have lost heart with Māori Television,' Mrs Turia said.*

Given this historical backdrop it could be said that *Native Affairs*' coverage of TKRNT and TPŌ events risked feeding into a long-standing stereotype of Māori organisations as financially mismanaged entities run by a cultural elite. A historical approach to the *NA–TKRNT* media event would therefore foreground the long role played by non-Māori media in establishing reductive and one-dimensional representations of things Māori, and the vested interests non-Māori media makers have in perpetuating these representations. Such an approach must also consider how contemporary Māori media makers must consistently wrestle with, or attempt to bypass or interrupt, these historically inflected sounds and images.

Another issue arising from a historically informed approach to the *NA–TKRNT* media event is an understanding of the contemporary climate under which news media practices are conducted. As we shall see in the discussion on the politics of culture framework for understanding this event, the language often used to describe the intentions of Māori news media (based on freedom, democracy and fairness) needs to also be historicised in relation to the changing conditions of production and reception facing Māori news media practitioners.

Questions of tikanga

At the heart of the *NA–TKRNT* media event is the issue of what gets to count as tikanga-based news media practices when dealing with Māori entities and leaders. When Turia claimed she had 'lost heart' with Māori Television, she drew on the kaupapa of mauri ora which is a concept linked to the wider idea of Māori wellbeing. In doing so, she implicitly drew on the historical harm done to te ao Māori through non-Māori media outlets, and implied that Māori Television's primary role is to heal this historical harm by promoting Māori wellbeing. Yet can there be a broad-based understanding of what constitutes wellbeing for those diverse groups and individuals who make up te ao Māori? A tikanga framework for thinking about the *NA–TKRNT* media event could consider:

---

*   Radio Waatea, 22 October 2013.

- competing ideas of tikanga-based media practices
- the wider forces conditioning who or what sets mediated tikanga.

Tariana Turia suggests that Māori media should be focused on mauri ora and on presenting images and stories from te ao Māori that balance out negative non-Māori media depictions. Radio Waatea host Dale Husband, in a subsequent interview with the general manager of Māori Television news and current affairs Julian Wilcox, also reflected on what a Māori approach to Māori matters might be:

> If we look into our Māori heart and we act as Māori people, often some of what mainstream media will throw across the networks should really be discussed behind closed doors, rather than splashed across the media, and I just wonder whether we're becoming whistle-blowers on our own bearing in mind there've been plenty of organisations prior to the development of Māori media that have been more than willing to discredit issues Māori, and there are many who are concerned that perhaps we're just allowing ourselves to drift down that path.*

Husband's comments once again underscore the importance of thinking historically about the media's role in perpetuating negative stereotypes of Māori, but these comments also refer to te ao Māori in terms that assume that there is a knowable 'Māori heart' familiar to all. This assumption contradicts Māori Television's diverse representations of things Māori and the differences within te ao Māori. Since 2004 Māori Television has expanded the available media representations of what constitutes a Māori world view, and such diversity of opinion and perspective was certainly ignited by the NA–TKRNT media event. Discussing the role of Māori Television programming more generally in 2012, former general manager of programming Haunui Royal noted:

> We still have a job though, I think, to ask the questions and to present the different points of view that exist within Māoridom as well – particularly because the reality is it stretches from 'send the Pākehās home' to 'oh you Māoris look at all the wonderful things Pākehā gave us like bulldozers'. That spectrum is getting wider every year and

---

* Radio Waatea, 23 October 2013.

the reality is philosophically when you say the word 'Māori' it's becoming more and more difficult to say what you mean by that word now. (H. Royal, interview, 2012)

It is important to think about the ways in which a post-2004 media culture offers more expansive images and stories that highlight the contested and diverse nature of te ao Māori. If it is impossible to talk about things Māori in monolithic terms, this includes discussions of correct tikanga. It is important to understand who or what sets the terms for understanding tikanga related to media.

For example, in the same radio interview with Julian Wilcox, Husband asked Wilcox if the *NA–TKRNT* coverage was driven by the need for ratings. Noting that 'some of our politicos' are critical of Māori Television's 'stylistic moves' that resemble a *20/20* or *60 Minutes* exposé approach, Husband asked: 'Isn't ratings what this is all about?'* Husband continued:

> We get the feeling that disgruntled [Kōhanga Reo] employees were at the back end of all of this and that's not uncommon. But we also know that a kuia who's given a great deal to the revival of our Māori language, is held in high esteem – it is in the ratings that her name has been besmirched for an amount of money that many would consider paltry. You can't deny, can you Jules, that the name of the Kōhanga Reo has been dragged through the media mud this past week and that the reputation and the mana of an esteemed kuia has been besmirched by the coverage, yet still no charges and yet still no proof of guilt.

In this comment, Husband clearly sides with TKRNT and considers *Native Affairs*' coverage as a breach of tikanga, related to the honour and mana of a long-standing leader in the Māori world. Yet Wilcox's response reflects an investment in tikanga related to the care and wellbeing of those whānau who came to Māori Television with their story. Wilcox responded by first restating how whānau from Mataatua and Tauranga Moana rohe had come to *Native Affairs* with their concerns, and how the news team had returned to these whānau once the first story had been aired to seek their views on the coverage. This consultative approach suggests that Māori Television followed a correct and tika process in relation to the whānau members involved. According to Wilcox, those interviewed felt vindicated by the story. Wilcox then expressed

---

* Radio Waatea, 23 October 2013.

concern at the fact that *Native Affairs*' coverage had now itself become a news story, instead of the focus being maintained on the experiences of these whānau. In relation to the amount of money concerned, Wilcox's response was to remind listeners, again, of the experiences of whānau at the grass roots:

> People have said a lot this week that we're only talking about $10,000 – well let me use the words of some of the Kōhanga Reo whānau: $10,000 means a van for a kōhanga, it means being able to feed kids for a long, long time actually within the kōhanga. What's at issue isn't the amount of money – what's at issue is the fact that the Kōhanga Reo movement, i.e. the kōhanga reo centres, have a strict set of policies that they must abide by. Now, how come those at the grass roots have a strict set of rules that they must adhere to and abide by, and yet others within the movement do not?*

Arguing that *Native Affairs* acted as a champion for whānau and communities at the grass roots (or, in Mihingarangi Forbes' words, 'we simply asked the questions of those who had no voice'), Wilcox and his team drew on orthodox journalistic practices and values to defend themselves against criticism. However, Wilcox's reference to the consultative and kanohi-ki-te-kanohi (face-to-face) approach to the whānau members who first raised the issue is also an expression of cultural norms attached to things Māori. Trying to find a balance between the professional norms of journalism and the cultural norms of Indigenous communities is a challenge shared by many Indigenous journalists (Hanusch, 2013). The issue of what a tikanga-based Māori media practice might look like is still a work in progress, and one not likely to be settled anytime soon. Indeed, the debate over who or what gets to decide on how 'Māori' Māori news media might be is a perpetual one due to the diverse interests and agendas of te ao Māori. At the forefront of such debates should be the issue of how mediated forms of tikanga are different from, say, marae-based tikanga practices, where the relationship between people, place and history determines the correct practices at each marae. In a mediated public sphere the protocols, linkages and lines of authority that set the tikanga become more questionable. In a post-2004 media era Māori Television has raised the status of te reo Māori, and also the diverse values, world views and political ideals of te ao Māori are more generally in New Zealand's public sphere. It could be argued that *Native Affairs*' coverage

---

* Radio Waatea, 23 October 2013.

of another Māori-language entity, and the debates about tikanga sparked by this coverage, signals the further emergence of a contested public sphere, based on Māori values and perspectives, long absent in New Zealand's larger media culture.

A programming approach

Viewing the *NA–TKRNT* media event through the lens of programming throws light on the challenges faced by Indigenous news media practitioners to find a balance between the norms of news journalism and Indigenous perspectives and cultural values (Hanusch, 2013). A programming approach might also ask: how could such a news story about TKRNT be told differently? A programming framework might examine:

- orthodox news media conventions and Indigenous news journalism
- demands for more innovative news media programming.

Orthodox approaches to the news media assume that journalists have the independence and freedom to mediate between the public and the state to report on issues of the day. In an interview with Radio New Zealand host Chris Laidlaw in 2010, former CEO Jim Mather described the importance of editorial independence in terms of news and current affairs programming in strengthening the credibility of Māori Television:

> For us it's about not telling 'the news' in the Māori language but it's actually broadcasting the news with a Māori perspective, and that really comes to the fore in specific news issues that Māori are facing. Mainstream media may report in a certain way and we will often say yes that's valid, but here is the Māori perspective of why this issue has developed. However for us it's a critical part of the credibility of Māori Television to have an editorially independent voice on news and current affairs – to hold our own leaders and other leaders to account in relation to what's occurring in the Māori domain particularly. One could really argue that without news and current affairs, and the credibility that that provides to the organisation, and the capacity to deliver the Māori perspective and our voice on issues, we would be an entertainment channel with a strong Māori influence.*

---

* http://www.radionz.co.nz/national/programmes/sunday/audio/2296138/jim-mather

Mather's comments underscore the important symbolic role that news and current affairs play in lending weight and significance to a newly emergent Māori media organisation. More than simply an entertainment medium, Māori media carry the dual role of having te reo as both language and voice, together with the larger role of presenting a range of Māori perspectives. Mather's comments also allude to the watchdog function of news media, and the role of Māori news media in not only mediating between the public and the state, but also in providing an objective and independent perspective on matters concerning Māori leadership. A programming approach to the *NA–TKRNT* media event would examine the tensions in maintaining journalistic independence and institutional integrity, at the same time as conveying diverse Māori perspectives.

New Zealand's prevailing television culture is driven by profit-making imperatives that privilege populist, briskly paced and emotionally appealing media content rather than more lengthy and complex modes of presentation (Horrocks, 2004). Critics of *Native Affairs'* coverage and pursuit of TKRNT likened their approach to *20/20* and *60 Minutes*, global news genres known for their tabloid-like approach. A programming-oriented approach to the *NA–TKRNT* media event might also compare and contrast the coverage provided by Māori Television with that of orthodox news media genres.

A programming approach to this event would also consider the calls made by Māori Television stakeholders for greater programming innovations, particularly in the area of news. Throughout the duration of this research project, many interviewees expressed disappointment at the lack of innovation in news media programming, and offered ideas for how news and current affairs programming might be redesigned in terms of format and structure.* Some of the suggestions included withdrawing the daily news bulletin and providing more in-depth and top-quality discussions of topics relevant to Māori every other day. People also suggested they offer more contextualising information about news items, and provide more coverage of iwi news and initiatives. They preferred news read by native speakers and kaumātua, who may not have the aesthetic appeal promoted by current television practices, but who have beautiful reo. Former general manager of Māori Television

---

* Many of these criticisms could be levelled at non-Māori news media practices as well, and should be seen in the light of the transformation in news media practices globally, such as the emergence of *The Daily Show* in the US or *The Conversation* in Australia.

programming and current Te Māngai Pāho executive Larry Parr suggested a nightly 8 pm current affairs programme that could discuss the 6 pm news on other channels (Parr, interview, 2012). Derek Fox suggested a studio-based 9 am to noon programme, where experts could have more than a 'sound bite' space to debate matters, and that such a programme could be simulcast across the iwi radio network (Fox, interview, 2014). Linda Tuhiwai Smith, reflecting on the kind of news and current affairs programming she would like to see, summed up a desire for innovation in this way:

> I want to see a Māori channel that reflects things in our way. Something that doesn't just reproduce [existing] methods – it's the same thing for research. Use the same news-gathering methods and then you reproduce that news and the opinions of the news of the mainstream media. I find that very irritating. I'd like them to think about what news means in a Māori framework. Otherwise you get the scandalous, news as defined really by the way mainstream TV defines Māori news. Whereas what happens in our communities, all the time, vibrant stuff, what happens here in conferences like this [He Manawa Whenua], to me, that's the news that I want to watch. (L. T. Smith, interview, 2013)

As these comments suggest, calling for more tikanga-aligned Māori news media practices does not necessarily mean that issues surrounding Māori cultural elites should not be addressed. Comments about the need for more innovation in news and current affairs suggest that orthodox news media formats established by non-Māori media practitioners need to be reshaped by Māori media practitioners in ways that enable tikanga-based practices to flourish. These practices include a more community-based approach that reveals the vibrancy of Māori life. A programming approach to the *NA–TKRNT* media event would take into account Māori Television's capacity for innovating news and current affairs media genres.

Audiences

Understanding the *NA–TKRNT* media event through the framework of audiences could reveal how particular sections of te ao Māori engaged with these media events, and the important role played by social media in voicing competing perspectives. Such an audience-oriented framework would take an expansive approach to the term 'audience' and could consider:

- social media's role in expressing diverse Māori perspectives
- non-Māori mediated responses to the *Native Affairs* coverage.

Mihingarangi Forbes described 'Feathering the Nest' as polarising the nation, and evidence for this can be found in Māori and non-Māori radio and television coverage of the *Native Affairs* story, and subsequent comments posted on Facebook, in the comments under online news stories, via Twitter accounts and on blogsites. Members of the public used these forums to offer a range of responses to *Native Affairs*' coverage of TKRNT and TPŌ, and *Native Affairs* journalist Mihingarangi Forbes and producer Annabelle Lee-Harris used Twitter to update their followers on any developments in the story. In response to TKRNT's refusal to give an interview to *Native Affairs*, Annabelle Lee-Harris posted this tweet:

> Why will Te Kohanga Reo National Trust still not give an interview to #NativeAffairs?? Worried we might ask the right questions?? Bad form.

Twitter appeared to be increasingly useful when *Native Affairs* staff were banned from attending the TKRNT press conference.

Native Affairs' use of social media allowed the team to continue to profile the story publicly even when they were barred from information routes such as the TKRNT press conference. However, another social media mechanism (the blogsphere) enabled members of the public to dispute the viewpoints and practices of *Native Affairs* staff. For example, blogger Ross Nepia Himona raised questions about the backstory behind *Native Affairs*' coverage of TKRNT and TPŌ, linking it to whānau and supporters who were now disaffected with TKRNT due to the dismissal of the Kōhanga Reo CEO.* This blogsite also raised questions about the professional behaviour of *Native Affairs* staff members who used Twitter accounts to make comments on events:

> Whilst the public broadcasting face of *Native Affairs* was presented as that of an objective investigative team, the fairly intense activity in Twitter revealed a subjective and personal face; the two faces of *Native Affairs*. . . . The tone of the *Native Affairs*' response on Twitter was self-righteous and triumphalist. It clearly showed that the

---

* *Te Pūtātara*, 13 June 2013, http://www.putatara.net/2014/06/anatomy-of-a-scandal/

Native Affairs team had gone beyond the bounds of objective investigative journalism and had joined the crusade. The *Native Affairs* team was conducting its own crusade through Twitter. It was a display of immaturity and a lack of professionalism. It wasn't very smart either.*

Meanwhile earlier tweets that encouraged their followers to watch *Native Affairs*' initial coverage of the TKRNT–TPŌ issue revealed a lingering perception of Māori news journalism as taking a less than independent approach to controversial Māori matters. For instance, long-standing non-Māori media commentator and blogger Russell Brown tweeted the following prior to the screening of 'Feathering the Nest':

> Russell Brown @publicaddress
> Watch #NativeAffairs on Maori TV at 8.30. It's a story they've fought to tell. Debunks the idea that Maori media don't hold Maori to account.

On the same day, another blogger issued a tweet that similarly framed the programme as a watershed moment in Māori news media:

> Duncan Stuart @duncan_stuart
> Evening all. To fellow NZers – be watching #NativeAffairs tonight. I think within Maoridom a landmark piece of journalism. Significant.

In a subsequent *Native Affairs* news story focused on an update on the first inquiry, Mihingarangi Forbes interviewed Member of Parliament Winston Peters, who, in the course of his kōrero, made the following statement:

> To be fair to this country, it's pleasing that Māori TV has raised this issue because in the past a lot of Māori commentators, when they see a thing like this, when something looks suspect, they have thought it best to serve their people's interests by shutting it down. It never does.

An audience approach to the *NA–TKRNT* media event could involve conducting a close analysis of select media discourses such as these, and placing these comments within a wider social, historical and political context. This

---

* http://www.putatara.net/2014/06/anatomy-of-a-scandal/

analysis could involve examining the presuppositions underpinning the claims made on these sites. The wider context in which these claims are made could also be a target of analysis, including the 'call and response' nature of media cultures where a headlining news story becomes the generator of social media comments and critiques that subsequently spawn other social media responses. Such an audience approach would be attuned to the context of each social media comment, as well as the prevailing discourses at play via these forums, including an alertness to claims made on behalf of 'Māori' as a homogenous category, naturalised assumptions as to what makes good journalism, and competing claims to tikanga-based news media practices. Social media's ability to provide public outlets for the many audiences, commentators and practitioners who have an investment in things Māori also accentuates, again, the varied nature of the multiple worlds that make up te ao Māori.

A politics of culture framework

A politics of culture framework is concerned with revealing the political and cultural hopes that some attach to Māori media practices, including Māori news journalism, and also the increase in representational power (both politically and culturally) enabled by Māori media. A politics of culture framework for addressing the *NA–TKRNT* media event could consider:

- the political and cultural hopes attached to Māori news journalism
- the potential political and cultural effects produced by innovations in Māori news media.

It would involve remaining attentive to the ways in which media commentators and practitioners frame Māori Television news media as a conveyer or vehicle for greater political and cultural representation, and would include the political and cultural debates opened up by *Native Affairs*' coverage. This means paying attention to the language used by some to describe Māori Television's journalistic practices, and the assumptions made about politics that are hidden in such language use. The language often assumes a naturalised relationship between the media, democracy and fairness. For example, in the wake of receiving an international journalism award for 'Feathering the Nest', Mihingarangi Forbes commented, 'This story was a game changer in the way that Indigenous journalists tell stories – it polarised the nation but it also gave voice to those who hadn't had one in the past.'* The voices Forbes refers to are those of three women from Mataatua and Tauranga Moana rohe who spoke publicly about their concerns for their tamariki and community:

> 'While we asked their questions, and told their story, it was these women who had the courage to demand democracy and fairness for our tamariki. . . . When *Native Affairs* set out to tell this story we knew it would rock the boat,' she said. 'It upset many within Māoridom who believed investigating Māori organisations was not the role of the Indigenous broadcaster. However, the role of a journalist is no different whether we're brown, white or pink – we simply asked the questions of those who had no voice,' said Ms Forbes.†

Forbes' statement foregrounds the role of journalists in holding organisations and elites to account, a role that complements the values of a mediated public sphere, where media provides the platform for citizens to rationally debate issues of the day. Forbes' comments implicitly champion the watchdog function of journalism, where journalists act on behalf of a particular 'public'. They also suggest that Indigenous journalism is no different from other forms of journalistic practice. A politics of culture approach to the *NA–TKRNT* media event would place critical pressure on the norms assumed to underpin contemporary New Zealand journalism, and Māori news journalism in particular.

The demise of public-service values in New Zealand media has long been diagnosed by media scholars alert to the impact of deregulation and market forces, and they now define television as a mechanism for delivering audiences to advertisers (Baker, 2007; Hope, 2012; P. Thompson, 2012). Commenting on the further decline in news and current affairs offerings off the back of *Campbell Live*'s cancellation in June 2015,‡ media scholar Peter Thompson argued:

> There's a social contract between the state and the public, and it needs to be mediated. We need a fourth estate that holds these people to account. If the news media aren't

---

* http://www.maoritelevision.com/news/national/native-affairs-wins-two-international-journalism-awards
† http://www.maoritelevision.com/news/national/native-affairs-wins-two-international-journalism-awards
‡ The June cancellation of *Campbell Live* coincided with the departure of Mihingarangi Forbes from Māori Television, sparking social media responses that alluded to a further decline in New Zealand news media values more generally.

able to reflect the society that we live in such that we can identify our issues, moral concerns, political policies, economic policies, we're impoverished.*

Thompson's viewpoint is compelling in light of the pervasiveness of ratings-driven news media globally, where the traditional role of media as the Fourth Estate is increasingly under threat. Yet how effective has this Fourth Estate been historically for members of te ao Māori? That is to say, non-Māori English speakers have historically defined the role of the Fourth Estate in New Zealand, and emphasis has been placed on the news media's role as a support for democratic politics and public-service ideals. Framing *Native Affairs* as part of a more general journalistic practice associated with the political norms of the Fourth Estate overlooks the ways in which New Zealand media has often functioned to negate Māori ideals of democracy, and Māori notions of 'public interest'. While the 1989 Broadcasting Act, NZ On Air and Te Māngai Pāho include provision for the representation of Māori, many have argued that the long-standing monolingualism of Aotearoa's media ecology, the marginal presence of Māori in the media sector, and anti-Māori media discourses have had lasting detrimental effects on the wellbeing and flourishing of Māori (Abel, 1997; Walker, 2002; Stephens, 2004; Nairn et al., 2012).

There are also more structural issues that need to be foregrounded when discussing notions of New Zealand's news media as an extension of democracy. For example, many argue that Te Tiriti o Waitangi included a form of power sharing between Crown and Māori that has never been implemented structurally (Fleras and Spoonley, 1999). For Māori leaders such as Whatarangi Winiata, signatories to the 1840 Te Tiriti o Waitangi understood that this Treaty would mobilise a persisting tension between kāwanatanga (Crown governorship) and tino rangatiratanga (Māori self-determination), a tension that Winiata argues could be resolved by developing a parliamentary democracy that better reflects the nature of the Treaty partnership (Hayward, 2012). For Māori lawyer Moana Jackson, the democratic ideal of 'majority rules' never had political currency when Māori were the majority at the signing of Te Tiriti, an observation that highlights the contingent, and politically expedient, nature of Western concepts and frameworks when confronted with Indigenous differences (Jackson, 2005). So, too, the concept of

---

* http://www.stuff.co.nz/entertainment/tv-radio/69031487/where-now-for-tv-current-affairs

'public-service television' which, as Haunui Royal suggests, stands in for a form of television that privileges a certain section of society:

> So you call it public broadcasting but the reality is, it's Pākehā TV and the unfortunate thing for [Pākehā] is that Māori are the only New Zealanders who are constitutionally guaranteed a TV channel. Nobody else is. (H. Royal, interview, 2012)

Based on these critiques, thinking about the political desires projected onto the *NA–TKRNT* media event would involve placing critical pressure on claims made on behalf of a 'public', the Fourth Estate, or democracy in general.

Understanding the *NA–TKRNT* media event through a politics of culture framework involves examining the political and cultural hopes attached to Māori news journalism, as well as the spaces created within the format of news media to retell Indigenous stories, from Indigenous perspectives. The possibilities of a structural realignment of television industrial practices based on te reo and tikanga as grounding norms have been raised throughout this book. While Māori Television has made significant and substantial contributions to telling Māori stories, for Māori, by Māori, and about Māori, the mixed reactions to *Native Affairs'* coverage of TKRNT suggests that some audiences want more tikanga-aligned news media practices, whatever these may be. As Linda Tuhiwai Smith asks, what does news media mean in a Māori framework? How can a Crown-funded entity such as Māori Television deliver on the ideals of a decolonising agenda that has Māori values, behaviours and world views at the centre of all practices?

A politics of culture approach to the *NA–TKRNT* media event could draw on the kōrero of Māori media practitioners like Quinton Hita, who has argued for a more devolved and flax-roots-based structure for the organisation, and for innovations in programme-making that can honour the integrity of te reo. What would news media look like from such a devolved perspective? In these discussions we see the seeds for a future Māori media organisation, one that is radically devolved, dialogical and responsive to the diverse needs of communities. In publicly contesting the status quo in terms of what Māori news media is, voices from te ao Māori lead the debate on what New Zealand audiences more generally might want from their free-to-air television providers, at a time when public-minded media content in this country is in decline. A politics of culture framework for understanding the *NA–TKRNT* media event would take such perspectives into account when discussing its impact and significance, including the role of social media in providing story spaces for diverse members of te ao Māori to express their viewpoints.

～

In providing a brief gloss of what a five-framework approach to the *Native Affairs*–Te Kōhanga Reo National Trust media event might look like, this chapter demonstrates the need for a site-specific and context-dependent approach to any Māori media event. *Native Affairs*' coverage of TKRNT, and the subsequent media events it inspired, demonstrates the perpetual debates surrounding Māori news values and practices, the prominence of Māori wellbeing in these debates, and the diverse nature of those who make up te ao Māori. By offering glimpses of how a five-framework approach might help to lay bare the dynamics underpinning this media event, the need to be attentive to context, actors, institutions and media, and underlying political and cultural norms, becomes apparent. Such a flexible, five-framework approach assumes that debates will be ongoing and perpetually contested. If a five-framework approach offers no easy answers, the value of such an approach is to provoke new lines of inquiry into the somewhat banal and everyday experience of the media cultures of Aotearoa.

The *Native Affairs* team consistently declared that their intent with the story was driven by general principles of good journalistic practice, as well as the broader notion of democracy, fairness and the wellbeing of the whānau involved. Asked if they were driven by ratings, Wilcox's response was to restate their guiding kaupapa, which was to act on behalf of flax-roots Māori communities. Meanwhile TKRNT invoked court proceedings, appealed to the Broadcasting Standards Authority, and banned *Native Affairs* staff from their press event. While TKRNT's actions might be interpreted as contrary to a democratic ethos, where public debate is a norm, they must be considered in light of the historical harm done by media outlets to Māori institutions. This historical perspective reveals the limits of ideals of democratic freedom that assume non-Māori as the norm. In the responses from the public to the NA–TKRNT media event we can see the return of a contested public sphere long absent in New Zealand's larger media culture. These debates signal the desire for forms of media that can contribute to Māori wellbeing, as well as to more informed New Zealand citizens, at a time when community-minded and politically oriented media is an increasing rarity.

Conclusion

Māori Television's 2004 emergence was the result of a sustained and flax-roots struggle by Māori for the Crown to fulfil its obligations to te reo and tikanga Māori, as ensured by Article II of Te Tiriti o Waitangi. Over the last twelve years Māori Television has built a niche audience for its Māori television programming, it has stimulated growth in the independent Māori media sector, and it has gained approval from politicians, media commentators and a broad non-Māori audience, who see Māori Television as a role model for public media provision.

The network contributes to greater political and cultural representations for te ao Māori, and has sparked debates about what different and diverse groups want from this Indigenous media entity. While Māori stakeholders suggest that seeing more Māori television programming on screen enhances individual and collective wellbeing, kōrero gathered together here also demonstrates how the network needs to develop closer and more expansive links with its Māori communities, to ensure it continues to be relevant and credible. In an era of digital plenty, where media outlets – both national and international – compete for the attention of viewers on multiple screens, Māori Television will continue to address the challenge of screening content that appeals to the large percentage of Māori who are rangatahi, as well as to those who fought for the network's emergence. Social media will play an increasingly important role in holding Māori Television to account, and will hopefully enable greater dialogue about things Māori in the mediated public sphere.

In terms of Māori Television's contribution to the protection and promotion of te reo and tikanga Māori, the organisation has certainly raised the profile of te reo Māori within New Zealand's mediated public sphere. It has added to the corpus of te reo Māori and it has provided many inspiring language role models for future generations to follow. While statistics on the number of te reo speakers have shown a 4.8 per cent decline since the 2006 census (Statistics New Zealand, 2013), the responsibility for increasing language acquisition is not the responsibility of Māori Television alone, because language revitalisation occurs when there is a wider ecology of language-support strategies.

Since the launch of the Māori Language Strategy in 2003 there has been no cohesive framework across the language sector of Te Taura Whiri i te Reo Māori, Māori Television, Te Māngai Pāho and the Ministry of Education. The 2013 review of the Māori Language Bill suggested developing a new structure involving a Māori–iwi Electoral College called Te Mātāwai, which would govern Te Taura Whiri, Te Māngai Pāho and Māori Television, replacing Te Pūtahi Pāoho as the governance structure (Freeman-Tayler, 2014). The 2016 Māori Language Act established Te Mātāwai to lead revitalisation strategies, a move that initially met with criticism from some communities and te reo experts, who questioned the wisdom of devolving the responsibility for language revitalisation back to iwi authorities.*

Meanwhile, as wider shifts in the Māori-language sector develop, between 2012 and 2013 funding agency Te Māngai Pāho devised new funding processes in the Māori media sector, based on recent research on language revitalisation. Given that 90 per cent of Māori Television's annual programme funding is 'managed, administered and controlled by Te Māngai Pāho', these shifts will have a significant impact on Māori Television's future programming strategies (Māori Television, 2014, p. 14). Te Māngai Pāho's adoption of Rawinia Higgins and Poia Rewi's ZePA model signals a shift in Te Tiriti o Waitangi-based arguments about the role of te reo in New Zealand society. While the initial arguments for Māori broadcasting rested on Article II of Te Tiriti (language as a taonga), the ZePA model is premised on the idea of te reo Māori as an integral aspect of New Zealand citizenship, for all New Zealanders. This means that Article III of Te Tiriti, with its emphasis on cultural citizenship, may become a guiding rationale for language revitalisation in the future. Under this framework, generating a positive attitude towards te reo among all New Zealanders becomes a key focus. To recall the categories of the ZePA model, Zero (kore) reflects individuals positioned in a dismissive or resistant attitude to the Māori language, Passive (pō) reflects a cohort that is relatively inert in relation to te reo Māori use but with a receptive and accommodating approach to Māori-language acquisition, and Active (awatea) describes those individuals who operationalise the language and who '[a]ctively strive to advance the language in all arenas' (Higgins and Rewi, 2014, p. 23). As stated by Higgins and Rewi:

---

* http://www.nzherald.co.nz/business/news/article.cfm?c_id=3&objectid=11236677

> Right-shifting demonstrates a transition across the three stages, from a state of Zero thinking or acting to a Passive position, which means a shift is at least made at a conscious level. We use 'conscious' here, as opposed to subconscious, because in terms of considering the existence of the Māori language, an individual or entity has moved from a point of zero-consideration and possibly zero knowledge, to entertaining a thought regarding it. The shift from Passive to Active means a commitment to operationalising the conscious: transferring the thought to action. (2014, p. 28)

In the 2014 *Briefing to the Incoming Minister*, Te Māngai Pāho noted that 'right-shifting' an audience from Zero to Passive can enhance awareness and support for language revitalisation. According to Te Māngai Pāho, once this awareness is improved, 'the subsequent right-shift from Passive to Active is then easier to achieve' (Te Māngai Pāho, 2014, p. 16). This shift in approach will have significant impact on Māori Television and the wider Māori media sector. One possible effect might be to increasingly appeal to individuals who have a dismissive or resistant attitude to te reo Māori. This approach might take precedence over Passive and Active audiences, particularly at a time when Māori Television needs to grow its audience share. If so, the concerns raised by the 2009 Te Kāhui o Māhutonga review about diluting the 'Māoriness of the message' due to broad appeal may be ignited again (Te Kāhui o Māhutonga, 2009, p. 13).

The impact of shifts in the wider language and media culture of Aotearoa New Zealand also raises some concerns for the independent Māori media sector. In light of Te Māngai Pāho's philosophical shift to the ZePA model, as well as in the wake of a National-led government's 'value for money' approach to the public sector, Te Māngai Pāho now requires independent Māori media producers to supply language plans when applying for funding. This requirement comes on top of an already demanding task list that includes finding Māori media professionals with competencies in te reo and tikanga Māori, delivering quality programming content with modest levels of funding, and providing professional development within the Māori media sector that fulfils the requirements of Te Pūni Kōkiri. Former independent producer and more recently Māori Television executive producer of current affairs Hone Edwards described the demands now facing Māori media producers:

> I feel a lot of concern for independent producers because they're being asked now to make language plans up. To show again, and illustrate how, their particular proposal

or language or programme – the extent to which that revitalises the language, and how do you measure that? Producers – we don't know that stuff. That's all linguistic stuff. We don't know how to do [that]. Okay, you could do it – qualitative audience research. Fine, there's ratings, and that tells you how many people are watching it, but it doesn't tell you the extent to which your particular programme or your particular strategy does that and how to measure that. Nor do we have enough funding as independent producers, when I was out there, to do qualitative research and know why people like or don't like your programmes. I think that responsibility lies between [the Māori Affairs] Select Committee and the funding agencies. I don't think it's fair to put that responsibility onto independent producers who are creative people. We know how to make programmes but we don't know how to do that stuff. (H. Edwards, interview, 2012)

In 2015, in the wake of TVNZ's decision to outsource Māori and Pacific programming, Ngā Aho Whakaari held a hui to discuss issues facing the sector. Radio Waatea reported the following summary of the event:

Māori working in screen and television are concerned that politicians and bureaucrats are loading them up with extra responsibilities without any extra resources. . . . Producers also complained they had to dig into already tight production budgets to tick the boxes of funding agency Te Māngai Pāho's new right shift te reo Māori strategy. Ngā Aho Whakaari chair Kim Muriwai says they're sick of being taken for granted. 'We've been subsidising the kaupapa for a long time now and it's getting to the level where, especially when producers are being asked to give up their online rights in perpetuity for the whole world, producers are now saying enough is enough,' she says.[*]

Kim Muriwai's comments allude to the Māori media sector's shared kaupapa – the health and wellbeing of te reo and tikanga Māori – and how this kaupapa is part of the funding model. On top of complying with measures to do with the quantity and quality of language, Māori producers and broadcasters must demonstrate that their product is viable by attracting audiences and making popular media that draws on an unpopular language. The rangatahi audience segment is vitally important, not only for building up audience share, but also for continuing the revitalising strategies of those who have

---

[*] Radio Waatea, 13 May 2015, retrieved from http://www.waateanews.com/waateanews/x_story_id/ODMxNw==/TV-producers-cry-enough

fought for te reo to be a living language. As the era of digital plenty offers more and more media content that captures the attention of rangatahi, the Māori media sector faces challenges on a range of fronts. Yet, as Rangi Matamua argues, the responsibility for the fate of te reo Māori does not lie solely with the Māori media sector:

> The role of Māori broadcasting is to encourage, to support and to be a resource for those willing to partake. It is true they must do all they can to help influence Māori to embrace the language and culture, but if Māori do not wish to participate, then the broadcasting arena cannot, and should not be held accountable. (Matamua, 2014, p. 346)

In some ways, Matamua's comments chime with the logic of Higgins and Rewi's ZePA model which suggests that the responsibility for the future of te reo Māori will need to be an increasingly shared one, involving all citizens of Aotearoa, if the language is to survive.

By drawing on kōrero from those who have a stake in Māori Television, this book has sought to gather together a range of voices whose perspectives might mutually inform one another, on the constraints and potentials of the Māori media sector. As is the case with many Māori initiatives focused on enhancing Māori wellbeing in relation to te reo me ngā tikanga Māori, the labour, time and energy to simply live, work and play as Māori faces constraints from multiple directions. Yet these constraints have also generated a great deal of innovative and informative Māori media. Charged with a legislative responsibility to promote and protect te reo and tikanga Māori after decades of Crown neglect, and in an era of digital plenty, marked by ever-eroding public-service media provisions, Māori Television, in its first ten years, laid the groundwork for imagining what state-funded New Zealand media might look like, from the perspective of te ao Māori, at the same time as it underscored the impossibility of thinking about things Māori in monolithic terms.

Appendix One

The Māori Television Service
(Te Aratuku Whakaata Irirangi Māori) Act 2003

Section 8
Functions of Service

(1) The principal function of the Service is to contribute to the protection and promotion of te reo Māori me ōna tikanga through the provision, in te reo Māori and English, of a high-quality, cost-effective television service that informs, educates, and entertains viewers, and enriches New Zealand's society, culture, and heritage.

(2) The Service must also—
    (a) ensure that during prime time it broadcasts mainly in te reo Māori; and
    (b) ensure that at other times it broadcasts a substantial proportion of its programmes in te reo Māori; and
    (c) ensure that, in its programming, the Service has regard to the needs and preferences of—
        (i) young people; and
        (ii) children participating in te reo Māori immersion education; and
        (iii) all persons learning te reo Māori; and
        (iv) persons whose first language is te reo Māori and persons with a high level of proficiency in te reo Māori; and
    (d) provide broadcast services that are technically available throughout New Zealand and practicably accessible to as many people as is reasonably possible.

(3) The Service may undertake other functions that contribute to the protection and promotion of te reo Māori.

(4) In performing its functions, the Service may provide a range of content and services on a choice of delivery platforms.

Section 8: replaced, on 28 November 2013, by section 7 of the Māori Television Service (Te Aratuku Whakaata Irirangi Māori) Amendment Act 2013 (2013 No 99).

Appendix Two

Funding Channels*

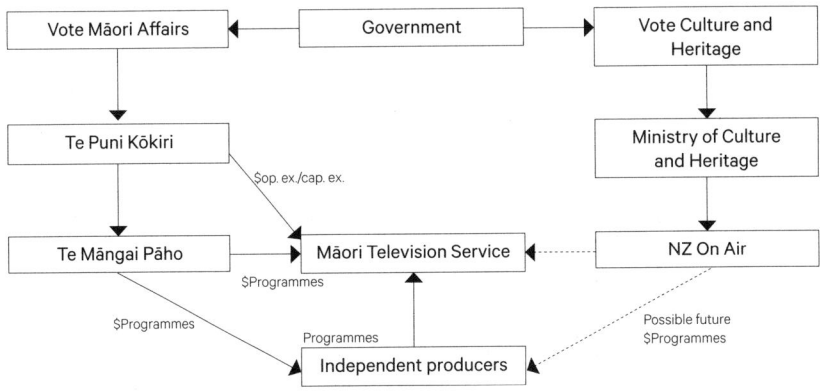

* From 2003–2004 Statement of Intent.

Appendix Three

Māori Television's Right of Reply

Māori Television – *The First 10 Years*

November 2015

Turuki, turuki! Paneke, paneke!
Tēnā koutou me ngā ahuatanga o te waa, ō tatou nei mate, noho mai i te ao wairua, tātou o te ao ora, otirā e te iwi whānui tēnā koutou katoa.

History and summary

As noted in Jo Smith's book, for many years, Māori broadcasting was lobbied for as a way to support Article II of the Treaty of Waitangi – to protect and promote *taonga Māori*. It was in the late nineties when Māori Television as an organisation started gaining momentum with the formation of the Te Reo and Māori Television Trust. After years of sustained lobbying for better funding and securing appropriate premises, Māori Television went to air for the first time on March 28, 2004. The establishment of Māori TV is a credit to the efforts of many, some since passed, who gave freely of their time and commitment to the cause of Māori broadcasting, *E kore e mimiti te mihi ki a koutou katoa.*

Since launching, Māori Television has focused its first ten years on establishing itself within New Zealand's competitive media industry by growing a loyal audience base. It remains a niche broadcaster with an important language growth mandate and has been described by politicians, iwi leaders and media commentators as one of the best examples of public broadcasting in the country. There is also no doubt that in commissioning, producing and broadcasting the wide array of programmes in both Māori and English that we have contributed to the sharing of a Māori perspective with a New Zealand and international audience. Some may debate at times the validity and the authenticity of those views but we believe it is a fair reflection of the diversity of the Māori world in the 21st century. Without Māori Television, this view would not necessarily be represented by other New Zealand broadcasters

Commitment to the kaupapa and future strategic direction

Māori Television's vision is unwavering in the *promotion and protection of te reo me ngā tikanga Māori,* and all that it does in support of this. The Board and Management are deeply committed to this vision and are unified in the view that for the next ten years that a sustained focus on this vision will require the right strategies in place to deliver on this objective. For that reason, the house that is Māori Television has **five strategic pillars** that hold up the vision:

Looking to the future, goals around **Partnership and Alliances** will see Māori Television aiming to generate increased new revenue streams from commercial partners and Crown agencies. This will be driven by advertising, sponsorship, product placement and content delivery partnerships. Increased revenue will also mean the ability to drive extended audience reach for clients. Ongoing partnership with the independent production community is also key to our success going forward.

Content will always be of the utmost importance in the growth and protection of *te reo me nga tikanga Māori*. Māori Television is striving to continually develop, update and deliver content which will engage audiences and thus help deliver on the organisation's strategic objectives. The core goal remains driving audience growth through entertaining and engaging content, with the aim of sustaining one million engagements per week. Engaging content will also assist in Māori Television developing as a meeting place for Māori youth.

At the heart of Māori Television are the **People**. The quality of staff is driven by a performance-based culture, improved staff engagement and collaboration and clearly understood role outcomes that connect to the vision. Together this will continue to enhance Māori Television's standing as an employment brand of choice. In 'walking the talk', Māori Television has set itself the aspirational goal of having a bilingual workforce by 2020.

Through audience growth, favourable media coverage and third party endorsements, the **Communications and Brand** strategy will enhance and protect Māori Television's corporate reputation.

As media technology and the way viewers consume content rapidly changes, Māori Television is working to continually stay updated and deliver **Multi-platform** content that connects with target audiences according to where and how they live. This has seen the launch of our channels available on the Freeview Plus platform and also the launch of the Māori Television app *Connect* in September 2015, which offers viewers a complimentary alternative to linear programming where they can consume content whenever and wherever they want. The on-demand content service is also offered on Māoritelevision.com.

Challenges faced by Māori Television

In an ever-changing media environment, Māori Television faces no shortage of challenges, including: funding; fragmented audiences; the need to invest in technology and attracting and retaining key talent. Regardless of the trials ahead, it is our collective dedication and belief in our *kaupapa* that drives us to meet and overcome these challenges in the years ahead.

Ki te tuohu koe, me maunga teitei – If you should bow your head let it be to a lofty mountain.

Nāku noa, nā,
Paora Maxwell (Te Tāhūhū Rangapū, CEO Māori TV)

Bibliography

Books and articles

Abel, Sue, 'Māori Television, Anzac Day, and Constructing "Nationhood"', in B. Hokowhitu and V. Devadas (eds), *The Fourth Eye: Māori Media in Aotearoa New Zealand*, University of Minnesota Press, Minneapolis, MN, 2013a, pp. 201–15.

Abel, Sue, 'Māori Television, Its Pākehā Audience and Issues of Decolonialization', *Studies in Australasian Cinema*, vol. 7, issues 2–3, 2013b, pp. 111–21.

Abel, Sue, *Shaping the News: Waitangi Day on Television*, Auckland University Press, Auckland, 1997.

Abel, Sue, 'The (Racial) Political Economy of Māori Television', *Australian Journal of Communication*, vol. 38, issue 3, 2011, pp. 125–38.

Alfred, Taiaiake, and Jeff Corntassel, 'Being Indigenous: Resurgences Against Contemporary Colonialism', *Government and Opposition*, vol. 40, issue 4, 2005, pp. 597–614.

Ang, Ien, *Desperately Seeking the Audience*, Routledge, London and New York, 1991.

Archie, Carol, *Pou Kōrero: a journalists' guide to Māori and current affairs*, NZ Journalists Training Organisation, Wellington, 2007.

Baker, Sarah, 'The Death of a Genre? Television Current Affairs Programmes on New Zealand Public Television', *Communications, Civics, Industry – ANZCA 2007 Conference Proceedings*, ANZCA and La Trobe University, Melbourne, 2007.

Barclay, Barry, 'Amongst Landscapes', in Jonathan Dennis and Jan Bieringa (eds), *Film in Aotearoa New Zealand*, Victoria University Press, Wellington, 2nd ed., 1996, pp. 116–29.

Barclay, Barry, *Our Own Image*, Longman Paul, Auckland, 1990.

Barnes, Angela M., 'Ngā Kai Para i te Kahikātoa: Māori Filmmaking, Forging a Path', unpublished doctoral thesis, University of Auckland, Auckland, 2011.

Barnes, Angela M., B. Borell, K. Taiapa, J. Rankine, R. Nairn, and T. McCreanor, 'Anti-Māori Themes in New Zealand Journalism: Toward Alternative Practice', *Pacific Journalism Review*, vol. 18, issue 1, 2012, pp. 195–216.

Barton, Chris, 'The Death of Public Service Television', *New Zealand Herald*, 4 October 2011. Retrieved 9 March 2015 from: http://www.nzherald.co.nz/business/news/article.cfm?c_id=3&objectid=10756281.

Bell, Allan, 'Advocating for a Threatened Language: The Case for Māori on Television in Aotearoa/New Zealand', *Te Reo*, vol. 53, 2010, pp. 3–26.

Bell, C., and C. Guyan, '"Bloody" Debate on Maori TV Expected', *The Dominion*, 18 February 1997.

Benton, Richard, '*The Maori Language 1985 and Beyond*', New Zealand Council for Educational Research/Te Wāhanga Māori, Wellington, 1985.

Borell, Belinda, 'Living in the City Ain't So Bad: Cultural Diversity of South Auckland Rangatahi', unpublished master's thesis, Massey University, Palmerston North, 2005.

Boyd-Bell, Robert, *New Zealand Television: The First 25 Years*, Methuen, Auckland, 1985.

Broadcasting Standards Authority, *Maori Worldviews and Broadcasting Standards: What Should Be the Relationship?*, Broadcasting Standards Authority, Wellington, 2009.

Brown Pages Collective, *The Brown Pages Directory 2008*, The Brown Pages, Auckland, 2008.

Burns, Derek, *Public Money Private Lives: Aotearoa Television – The Inside Story*, Reed Books, Auckland, 1997.

Cleave, Peter, *Iwi Station: A Discussion of Print, Radio and Television in Aotearoa/New Zealand*, Campus Press, Palmerston North, 2008.

Comrie, Margie, 'Double Vision: Election News Coverage on Mainstream and Indigenous Television in New Zealand', *The International Journal of Press/Politics*, vol. 17, issue 3, 2012, pp. 275–93.

Cormack, Mike, 'The Media and Language Maintenance', in M. J. Cormack and N. Hourigan (eds), *Minority Language Media: Concepts, Critiques and Case Studies*, Multilingual Matters, New York, NY, 2007, pp. 52–68.

Dahlberg, Lincoln, and Eugenia Siapera, *Radical Democracy and the Internet*, Palgrave, Basingstoke, UK, 2007.

Debrett, Mary, *Reinventing Public Service Television for the Digital Future*, Intellect Books, Bristol and Chicago, 2010.

Devadas, Vijay, '15 October 2007, Aotearoa: Race, terror and sovereignty', *Sites*, vol. 5, issue 1, 2008, pp. 124–51.

Drinnan, John, 'TVNZ to Outsource Most of Māori Unit', *New Zealand Herald*, 2014. Retrieved 4 March 2015 from: http://www.nzherald.co.nz/business/news/article.cfm?c_id=3&objectid=11347114.

Dunleavy, Trisha, 'Maximising Public Value in Costly Areas of TV Production: Drama, Comedy, and the "New Zealand On Air" Model', *RIPE*, 2012. Retrieved 13 December 2013 from: http://www.ripeat.org.

Dunleavy, Trisha, 'New Zealand Television and the Struggle for "Public Service"', *Media, Culture and Society*, vol. 30, issue 6, 2008, pp. 795–811.

Dunleavy, Trisha, *Ourselves in Primetime: A History of New Zealand Television Drama*, Auckland University Press, Auckland, 2005.

Dunleavy, Trisha, 'Public Television in a Small Country: The New Zealand "Experiment" 20 Years On', *FlowTV*, 2009. Retrieved 4 March 2015 from: http://flowtv.org/2009/05/.

Dunleavy, Trisha, 'Television – Māori Television', *Te Ara – The Encyclopedia of New Zealand*, 2014. Updated 29-Oct-14. Retrieved from: http://www.TeAra.govt.nz/en/television/page-3.

Dunleavy, Trisha, and Hester Joyce, *New Zealand Film and Television: Institution, Industry and Cultural Change*, Intellect Books in association with Chicago University Press, Bristol and Chicago, 2011.

Easton, Brian, 'The Broadcasting Reforms', in J. Farnsworth and I. Hutchison (eds), *New Zealand Television: A Reader*, Dunmore Press, Palmerston North, 2001, pp. 225–30.

Easton, Brian, *The Commercialisation of New Zealand*, Auckland University Press, Auckland, 1997.

Edge, Alexandra, 'Indigenous Journalism in Aotearoa New Zealand: A Case Study of Māori Television's News and Current Affairs', unpublished master's thesis, University of Auckland, Auckland, 2013.

Ellis, John, *Seeing Things*, I. B. Tauris and Co., London and New York, 2000.

Fishman, Joshua, *Reversing Language Shifts: Theoretical and Empirical Foundations of Assistance to Threatened Languages*, Multilingual Matters, Clevedon and Philadelphia, PA, 1991.

Fleras, Augie, and Paul Spoonley, *Recalling Aotearoa: Indigenous Politics and Ethnic Relations in New Zealand*, Oxford University Press, Auckland, 1999.

Fox, Derek, 'Aotearoa Broadcasting System, Inc.', in P. Spoonley and W. Hirsch (eds), *Between the Lines: Racism and the New Zealand Media*, Heinemann Reed, Auckland, 1990a, pp. 128–33.

Fox, Derek, 'Honouring the Treaty: Indigenous Television in Aotearoa', in J. Farnsworth and I. Hutchison (eds), *New Zealand Television: A Reader*, Dunmore Press, Palmerston North, 2001, pp. 260–69.

Fox, Derek, 'Te Karere: The Struggle for Maori News', in P. Spoonley and W. Hirsch (eds), *Between the Lines: Racism and the New Zealand Media*, Heinemann Reed, Auckland, 1990b, pp. 103–7.

Fox, Derek, 'The Battle for Māori Television', *Mana*, vol. 87, April–May 2009, pp. 14–15.

Fox, Derek, 'The Maori Perspective of the News', in M. Comrie and J. McGregor (eds), *Whose News?*, Dunmore Press, Palmerston North, 1992, pp. 170–80.

Fox, Derek, 'The Mass Media: A Maori Perspective', in *Royal Commission on Social Policy. The April Report: Volume IV Social Perspectives,* Royal Commission on Social Policy, Wellington, 1988, pp. 481–503.

Freeman-Tayler, Kate, 'Understanding the Māori Television Service's Policy and Legislation: The First Ten Years', unpublished master's thesis, Victoria University of Wellington, Wellington, 2014.

Gregory, A., B. Borell, T. McCreanor, A. M. Barnes, R. Nairn, J. Rankine, S. Abel, K. Taiapa, and H. Kaiwai, 'Reading News About Māori', *AlterNative: An International Journal of Indigenous Peoples,* vol. 7, issue 1, 2011, pp. 51–64.

Grin, Francois, and F. Vaillancourt, *Language Revitalisation Policy: An Analytical Survey, Theoretical Framework, Policy Experience and Application to te Reo Maori,* New Zealand Treasury, Wellington, 1998. Retrieved 27 November 2014 from: http://ideas.repec.org/p/nzt/nztwps/98-06.html.

Haami, Bradford, *Te Urutahi Koataata Māori: Working with Māori in Film and Television,* Ngā Aho Whakaari, Auckland, 2008.

Hanusch, Folker, 'Charting a Theoretical Framework for Examining Indigenous Journalism Culture', *Media International Australia Incorporating Culture and Policy: Quarterly journal of media research and resources,* 2013, pp. 82–91.

Harawira, Wena, 'Challenges Facing Indigenous Broadcasters', address at Pacific Media Summit, Apia, 16 April 2008. Retrieved from: http://www.hrc.co.nz/hrc_new/hrc/cms/files/documents/23-Apr-2008_11-50-04_Challenges_facing_Indigenous_broadcasters-Wena_Harawira.doc.

Havens, Timothy, *Global Television Marketplace,* British Film Institute, London, 2006.

Hay, David, 'Giving/Taking, Selling/Buying, Speaking/Silence: Te Reo Maori in Primetime', *Continuum,* vol. 10, issue 1, 1996, pp. 94–107.

Hayward, Janine, 'Biculturalism – Continuing Debates', *Te Ara – The Encyclopedia of New Zealand,* 2012. Updated 13-Jul-12. Retrieved from: http//www.TeAra.govt.nz/en/biculturalism/page-3.

Hearn, Alison, 'Reality Television, *The Hills* and the Limits of Immaterial Labour Thesis', *TripleC: Communication, Capitalism and Critique,* vol. 8, issue 1, 2010, pp. 60–76.

Henry, Ella, 'Te Wairua Auaha: Emancipatory Māori Entrepreneurship in Screen Production', unpublished doctoral thesis, Auckland University of Technology, Auckland, 2012.

Henry, Ella, and Melissa Wikaire, *The Brown Book,* Ngā Aho Whakaari, Auckland, 2013.

Higgins, Rawinia, and Poia Rewi, 'ZePA – Right-shifting: Reorientation towards Normalisation', in R. Higgins, P. Rewi and V. Olsen-Reeder (eds), *The Value of the Māori Language: Te Hua o te Reo Māori,* Huia Publishers, Wellington, 2014, pp. 7–32.

Hill, Richard S., 'Maori Urban Migration and the Assertion of Indigeneity in Aotearoa/New Zealand, 1945–1975', *Interventions,* vol. 14, issue 2, 2012, pp. 256–78.

Hill, Richard S., and Brigitte Bönisch-Brednich, 'Fitting Aotearoa into New Zealand: Politico-Cultural Change in a Modern Bicultural Nation', in M. Berg and B. Schaefer (eds), *Historical Justice in International Perspectives,* Cambridge University Press, Cambridge, UK, 2009, pp. 239–63.

Hodgetts, Darrin, A. Barnett, A. Duirs, J. Henry, and A. Schwanen, 'Maori Media Production, Civic Journalism and the Foreshore and Seabed Controversy in Aotearoa', *Pacific Journalism Review,* vol. 11, issue 2, 2005, pp. 191–208.

Hokowhitu, Brendan, and Vijay Devadas (eds), *The Fourth Eye: Māori Media in Aotearoa New Zealand,* University of Minnesota Press, Minneapolis, MN, 2013.

Hollings, Mike, 'Māori Language Broadcasting: Panacea or Pipedream', in A. Bell, R. Harlow, and D. Starks (eds), *Languages of New Zealand,* Victoria University Press, Wellington, 2005, pp. 111–30.

Hope, Wayne, 'New Thoughts on the Public Sphere in Aotearoa/New Zealand', in M. Hirst, S. Phelan, and V. Rupar (eds), *Scooped: The Politics and Power of Journalism in Aotearoa/New Zealand,* AUT Media, Auckland, 2012, pp. 27–47.

Horomia, Parekura, *Second reading of the Māori Television Service (Te Aratuku Whakaata Irirangi Māori) Bill* 2003, New Zealand Parliamentary Debates, vol. 607, p. 4908.

Horrocks, Roger, 'New Zealand Cinema: Culture, Policies, Film', in D. Verhoeven (ed.), *Twin Peeks: Australian and New Zealand Feature Films,* Damned Publishing, Melbourne, 1999, pp. 129–37.

Horrocks, Roger, 'The History of New Zealand Television: An Expensive Medium for a Small Country', in R. Horrocks and N. Perry (eds), *Television in New Zealand: Programming the Nation*, Oxford University Press, Melbourne, 2004, pp. 20–43.

Hubbard, Anthony, 'From Political Football to Part of the Furniture', *Dominion Post*, 4 May 2013, p. A6.

Hunkin, Joanna, '*Campbell Live*'s Future Depends on Ratings. But How Do They Work?', *New Zealand Herald*, 11 April 2015. Retrieved 31 July 2015 from: http://www.nzherald.co.nz/entertainment/news/article.cfm?c_id=1501119&objectid=11430927.

Hunn, Jack, *Report on the Department of Maori Affairs*, Government Printer, Wellington, 1961.

Hutchings, Jessica, 'Decolonisation and Aotearoa – A Pathway to Right Livelihood', 2002. Retrieved 19 January 2015 from: http://www.swaraj.org/shikshantar/ls3_jessica.htm.

Hutchings, Jessica, A. Barnes, K. Taupo, N. Bright, L. Pihama, and J. Lee, *Kia Puāwaitia Ngā Tūmanako: Critical Issues for Whānau in Māori Education*, NZCER Press, Wellington, 2012.

Hutchison, I., and Geoff Lealand (eds), *Aotearoa/New Zealand: A New Mediascape*, Department of Media Studies, Edith Cowan University, Mt Lawley, WA, 1996.

Jackson, Moana, 'Hui Reflections: Research and the Consolations of Bravery', in J. Hutchings, H. Potter, and K. Taupo (eds), *Kei Tua o te Pae Hui Proceedings – The Challenges of Kaupapa Māori Research in the 21st Century*, NZCER Press, Wellington, 2011.

Jackson, Moana, 'The Face Behind the Law: The United Nations and the Rights of Indigenous Peoples', in A. Mikaere (ed.) *Yearbook of New Zealand Jurisprudence: Special Issue Te Purenga*, University of Waikato School of Law, Hamilton, 2005, pp. 10–30.

Johnson, Sophie, 'Ngā Kaikawekōrero: Producing Māori Television Documentary in Aotearoa New Zealand', unpublished master's thesis, Auckland University of Technology, Auckland, 2013. Retrieved 1 May 2016 from: http://hdl.handle.net/10292/5290.

Kāretu, Tīmoti, 'Solutions for Maori Broadcasting', in P. Norris and J. Farnsworth (eds), *Keeping it Ours – Issues of Television Broadcasting in New Zealand*, Christchurch Polytechnic, Christchurch, 1997, pp. 95–100.

Kiriona, Renee, 'Doubters Told to Wait for Maori TV Launch', *New Zealand Herald*, 20 March 2004. Retrieved 1 May 2016 from: http://www.nzherald.co.nz/nz/news/article.cfm?c_id=1&objectid=3555817.

Laenui, Poka (aka Burgess, H. F.), 'Processes of Decolonization', in M. Battiste (ed.) *Reclaiming Indigenous Voice and Vision*, University of British Columbia Press, Vancouver, BC, 2011, pp. 150–60.

Lawn, Jennifer, *Neoliberalism and Cultural Transition in New Zealand Literature, 1984–2008: Market Fictions*, Lexington Books, Lanham, MD, 2016.

Lealand, Geoff, 'New Zealand Television and the Dominance of Foreign Content', in P. Spoonley and W. Hirsch (eds), *Between the Lines: Racism and the New Zealand Media*, Heinemann Reed, Auckland, 1990, pp. 69–75.

Lealand, Geoff, 'Ratings and More Damn Ratings: Measuring Television Viewing in New Zealand', *New Zealand Journal of Media Studies*, vol. 5, issue 1, 1998, pp. 36–50.

Lealand, Geoff, 'Television Ratings and Other Myths of the Modern Age', *New Zealand Business Times*, 9 March 2001.

Lee, Jenny, 'Decolonising Māori Narratives: Pūrākau as a Method', *MAI Review*, vol. 2, 2009, pp. 1–12.

Lysaght, Ruth, 'Language Image in National Minority Language Television Idents: TG4 (Teilifís na Gaeilge, Ireland) and Whakaata Māori (Māori Television, New Zealand)', *Estudios Irlandeses*, vol. 4, 2009, pp. 45–57.

Lysaght, Ruth, 'Teanga and Tikanga: A Comparative Study of National Broadcasting in a

Minority Language on Māori Television and Teilifís na Gaeilge', unpublished doctoral thesis, University of Auckland, Auckland, 2010.

Mallard, Trevor, *Māori Television Service (Te Aratuku Whakaata Irirangi Māori) Amendment Bill,* New Zealand Parliamentary Debates, vol. 688, 2013, p. 8792.

Mane, Jo, 'Pāho Māori: The Impact of Māori Language Broadcasting on Māori Language Survival', unpublished doctoral thesis, University of Auckland, Auckland, 2009.

Mane-Wheoki, Te Aroha, 'In Terms of Māori-medium Television Programmes, are Government Agencies Meeting Their Objectives and Fulfilling Their Responsibilities and Commitments to the Treaty of Waitangi?', Ngā Pae o te Māramatanga, Auckland University, Auckland, 2005, pp. 61–80.

Māori Television Service, *Briefing to the Incoming Ministers of Māori Development and Finance,* Auckland, 2014a.

Māori Television Service, *Pānui Whāinga: Statement of Intent 2004–2005,* Auckland, 2005; *2005–2006,* Auckland, 2005a; *2009–2010,* Auckland, 2008; *2011–2014,* Auckland, 2010a; *2013–2016,* Auckland, 2012; *2014–2017,* Auckland, 2014.

Māori Television Service, *Pūrongo-ā-tau: Annual Report 2005,* Auckland, 2005b; *2006,* Auckland, 2006; *2009,* Auckland, 2009; *2010,* Auckland, 2010b; *2013,* Auckland, 2013; *2014,* Auckland, 2014b.

Māori Television Service, *Te Reo Māori me Ngā Tikanga Guidelines.* Retrieved 22 May 2014 from: http://www.maoritelevision.com/sites/default/files/attachments/Te percent20Reo percent20Ma percentC5 percent8Dri percent20me percent20ng percentC4 percent81 percent20Tikanga percent20Guidelines.pdf.

Matahaere, Donna, 'Māori the "Eternally Compromised Noun": Complicity, Contradictions and Postcolonial Identities in the Age of Biculturalism', *Women's Studies Journal,* vol. 11, issues 1 and 2, 1995, pp. 15–24.

Matamua, Rangi, 'Te Reo Pāho: Māori Radio and Language Revitalisation', unpublished doctoral thesis, Massey University, Palmerston North, 2006.

Matamua, Rangi, 'Te Reo Pāpāho me te Reo Māori – Māori Broadcasting and te Reo Māori', in R. Higgins, P. Rewi, and V. Olsen-Reeder (eds), *The Value of the Māori Language: Te Hua o te Reo Māori,* Huia Publishers, Wellington, 2014, pp. 331–348.

McCombs, Maxwell, and D. Shaw, 'The Agenda-Setting Function of Mass Media', *Public Opinion Quarterly,* vol. 36, issue 2, 1972, pp. 176–87.

McCurdy, Diana, and R. Kiriona, 'Te Reo Comes to Prime Time', *New Zealand Herald,* 8 March 2004. Retrieved from: http://www.nzherald.co.nz/nz/news/article.cfm?c_id=1&objectid=3557270.

McGregor, Judy, *News Values and the Reporting of Maori News,* Department of Human Resource Management, Faculty of Business Studies, Massey University, 1991.

McGregor, Judy, and J. Te Awa, 'Racism and the News Media', in P. Spoonley, C. MacPherson, and D. Pearson (eds), *Nga Patai: Racism and Ethnic Relations in Aotearoa New Zealand,* Dunmore Press, Palmerston North, 1996, pp. 235–46.

McLeod, Jonathan, *New Zealand Public Television, Public Service and Everything in Between: The Success and Struggles of New Zealand on Air and Public Television,* unpublished master's thesis, Victoria University of Wellington, Wellington, 2014.

Metge, Joan, *Rautahi: The Maoris of New Zealand,* Routledge, London, 1976.

Middleton, Julie, 'Ka Rangona te Reo: The Development of Māori-Language Television Broadcasting in Aotearoa New Zealand', *Te Kaharoa,* vol. 3, issue 1, 2010, pp. 146–76.

Mita, Merata, 'Head and Shoulders', *Te Ao Mārama,* vol. 2, 1993a, pp. 278–82.

Mita, Merata, 'Storytelling: A Process of Decolonisation', in L. Pihama (ed.), *The Journal of Puawaitanga. Special Issue: Indigenous Women and Representation,* Te Whare Wānanga o Tāmaki Makaurau, Auckland, 2000, pp. 7–9.

Mita, Merata, 'The Politics of Culture: Indigenous Literature in a Colonial Society', in W. T. Ihimaera, H. Williams, I. Ramsden, and D. S. Long (eds), *He Whakaatanga o te Ao: The Reality,* Reed Books, Auckland, 1993b, pp. 310–14.

Mita, Merata, 'The Soul and the Image', in J. Bieringa and J. Dennis (eds), *Film In Aotearoa New Zealand*, Victoria University Press, Wellington, 1992, pp. 36–56.

Moran, Albert, 'National Broadcasting and Cultural Identity: New Zealand Television and Shortland Street', *Continuum*, vol. 10, issue 1, 1996, pp. 168–86.

Morozov, Evgeny, 'Tunisia, Social Media and the Politics of Attention', *Foreign Policy*, 14 January 2011.

Murray, Stuart, *Images of Dignity: Barry Barclay and Fourth Cinema*, Huia Press, Wellington, 2008.

Nairn, Ray, A. M. Barnes, B. Borell, J. Rankine, A. Gregory, and T. McCreanor, 'Māori News Is Bad News: That's Certainly So on Television', *MAI Journal*, vol. 1, issue 1, 2012, pp. 38–49.

New Zealand House of Representatives, *Māori Television Service (Te Aratuku Whakaata Irirangi Māori) Amendment Bill – First Reading*, vol. 688, 2013a, p. 8787.

New Zealand House of Representatives, *Māori Television Service (Te Aratuku Whakaata Irirangi Māori) Amendment Bill – Second Reading, Instruction to Committee, in Committee, Third Reading*, vol. 695, 2013b, p. 14921.

Norris, Paul, *Reshaping Public Broadcasting: The New Zealand Experience 1988–2003*. Institute for Public Policy Research, 2004. Retrieved 1 May 2016 from: http://www.slideserve.com/nero-cross/reshaping-public-broadcasting-the-new-zealand-experience-1988-2003.

Norris, Paul, 'The Progress to Digital Television in New Zealand: An Update', *International Journal of Digital Television*, vol. 1, issue 3, 2010, pp. 345–49.

Norris, Paul, and Brian Pauling, *NZ On Air: An Evaluative Study 1989–2011*, NZ On Air, Wellington, 2012.

Norris, Paul, and Brian Pauling, *The Digital Future and Public Broadcasting: A Research Report Prepared for NZ On Air*, NZ On Air, Wellington, 2008.

NZ On Air, *Local Content: New Zealand Television*, Wellington, 2014b.

NZ On Air, *Ngā Matakiirea: Report on Mainstream Māori Programming*, Wellington, 2010.

NZ On Air, *Where Are the Audiences?: Benchmark Survey of New Zealanders' Media Consumption*, Wellington, 2014a.

O'Carroll, Acushla Dee, 'An Analysis of How Rangatahi Māori Use Social Networking Sites', *MAI Journal*, vol. 2, issue 1, 2013a, pp. 46–59.

O'Carroll, Acushla Dee, 'Kanohi ki te Kanohi – A Thing of the Past?: An Examination of Māori use of Social Networking Sites and the Implications for Māori Culture and Society', unpublished doctoral thesis, Massey University, Auckland, 2013b.

O'Carroll, Acushla Dee, 'Kanohi ki te Kanohi – A Thing of the Past?: Examining the Notion of "Virtual" Ahikā and the Implications for Kanohi ki te Kanohi', *Pimatisiwin: A Journal of Aboriginal and Indigenous Community Health*, vol. 11, issue 3, 2013c, pp. 441–55.

O'Carroll, Acushla Dee, 'Māori Identity Construction in Social Networking Sites', *International Journal of Critical Indigenous Studies*, vol. 6, issue 2, 2013d, pp. 2–16.

O'Carroll, Acushla Dee, 'Virtual Whanaungatanga – Māori Utilising Social Networking Sites to Attain and Maintain Relationships', *AlterNative*, vol. 9, issue 3, 2013e. pp. 230–45.

Oren, Tasha, and S. Shahaf, *Global Television Formats: Understanding Television Across Borders*, Routledge, London and New York, 2012.

Pacific Media Centre, 'NZ: TVNZ Programme Outsourcing Plan "Catastrophic" for Pasifika, says PIMA', *Pacific Media Centre*, 2014. Retrieved 4 March 2015 from: http://www.pmc.aut.ac.nz/pacific-media-watch/nz-tvnz-programme-outsourcing-plan-catastrophic-pasifika-says-pima-9028.

Paul, Joanna, 'Challenges Lie Ahead for MTS in the Aotearoa Public Sphere', *Pacific Journalism Review*, vol. 11, issue 1, 2005, pp. 42–46.

Penetito, Wally, 'Kaupapa Māori Education: Research as the Exposed Edge', in J. Hutchings, H. Potter and K. Taupo (eds), *Kei Tua o Te Pae Hui Proceedings – The Challenges of Kaupapa Māori Research in the 21st Century*, NZCER Press, Wellington, 2011, pp. 38–43.

Petersen, Søren M., 'Loser Generated Content: From Participation to Exploitation', *First Monday*, vol. 13, issue 3, 2008. Retrieved 4 March 2015 from: http://firstmonday.org/article/view/2141/1948.

Pihama, Leonie, 'Report to Te Mangai Paho and Aotearoa Television Network, From the Research Unit for Maori Education, In Regard to the Monitoring and Evaluation of the Maori Television Pilot Project', International Research Institute for Maori and Indigenous Education and University of Auckland, Auckland, 1996.

Pihama, Leonie, 'Re-presenting Maori: Broadcasting and Knowledge Selection', in L. Pihama and Cherryl W. Smith (eds), *Cultural and Intellectual Property Rights: Economics, Politics and Colonisation*, International Research Institute for Maori and Indigenous Education, Auckland, 1997, pp. 57–63.

Pihama, Leonie, and Carl Mika, 'The Treaty of Waitangi and Policy in Māori Broadcasting', in V. Tawhai and K. Gray-Sharp (eds), *Always Speaking*, Huia Publishers, Wellington, 2012, pp. 175–91.

Poihipi, Vanessa, 'The Impact of Māori Television on Being Māori: A Geographical Approach', *MAI Review*, vol. 1, 2007, pp. 1–21.

Prentice, Chris, 'Reorienting Culture for Decolonization', *Continuum: Journal of Media and Cultural Studies*, vol. 27, issue 1, 2013, pp. 4–17.

Prentice, Chris, 'The Māori Television Service and Questions of Culture', in B. Hokowhitu and V. Devadas (eds), *The Fourth Eye: Māori Media in Aotearoa New Zealand*, University of Minnesota Press, Minneapolis, MN, 2013, pp. 181–200.

Puriri, Nau, 'The Maori on TV', *Te Ao Hou*, March, vol. 58, 1967. Retrieved 1 May 2016 from: http://teaohou.natlib.govt.nz/journals/teaohou/issue/Mao58TeA/c17.html.

Rahoi-Gilchrest, Rita, 'Examining the Successes and Struggles of New Zealand's Māori TV', in K. Howley (ed), *Understanding Community Media*, Sage, Los Angeles, CA, 2010, pp. 161–71.

Rangihau, T., 'Solutions for Maori Broadcasting', in P. Norris and J. Farnsworth (eds), *Keeping it Ours: Issues of Television Broadcasting in New Zealand: Papers from the New Zealand Broadcasting School Seminar*, Christchurch Polytechnic, Christchurch, 1997, pp. 106–9.

Rankine, Jenny, R. Nairn, A. M. Barnes, M. Gregory, H. Kaiwai, and B. Borell, *Media and Te Tiriti o Waitangi 2007*, Kupu Taea: Media and Te Tiriti Project, Auckland, 2008.

Reid, Donald, 'Public Broadcasting in New Zealand: Is State Media Inclusive Media?', in J. Chapple (ed.), *Boundaries: Dichotomies of Keeping in and Keeping Out,* Inter-Disciplinary Press, Oxford, 2010, pp. 133–39.

Reweti, Debra, 'Māori and Broadcasting', in Mulholland and contributors (eds), *State of the Māori Nation: Twenty-First-Century Issues in Aotearoa*, Reed Books, Auckland, 2006, pp. 179–86.

Royal, T. Charles, 'Some Speculations on Māori Identity in the New Zealand of Tomorrow', paper presented at Concepts of Nationhood: Marking 100 Years Since the Proclamation of Dominion Status for New Zealand, Legislative Council Chamber, Parliament Buildings, Wellington, 26 September 2007.

Sharples, Pita, *Maori Television Service (Te Aratuku Whakaata Irirangi Māori) Amendment Bill*, 2013, New Zealand Parliamentary Debates, vol. 688, p. 8787.

Smith, Graham H. 'Protecting and Respecting Indigenous Knowledge', in M. Battiste (ed.), *Reclaiming Indigenous Voice and Vision*, University of British Columbia Press, Vancouver, BC, 2000, pp. 209–24.

Smith, Jo, 'Māori Television's Indigenous Insistence', *Studies in Australasian Cinema*, vol. 7, issue 2–3, 2013, pp. 101–10.

Smith, Jo, 'Māori Television's Service to its Publics in an Era of Digital Plenty', *International Journal of Digital Television*, vol. 6, issue 2, 2015, pp. 185–201.

Smith, Jo, 'Parallel Quotidian Flows: Māori Television on Air', *New Zealand Journal of Media Studies*, vol. 9, 2006, pp. 27–35.

Smith, Jo, 'Postcolonial Māori Television?: The Dirty Politics of Indigenous Cultural Production', *Continuum*, vol. 25, issue 5, 2011, pp. 719–29.
Smith, Jo, and Sue Abel, 'Ka Whawhai Tonu Matou: Indigenous Television in Aotearoa New Zealand', *New Zealand Journal of Media Studies*, vol. 11, issue 1, 2008, pp. 1–14.
Smith, Jo, and Sue Abel, 'Three Years On: Maori Television', *Take: The SDGNZ Film and Television Quarterly*, vol. 48, 2007, pp. 16–19.
Smith, Jo, and Joost de Bruin, '*Survivor*-styled Indigeneity in Two Reality Television Programmes from Aotearoa/New Zealand', *Australasian Journal of Popular Culture*, vol. 1, issue 3, 2011, pp. 297–311.
Smith, Linda Tuhiwai, *Decolonizing Methodologies: Research and Indigenous Peoples*, Zed Books, London, 1999.
Spoonley, Paul, 'Racism, Race Relations and the Media', in P. Spoonley and W. Hirsch (eds), *Between the Lines: Racism and the New Zealand Media*, Heinemann Reed, Auckland, 1990, pp. 26–37.
Statistics New Zealand, *2013 QuickStats About Māori*. Wellington, 2013. Retrieved 1 May 2016 from http://www.stats.govt.nz/Census/2013-census/profile-and-summary-reports/quickstats-about-maori-english.aspx.
Stephens, Tainui, 'Māori Television', in R. Horrocks and N. Perry (eds), *Television in New Zealand: Programming the Nation*, Oxford, Melbourne, VIC, 2004, pp. 107–14.
Strickland, April, 'Barry Barclay's *Te Rua*: The Unmanned Camera and Māori Political Activism', in B. Hokowhitu and V. Devadas (eds), *The Fourth Eye: Māori Media in Aotearoa New Zealand*, University of Minnesota Press, Minneapolis, MN, 2013, pp. 143–61.
Strickland, April, 'Mediating Māoritanga: Film, Television, and Indigenous Sovereignty in Aotearoa New Zealand', unpublished doctoral thesis, New York University, New York, 2014.
Stuart, Ian, 'The Construction of a National Maori Identity by Maori Media', *Pacific Journalism Review*, vol. 9, issue 1, 2003, pp. 45–58.
Sunday Star-Times, 'The Little Station that Could', 23 March 2014. Retrieved 26 May 2016 from: http://www.stuff.co.nz/entertainment/tv-radio/9854340/The-little-station-that-could.
Tamahori, Lee, 'Directing Warriors', *Midwest*, vol. 6, 1994, pp. 15–17.
Taylor, Rangimoana, and John Miller, 'Kimihia – Still Looking', *Illusions*, vol. 11, July 1989.
Te Awa, Joanne, 'Mana News: A Case Study', *Sites*, vol. 33, 1996, pp. 168–75.
Te Kāhui o Māhutonga, *He Arotakenga i te Ture Whakaata Irirangi Māori 2003 / Māori Television Service Act 2003 Independent Review. A Report to the Ministers of Māori Affairs and Finance*, Te Puni Kōkiri, Wellington, 2009.
Te Kawa a Māui Media Research Team, *Portrayal of Māori and Te Ao Māori in Broadcasting: The Foreshore and Seabed Issue*, Broadcasting Standards Authority, Wellington, 2005.
Te Māngai Pāho, *Annual Report*, Wellington, 2005.
Te Māngai Pāho, *Briefing to the Incoming Minister of Māori Development and Finance*, Wellington, 2014.
Te Puni Kōkiri, *Attitudes Toward the Māori Language*, Wellington, 2006a.
Te Puni Kōkiri, *Impact of Iwi Radio on the Māori Language*, Wellington, 2011b.
Te Puni Kōkiri, *Impact of Māori Television on the Māori Language*, Wellington, 2011c.
Te Puni Kōkiri, *Māori Broadcasting and e-Media*, Wellington, 2007.
Te Puni Kōkiri, *Report of the Māori Broadcasting Advisory Committee (MBAC)*, Wellington, 2000.
Te Puni Kōkiri, *Te Paepae Motuhake: Te Reo Mauriora: Te Arotakenga o te Rāngai Reo Māori me te Rautaki Reo Māori*, Wellington, 2011d.
Te Puni Kōkiri, *Te Reo Mauriora: Review of the Māori Language Sector and the Māori Language Strategy*, Wellington, 2011a.
Te Puni Kōkiri, *The Health of the Māori Language in the Broadcast Sector 2006*, Wellington, 2006b.

Te Puni Kōkiri, *Use of Broadcasting and e-Media, Māori Language and Culture*, Wellington, 2010.
Te Puni Kōkiri and Te Taura Whiri i te Reo Māori, *Report to the Minister of Māori Affairs: Review of the Māori Language Strategy*, Wellington, 2009.
Te Puni Kōkiri and Te Taura Whiri i te Reo Māori, *Te Rautaki Reo Māori: The Māori Language Strategy*, Wellington, 2003.
Te Rito, Joe, 'Struggles for the Māori Language: He Whawhai Mo Te Reo Māori', *MAI Review*, vol. 2, 2008, pp. 1–8.
Te Taura Whiri i te Reo Māori, Te Puni Kōkiri and Statistics New Zealand, *National Māori Language Survey*, Te Puni Kōkiri, Wellington, 1995.
Thiong'o, Ngũgĩ, *Decolonising the Mind: The Politics of Language in African Literature*, Heinemann, New Hampshire, 1986.
Thomas, Huw, 'S4C: Annual Report Shows Viewing Figures Fall', *BBC News*, 17 July 2013. Retrieved 13 December 2013 from: http://www.bbc.com/news/uk-wales-23343492.
Thompson, Peter, 'Digital Age or Dark Ages?: The Refeudalisation of Media Politics in New Zealand', *Take*, vol. 64, Autumn, 2012, pp. 5–6.
Thompson, Peter, 'National's Broadcasting Policy: Expedient Fictions, Inconvenient Truths', 2009. Retrieved 4 March 2015 from: www.scoop.co.nz/stories/HL0904/S00090.htm.
Thompson, Peter, 'Show Me the Money: Funding Possibilities for Public Television in New Zealand', paper presented at SPADA conference, Auckland, New Zealand, 2011.
Thompson, Richard, 'Maori Affairs and the New Zealand Press: I', *The Journal of the Polynesian Society*, vol. 62, issue 4, 1954, pp. 366–83.
Thompson, Richard, 'Maori Affairs and the New Zealand Press: II', *The Journal of the Polynesian Society*, vol. 63, issue 1, 1954, pp. 1–16.
Thompson, Richard, 'Maori Affairs and the New Zealand Press: III', *The Journal of the Polynesian Society*, vol. 63, issue 3/4, 1954, pp. 216–27.
Thompson, Richard, 'Maori Affairs and the New Zealand Press: IV', *The Journal of the Polynesian Society*, vol. 64, issue 1, 1955, pp. 22–34.
Turei, Metiria, *Māori Television Service (Te Aratuku Whakaata Irirangi Māori) Amendment Bill*, New Zealand Parliamentary Debates, vol. 685, 2013, p. 14921.
Turner, Graeme, and J. Tay, *Television Studies After TV: Understanding Television in the Post-broadcast Era*, Routledge, New York, NY, 2009.
Turner, Richard, 'Non-Māori Viewing of Māori Television: An Empirical Analysis of the New Zealand Broadcast System', unpublished master's thesis, Massey University, Albany, 2010.
Van Dijck, José, 'Users Like You?: Theorizing Agency in User-Generated Content', *Media, Culture and Society*, vol. 31, issue 1, 2009, pp. 41–58.
Waitangi Tribunal, *Report of the Waitangi Tribunal on the Te Reo Maori Claim (Wai 11)*, Wellington, 1986.
Waitoa, Joanne, 'E-whanaungatanga: The Role of Social Media in Māori Political Engagement', unpublished master's thesis, Te Kunenga ki Pūrehuroa, Massey University, Palmerston North, 2013.
Walker, Ranginui, 'Māori News is Bad News', in J. McGregor and M. Comrie (eds), *What's News?: Reclaiming Journalism in New Zealand*, Dunmore Press, Palmerston North, 2002, pp. 215–32.
Walker, Ranginui, 'The Role of the Press in Defining Pakeha Perceptions of the Maori', in P. Spoonley and W. Hirsch (eds), *Between the Lines: Racism and the New Zealand Media*, Heinemann Reed, Auckland, 1990, pp. 38–46.
Wall, Melanie, '"Being A Maori Is. . .": Media Constructions of the Maori "Race" As the Black Other', unpublished master's thesis, University of Auckland, Auckland, 1995. Retrieved from http://victoria.lconz.ac.nz/vwebv/holdingsInfo?bibId=1058151.
Wall, Melanie, 'Stereotypical Constructions of the Maori "Race" in the Media', *New Zealand Geographer*, vol. 53, issue 2, 1997, pp. 40–45.
Williams, H., 'Broadcasting and the Maori Language', in J. Farnsworth and I. Hutchison

(eds), *New Zealand Television: A Reader*, Dunmore Press, Palmerston North, 1987.
Wilson, Jani, 'Whiripapa: Tāniko, Whānau and Kōrero-Based Film Analysis', unpublished doctoral thesis, University of Auckland, Auckland, 2013.
Winitana, Chris, *My Language, My Inspiration: The Struggle Continues / Tōku Reo, Tōku Ohohō: Ka Whawhai Tonu Mātou,* Huia Publishers, Wellington, 2011.
Zanker, Ruth, and Geoff Lealand, 'In Search of the Audience', in L. Goode and N. Zuberi (eds), *Media Studies in Aotearoa New Zealand*, Pearson, New Zealand, 2010, pp. 23–33.
Zavala, Miguel, 'What Do We Mean By Decolonizing Research Strategies?', *Decolonization: Indigeneity, Education and Society*, vol. 2, issue 1, 2013, pp. 55–71.

Interviews

Akuhata-Brown, K. 5 September 2012, by Sue Abel and Jo Smith
Amoamo, M. 25 January 2013, by Sue Abel and Jo Smith
Bargh, M. 6 September 2012, by Sue Abel and Jo Smith
Bishara, J. 6 September 2012, by Sue Abel and Jo Smith
Britow, D. 25 January 2013, by Sue Abel and Jo Smith
Bullen, M. 23 January 2013, by Sue Abel and Jo Smith
Chapman, H. 8 February 2013, by Sue Abel
Curtis, P. 13 February 2014, by Sue Abel and Jo Smith
Dewes, C. 17 December 2012, by Ross Burden
Dunleavy, T. 13 September 2013, by Sue Abel and Jo Smith
Edwards, H. 14 December 2012, by Sue Abel and Jo Smith
Ellmers, K. 1 August 2012, by Sue Abel
Flavell, T. U. 27 March 2013, by Sue Abel and Jo Smith
Forbes, M. 21 January 2013, by Sue Abel and Jo Smith
Fox, D. 15 December 2014, by Sue Abel
Graham, K. 30 November 2012, by Sue Abel
Haggie, S. 15 November 2012, by Sue Abel
Harawira, H. 2 May 2013, by Sue Abel
Harawira, W. 17 February 2013, by Sue Abel
Hawke, S. 15 October 2012, by Sue Abel
Henry, E. 23 August 2012, by Sue Abel
Higgins, R. 16 September 2014, by Jo Smith
Hita, Q. 7 February 2014, by Sue Abel
Hoey, N. 26 August 2013, by Sue Abel and Jo Smith
Jackson, W. 24 August 2013, by Sue Abel and Jo Smith
Mackey, B. 23 August 2013, by Sue Abel and Jo Smith
Mane, J. 8 February 2013, by Sue Abel
Mather, J. 2007, by Sue Abel; 2012, by Sue Abel and Jo Smith; 2013, by Sue Abel and Jo Smith
McRae, C. 7 October 2013, by Sue Abel
Metge, J. 23 August 2013, by Sue Abel
Mohi, H. 15 October 2014, by Jo Smith
Morgan, E. 13 June 2014, by Sue Abel
Muriwai, K. 16 October 2014, by Sue Abel and Jo Smith
Murray, A. 22 January 2013, by Sue Abel and Jo Smith
Mutu, M. 27 July 2012, by Sue Abel
Nathan, D. 8 September 2014, by Sue Abel
Nathan, T. 24 June 2013, by Sue Abel
Ngata, W. 5 November 2012, by Sue Abel
Northcroft, L. 15 February 2014, by Sue Abel and Jo Smith

Palmer, C. 23 November 2012, by Sue Abel and Jo Smith
Parr, L. 6 September 2012, by Sue Abel and Jo Smith
Paul, J., 25 September 2012, by Sue Abel
Rangihau, T. 19 February 2014, by Sue Abel
Reid, B. 24 February 2014, by Sue Abel and Jo Smith
Reid, P. 24 September 2012, by Sue Abel
Royal, H. 14 December 2012, by Sue Abel and Jo Smith
Sharples, P. 26 March 2013, by Sue Abel and Jo Smith
Smith, L. T. 2 July 2013, by Jo Smith
Smith, S. 1 October 2013, by Jo Smith
Taylor, I. 30 July 2013 by Jo Smith
Te Rito, J. 30 July 2012, by Sue Abel
Traill, G. 22 November 2012, by Sue Abel and Jo Smith
Usmar, G. 26 February 2014, by Sue Abel
Walker, P. 27 March 2013, by Sue Abel and Jo Smith
Walker, R. 11 October 2012, by Sue Abel
Wilcox, J. 21 November 2012, by Sue Abel and Jo Smith
Wilson, G. 29 November 2012, by Sue Abel
Witherington, A. 22 January 2013, by Sue Abel and Jo Smith

Index

Abel, Sue 72, 93, 121, 134, 146, 158
activism 4, 8, 13–14, 23, 118, 120
advertising revenue 1, 26, 71, 81, 169
AGB Nielsen ratings statistics 91–92, 141
Ako 75, 89, 95, 102
Akuhata-Brown, Kath 12, 134
Amoamo, Mahuta 50–51
Ang, Ien 92
Animation Research Ltd 78
Anzac Day 71, 73, 86, 93, 94, 108, 133–34
Aotearoa Broadcasting Systems 16
Aotearoa Television Network (ATN) 19–20, 21
Archie, Carol 144
Ask Your Auntie 47–48, 74
assimilationist policies 12–13
audience research, Māori Television 92–95
audiences 3; broad audience appeal 2, 11, 15, 22, 33–34, 38, 64, 66–71, 80, 88–89, 135–36, 137; consumer sovereignty 48; expectations 38, 41, 48, 63, 87; feedback 140–42; inclusive approach 120, 135–36; links with producers 56–57, 58; Māori audiences 10, 28–29, 48, 102–03, 118, 120–21; Māori Television target audiences 64, 65–71, 80; *Native Affairs* coverage of Te Kōhanga Reo National Trust 153–56; non-Māori audiences 1, 9–11, 29, 34–37, 73, 92–93, 103, 104, 108–09, 118, 121, 123, 134, 135, 137, 161; quantitative data collection processes 91–92, 137; share and ratings 67, 68, 73, 79, 81, 86–87, 91–92, 118, 132, 135, 136–38, 141, 149, 164; tracking 84; viewing habits and practices 92–93, 94–95; youth 67, 70, 81, 84–85, 87–88, 126, 161, 164–65
August, Te Maumoko 20

Baker, Tungia 58
Barclay, Barry 15, 25, 38, 56
Bargh, Maria 34–35, 121
Bell, Allan 30, 33
Benton, Richard 16–17
Berryman, Charles 52
Bishara, John 58, 135, 136
Blue Bach Productions 76
Boil Up 106
Borell, Belinda 126
Broadcasting Act 1989 25, 158

Broadcasting Amendment Act 1993 19
Broadcasting Corporation of New Zealand (BCNZ) 16, 24; court proceedings by Māori 16, 18, 20, 25; *see also* New Zealand Broadcasting Corporation; TVNZ
Broadcasting Standards Authority 145, 160
The Brown Book: Working with Māori in Screen Production 57
Brown, Russell 155
Burns, Derek 20

Campbell Live 157–58
capacity building, Māori Television 60–61
children's programmes 65, 73, 74, 78, 81, 84
Cinco Cine Film Productions 60–61, 73
The Circuit 78
citizenship, Māori cultural 33, 37, 126, 162
CODE sports show 73, 76, 94, 141
commercial media climate 1, 24, 26, 27, 64, 68–69, 76, 93, 152
community engagement, Māori Television 46–51, 56–57, 58, 76, 77–78, 103, 112, 113–15, 118, 119, 140–42, 161; news and current affairs programmes 153, 159; portal for community-based Māori media initiatives 49–50; *see also* whanaungatanga, Māori Television's contribution
consumer sovereignty 48
Cooper, Dame Whina 14
Cormack, Mike 30–31, 33
culture 25; *see also* tikanga Māori
current affairs programming 2, 55, 70, 74, 89, 140, 144–60; *see also* names of individual programmes, e.g. *Native Affairs*
Curtis, Piripi 31, 46, 67

Daniels, Stacey *see* Morrison, Stacey Daniels
Davis, Esther 41
Davy, John 21
de Bres, Joris 9
Debrett, Mary 63
decolonisation 36, 120, 121–22, 131, 133, 135, 137, 140, 142, 143, 159
Devadas, Vijay 10, 123
Dewes, Cathy 8–9, 11, 48, 51, 52
digital media 4, 26–27, 64, 83–85, 86, 87, 104, 115, 119, 131–32, 142, 165; Māori Television strategy 10, 82–85, 86, 87,

182

89, 115, 131–32, 161, 169; *see also* DSO (digital switch over) 2013
Marae DIY 58, 73, 94, 113–14
DSO (digital switch over) 2013 27, 82, 131–32
documentaries 2, 90, 109, 124
Dunleavy, Trisha 18, 19, 24, 86

East West 101 78
educational role of Māori Television 11; cultural knowledge 97–102; language learning 29–30, 31, 95–97, 105, 119; non-Māori audiences 108–09
Edwards, Hone 20, 43, 52–53, 72–73, 86–87, 163–64
electronic programming guide (EPG) 131–32
Ellmers, Kay 43, 60, 66, 76–77
entertainment imperative 11, 36

FACE TV 27; *see also* Triangle TV; Stratos Television
Fala, Whetu 25
family-style programming 70
films 2, 70, 90, 109, 112, 119
Fishman, Joshua 12
five-framework approach 3–4, 146–60
Flavell, Te Ururoa 35, 39
Forbes, Mihingarangi 16, 146, 150, 154, 155, 156–57
Foreshore and Seabed Act 4
Fox, Derek 15, 20, 21, 153
Freeview digital platform 26, 27, 77, 131–32, 169
funding: funding channels 167; Māori programming 18–19, 163–64; Māori Television 1, 11, 21, 22, 40, 41, 48, 51, 52, 58–60, 62, 63, 65, 71, 73, 79–80, 81, 135–36, 162–64, 167, 169; public broadcasting 26; and ratings statistics 91
Fusion Feast 76
future challenges and improvements, Māori Television 85–89, 111–19, 169–70

Gage, Rikirangi 48
Godfery, Morgan 124
governance structures, Māori Television 38, 39, 40–46, 162
government policy 11, 18–23, 79, 82, 135–36, 163; global financial crisis impact 41, 74; public service broadcasting 26–27, 72, 86; te reo Māori 12–14, 18, 19, 21, 28, 30, 31; tikanga Māori 18, 19

Grace-Smith, Briar 78
Grey, George 13

Hakaraia, Libby 76
Harawira, Hone 20, 40, 45
Harawira, Wena 15, 74
Hari, Bevan 127
Harrison, Kevin 85
Hawke, Sharon 58
Heartland 27
Henare, James 12
Henry, Ella 22–23, 27, 121
Hide, Rodney 21
Higgins, Rawinia 32–34, 37, 162–63, 165
Himona, Ross Nepia 154
Hirschfeld, Carol 71
history of Māori Television establishment 11, 12–23, 124, 168
Hita, Quinton 49, 53–54, 62, 75, 99, 121, 132–33, 159
Hoey, Nicole 60–61
Hohepa, Patu 97
Hokowhitu, Brendan 10
Holmes, Huata 41
Hōmai te Pakipaki 48, 56, 70, 76, 103–04, 117
Horomia, Parekura 18, 21
Horrocks, Roger 18, 24, 25, 26
Hunn, Jack 13
Hunting Aotearoa 31, 46, 67, 74, 76
Huria, Gabrielle 25
Huria, Jane 43
Husband, Dale 148, 149

identity, Māori 12, 17, 93, 100, 112–3, 125–30
IGLOO 27
Ihaka, Kingi 41
Indigenous identities 126, 127
Indigenous Insight 130
Indigenous media 64; Indigenous television movement 1; Māori Television programming and connections 78, 109, 129–31; World Indigenous Television Broadcaster's Network 78, 130
integration policies 13
intergenerational linking, Māori Television 98–102, 119
international programmes 4, 24, 27, 38, 76, 78, 88–89, 90; Māori Television as a source 64
Iti, Tame 123
It's in the Bag 70, 76

It's in the Kete 94, 117
Iwi Anthems 94, 97–98, 128–29

Jackson, Hana 8, 14
Jackson, Moana 10, 142, 158
Jackson, Willie 44–45
Jonathan, Te Kaha 85
Joyce, Hester 18, 19, 24, 86

Kaa, Wi Kuki 25
Kai Ora 76
Kai Time on the Road 68, 69, 70, 73, 76, 94, 123
Kaitangata Twitch (Margaret Mahy) 78
Kanikani Mai 76
Kapa Haka: Behind the Faces 61
Kaunihera Kaumātua 41–42, 45–46
Key, John 79
Kidzone 27
Kimihia training scheme 25
King, Michael 15
Ko Tawa 77
Koha 8, 9, 15, 24, 132
kōhanga reo 14, 48, 49, 88, 100, 119, 145, 146, 150; *see also* Te Kōhanga Reo National Trust
Kōrero Mai 73, 89, 95
Kōwhao Rau 75, 89, 94, 99, 132–33
kura kaupapa Māori 48, 88, 100, 119

Laidlaw, Chris 151
language: impact of television on use 33; minority languages 30–31, 36; rights 9; *see also* te reo Māori
Latimer, Graham 14
launch of Māori Television 3, 4, 123–24
Lawn, Jennifer 123
Lee-Harris, Annabelle 154
Leonard, Ernie 15, 24
Lightbox 85
local content 7, 24, 41, 64, 76, 93, 136
Lysaght, Ruth 30, 33, 46, 52

Mace, Huia 85
Mackey, Bailey 138–39
Mahuika, Apirana 41
Mahy, Margaret, *Kaitangata Twitch* 78
Mair, Gilbert 77
Mallard, Trevor 22
Mane, Jo 31
Maniapoto, Ngawaero 84–85
Māori Affairs Select Committee 80, 164
Māori Boy Genius 56–57

Māori Broadcasting Advisory Committee 20–21
Māori Broadcasting: Principles for the Future 19
Māori–Crown Working Group on Broadcasting Policy 19
Māori Economic Development Commission 16
Māori Land March 14
Māori language *see* te reo Māori
Māori Language Act 1987 17
Māori Language Act 2016 162
Māori Language Bill review, 2013 31, 49, 162
Māori Language Commission (Te Taura Whiri i te Reo Māori) 17, 32, 72, 162
Māori Language Strategy 13, 162
Māori Language Week 9, 14, 15
Māori media sector 11, 32, 38, 50, 59–60, 63, 72, 75, 79, 114, 115, 120, 136, 139, 142, 144, 161, 162, 163–64, 165
Māori Programmes Innovation Fund 19
Māori Television *see* programming, Māori Television; and under topics such as funding; specific topics, e.g. history of Māori Television establishment
Māori Television Board 43, 45, 52, 80–81, 90
Māori Television Establishment Board 21
Māori Television Service (Te Aratuku Whakaata Irirangi Māori) Act 2003 2, 3, 38, 42, 65, 72, 80–81, 82, 90, 135; Section 8, Functions of Service 166
Māori Television Service Amendment Bill 2013 123–24
Māori Women's Welfare League 16, 42
Māorioke 76
Marae 10
Marae DIY 58, 73, 94, 113–14
Marae Kai Masters 69, 76–77
Mataira, Kāterina Te Heikōkō 14, 98
Matamua, Rangi 17–18, 29, 30, 165
Mataora 81, 89
Mather, Jim 10, 11, 21, 23, 40–41, 44, 45, 51, 52, 55, 64, 79, 83, 87, 121, 151–52
Mauri (film, 1988) 25
Maxwell, Paora 22, 25, 45, 80, 81, 168–70
media environment and culture, New Zealand 15, 17, 21, 38–39, 147; agenda-setting function 34; commercial climate 1, 24, 26, 27, 64, 68–69, 76, 93, 152; cross-media ownership 27; depiction of Māori by non-Māori media 3, 25, 34–35, 39, 106, 107, 108, 123, 146–47, 148–49, 158, 160; international

media content 4, 24, 27, 38, 64, 76, 78, 88–89, 90; local content 7, 24, 41, 64, 76, 93, 136; norms 11, 12, 38, 45, 49–50, 53–56, 68–69, 135, 144; *see also* Māori media sector; television industry, New Zealand
MediaWorks 11, 27, 136, 142
Metge, Joan 14
Mīharo 74, 89
Miller, John 25
Ministry of Education 145, 162
Mita, Merata 15, 25, 38, 58
Mohi, Hinewehi 88
Morehu, Te Ariki 41
Morgan, Eruera 77–78, 81
Morrison, Scotty 30
Morrison, Stacey Daniels 76
Muriwai, Kim 47–48, 164
Murray, Annie 31, 59
Mutu, Margaret 128

national identity and nationhood 31, 72, 78, 89, 134; *see also* identity, Māori
National Māori Congress 42, 43
Native Affairs 7, 16, 56, 70, 74, 89, 94, 104, 106–07, 123, 140; *Kōwhiri* programming 123; Te Kōhanga Reo National Trust coverage 144–60
Netflix 85
New Zealand Broadcasting Corporation 14–15, 24; *see also* Broadcasting Corporation of New Zealand (BCNZ)
New Zealand Council for Educational Research, Māori Unit 16–17
New Zealand Māori Council 14, 16, 18
Newmarket, location for Māori Television 46, 47
news programmes 2, 15, 34, 46, 55–56, 71, 73, 74, 123, 140, 144–60; regional coverage 50; *see also* names of individual programmes, e.g. *Native Affairs*
Ngā Aho Whakaari 21–22, 25, 42, 43, 57, 121, 164
Ngā Kaiwhakapūmau i te Reo Māori (Guardians of the Language) 16, 18, 20, 42
Ngā Matakiirea report (NZ On Air) 74
Ngā Pari Kārangaranga o te Motu 77, 129
Ngā Tamatoa 14
Ngā Taonga Sound and Vision 132
Ngā Taonga Whitiāhua 132
Ngaropo, Pouroto 127
Ngata, Whai 24, 38

Ngati (film, 1987) 25
Nielsen ratings statistics 91–92, 141
Northcroft, Lara 61–62
The Nutter's Club 115
NZ On Air 19, 24, 26, 58–59, 81, 136, 158; *Ngā Matakiirea* report 74, 122; Rautaki Māori content strategy 19

on-screen Indigeneity 2–3
open-door policy, Māori Television 46, 47

Pakehas against Racism 16
Palmer, Coral 86, 88, 140–41
Palmer, Hauata 41
Papa, Pānia 30, 75, 105
Parr, Larry 73, 153
Paul, Joanna 20, 28, 47, 56–57
Penetito, Wally 125, 127
Penfold, Merimeri 41
people-meter panels 91–92
Peri, Timi 41
Peters, Winston 155
Pēwhairangi, Te Kumeroa Ngoingoi 14
Pihama, Leonie 16
Platinum Fund 26
Poananga, Atareta 10
Poata, Tama 25, 58
Police Ten 7 106, 108
political function of Māori Television 28, 121–22; greater representation 122–31; Māori agendas for social and political change 135–40; politicians' views 123–24; politics of culture framework, news journalism 156–60
Pouwhare, Robert 20
Prime TV channel 27, 79
Production Company Overhead (PCO) 59
production, Māori Television: engagement with Māori communities 113–14; non-Māori personnel 53–54, 118; proposals 59, 79, 163–64; set design 116; tikanga-based practices 56–62, 63
programming: MediaWorks 11; scheduling 69; sports 26, 27; TVNZ 7, 10, 11, 15, 24, 26, 41, 64, 74, 76, 93, 136, 164; *see also* international programmes; public service broadcasting
programming, Māori Television 2, 3, 22, 46, 48–51, 53–63, 64; broad audience appeal 2, 11, 22, 33–34, 38, 64, 66–71, 80, 88–89, 135–36, 137; culturally diverse 109; framework 4; funding change impact 162; future challenges and improvements

85–89, 111–19; history 71–85; news and current affairs 151–53; public-service content 1; reworking of existing television formats 76–77; scheduling 68–71; sports 26, 27, 69, 70, 71, 73, 74, 76, 78–79; *see also* te reo Māori programming; names of individual programmes, e.g. *Koha;* and under tikanga Māori
public service broadcasting 24, 26–27, 72, 157, 159; Māori Television 1, 3, 22–23, 27–28, 64, 71, 93, 124, 159, 161
Pūkana 94, 95, 97

qualitative measures of Māori Television success 137–38, 141, 164
'quality' television 48, 63, 75, 90
quantitative audience data collection processes 91–92, 137

radio, Māori-controlled 18, 29, 30, 50, 113, 114–15, 119, 136
Radio New Zealand 140
Radio Waatea 146–47, 148
rangatahi audiences and programming 67, 70, 81, 84–85, 87–88, 126, 161, 164–65
ratings 67, 68, 79, 81, 86–87, 91–92, 118, 132, 135, 136–38, 141, 149, 164
Rautaki Reo plan 45–46
representations of Māori by non-Māori 3, 25, 34–35, 39, 106, 107, 108, 123, 146–47, 148–49, 158, 160
review of Māori Television, 2009 (Te Kāhui o Māhutonga) 43, 65, 67–68, 74–75, 80, 163
revitalisation of Māori culture and language 8, 10
Reweti, Debra 15
Rewi, Poia 32–34, 37, 162–63, 165
Rise Up telethon for Christchurch 78
Rogers, Nevak 76
role models, Māori 30, 107
Royal Commission on Broadcasting 1986 17–18
Royal, Haunui 5, 25, 29, 68–69, 83–84, 141–42, 148–49, 159
Royal, Te Ahukaramū Charles 5–6
Rugby World Cup 2011 71, 78–79, 86–87, 89, 110, 115

self-determination (tino rangatiratanga): Māori Television role 23, 121, 137, 158; Ngā Whare Rua or 'two-house' model 10; and Te Tiriti o Waitangi 158

Selwyn, Don 38, 41, 58
Serious Fraud Office 145
Sharples, Pita 79, 123–24
Sky 26, 27, 71, 77, 85, 132
Smith, Lee 14
Smith, Linda Tuhiwai 36, 121–22, 134, 137–38, 153, 159
Smith, Stephen 82
social change, Māori agendas 135–40
social media 84–85, 103, 104, 126–27, 153–56, 160, 161
Songs from the Inside 94
South Pacific Television (SPTV) 24
sports programmes 26, 27, 69, 70, 71, 73, 74, 76, 78–79
stakeholders, Māori Television 2, 3, 42, 43, 63, 74–75, 140, 143, 144
Stephens, Tainui 15, 20, 25, 43, 57, 76
stereotypes, Māori 106–07, 117, 118, 123, 147, 148
storytelling, Māori 131–34
Stratos Television 27; *see also* FACE TV; Triangle TV
studio and office spaces, Māori Television 46–48
Swagger 84–85, 88

Takatāpui 73
Tangata Whenua documentary series 15, 99
Taniwha Rau 75
taonga: te reo Māori 8, 16, 17, 29, 32, 33, 36, 80–81, 162; tikanga Māori 8, 80–81
Tātai Hono 126–28
Tautohetohe 94
Taylor, Ian 71, 78
Taylor, Rangimoana 25
Te Ataarangi language-learning movement 14
Te Hētere 74
Te Kāea 73, 74, 123, 140
Te Kāhui o Māhutonga 43, 44, 54, 65, 67–68, 74–75, 80, 163
Te Karere 10, 15, 16, 24
Te Kōhanga Reo National Trust 7, 42, 56, 106–07, 144–60
Te Kokonga Kōrero (Speaker's Corner) 47
Te Māngai Pāho 1, 18–19, 22, 40, 58–59, 60, 62, 69, 72, 73, 99, 135, 136–37, 158; purchase and funding framework: language content 66, 67; ZePA model use 79–80, 90, 162–63, 164
Te Manu Aute 25
Te Matatini festival 74, 86, 97

Te Pātaka Kōrero 77
Te Pātaka Ōhanga 56, 144–47
Te Punga Net 50
Te Puni Kōkiri 20, 32, 60, 71–72, 79, 163
Te Pūtahi Pāoho Electoral College (TPP) 3, 42–46, 63, 80, 140, 162
Te Rautaki Reo Māori, the Māori Language Strategy 72, 90
Te Reo channel 43–45, 77–78, 81–82, 97, 115
te reo Māori: citizenship 33, 37, 162; government policies 12–14, 18, 19, 21, 28, 30, 31; language plans 59, 63, 75, 79, 163–64; and Māori identity 12, 17, 93; Māori speakers 28, 29–30, 32, 33, 37, 38, 51–53, 89; in Māori Television workplace 51–53; Māori Television's promotion and protection 1, 2, 3, 9, 11, 80, 161, 165, 166, 168–69; media organisations' use and pronunciation 109–10, 119, 140; non-Māori engagement 9–10, 33, 34–37, 73; official language of New Zealand 17, 32; research 32–33; role models 30; Royal Commission on Broadcasting recommendations 17–18; taonga status 8, 16, 17, 29, 32, 33, 36, 80–81, 162; Te Reo Claim (WAI 11) 16–18, 29; and television industry norms 53–56; *see also* Māori Language Week
te reo Māori me ngā tikanga 2, 51, 65, 80–81, 90, 165, 168
te reo Māori me ōna tikanga 2, 80, 90, 143, 166
te reo Māori programming 17, 19, 28–32, 33–37, 42, 43–45, 59–60, 64–65, 161; balance of language responsibility and audience appeal 67–71, 80, 88–89, 135–36; comparison of mainstream and Māori Television 122–23; early days of Māori Television 22, 23, 28, 72–75, 90; framework for understanding Māori Television 4; language outcomes role of international films and documentaries 89–90; Māori Television contribution to language learning 29–30, 31, 95–97, 105, 119; Māori Television legislative responsibility 2, 38, 166; measures of success 137–38; non-fluent viewers 73, 89; quality 48, 63, 75, 90, 163; Rugby World Cup 2011 79; scheduling 68–71; Te Māngai Pāho purchase and funding framework: language content 66, 67
te reo Māori revitalisation 8, 10, 12, 14, 36–37, 54, 62, 135, 161; digital media opportunities 83–84, 89; Māori Television's role and impact 11, 23, 28–36, 38, 39, 51, 55, 65, 67, 72, 73, 75; national events coverage 89; youth market 67, 164–65; ZePA model 32–34, 79–80, 90, 162–63
Te Reo Māori Society 14–15
Te Reo Māori Television Trust (Te Awhiorangi) 20, 21
Te Reo Mauriora 12–13
Te Reo Whakapuaki Irirangi 18–19; *see also* Te Māngai Pāho
Te Rito, Joe 54
Te Taura Whiri i te Reo Māori (Māori Language Commission) 17, 32, 72, 162
Te Tēpu 89, 123
Te Tiriti o Waitangi 3, 8, 9, 11, 12, 13, 16, 17, 23, 33, 37, 118, 124, 158, 161
Te Wānanga o Raukawa 81
television industry, New Zealand: Māori Television's challenges to other institutions 109–11, 119; New Zealand overview 24–28; norms 11, 12, 38, 45, 49–50, 53–56, 68–69, 135, 144; *see also* media environment and culture, New Zealand
Television New Zealand Act 2003 26
Terei, Pio 76
Terei, Teina 85
Thompson, Peter 27, 86, 157–58
Through the Lens 124
tikanga Māori: cultural representation 122–31; framework for understanding Māori Television 4; government policies 18, 19; informing non-Māori 108–09; Māori Television contribution to cultural knowledge 10, 11, 97–102, 125–28, 132; Māori Television's promotion and protection 1, 2, 3, 39, 80, 81, 161, 165, 166, 168–69; news media practices 147–51; production practices, Māori Television 56–62; programming 17, 19, 23, 29, 30, 32, 34–35, 39–40, 42, 67–71, 80–81, 97–102, 117–18, 119, 126–29, 132; and public studio tours 47–48; Rautaki Reo plan 45–46; revitalisation 8, 23, 38, 62, 83–84, 89; Royal Commission on Broadcasting recommendations 17–18; taonga status 8, 80–81; and television industry norms 53–56, 68–69
tino rangatiratanga (self-determination) 23, 121, 137, 158
Tōku Reo 89, 95

INDEX

Traill, Greg 68, 70
Treaty of Waitangi *see* Te Tiriti o Waitangi
Triangle TV 27; *see also* FACE TV; Stratos Television
Tuhaka, Te Kohe 76
Tūmanako Productions 60, 76–77
Turia, Tariana 146–47, 148
TV One 24, 27
TV One Plus 1 26
TV2 24, 27, 70
TV3 25, 27, 68, 71, 79
TV4 70
TVNZ 24, 25–26, 71, 74, 79, 82, 136, 142; Kimihia training scheme 25; Māori Production Unit 15, 24; Māori Programmes Department 15, 24; Māori programming 10, 11, 15, 74, 164; negative attitudes to Māori programmes 15–16; Pacific programming 164
TVNZ U 26
TVNZ6 26–27
TVNZ7 26–27

urbanisation of Māori 13
Urutahi Koataata Māori / Working with Māori in Film and Television 57
user-generated media content 84–85

Velvet Stone Media 62
Vimeo 115
Vodafone 27
Vote Māori Affairs 1

Waaka, Ani 21

Waho, Toni 146
Waikerepuru, Te Huirangi 16, 41
Wairua 97
Waitangi Day 71, 74, 124
Waitangi Tribunal 6, 14, 16, 30, 81; Te Reo Claim (WAI 11) 16–18, 29
Waka, Hemana 20
Waka Huia 24, 94, 97, 98, 99, 132
Walden, Wayne 21
Walker, Piripi 20, 28, 35, 42, 54–55, 121
Waru, Ray 15, 24
website, Māori Television 83
wellbeing, Māori Television contribution 105–08, 116–17, 119, 121, 125, 147–48, 160, 161
Whānau Forum 141
whanaungatanga, Māori Television's contribution 102–05, 119
Wiki, Bill 41
Wilcox, Julian 30, 50, 55, 74, 81–82, 148, 149–50, 160
Williamson, Maurice 19
Winiata, Whatarangi 158
Winitana, Chris 22, 39, 44
Witherington, Alan 131–32
Working with Māori in Screen Production 57
World Indigenous Television Broadcaster's Network 78, 130

youth audiences and programming 67, 70, 81, 84–85, 87–88, 126, 161, 164–65

ZePA model of language revitalisation 32–34, 79–80, 90, 162–63, 165